D1826624

SCHOOLING IN TURMOIL

Schooling in Turmoil

Edited by Geoffrey Walford

CROOM HELM
London • Sydney • Dover, New Hampshire

© 1985 Geoffrey Walford
Croom Helm Ltd, Provident House, Burrell Row,
Beckenham, Kent BR3 1AT
Croom Helm Australia Pty Ltd, First Floor,
139 King Street, Sydney, NSW 2001, Australia

British Library Cataloguing in Publication Data

Schooling in turmoil.
   1. Education—Great Britain
   I. Walford, Geoffrey
   370'.941   LA632
   ISBN 0-7099-3618-4
   ISBN 0-7099-3648-6 Pbk

Croom Helm, 51 Washington Street, Dover,
New Hampshire 03820, USA

Library of Congress Cataloging in Publication Data
Main entry under title:

Schooling in Turmoil.

   Includes Index.
   1. Education—Great Britain—Addresses, Essays,
Lectures. I. Walford, Geoffrey.
LA632.S33   1985   370'.941   85-4101
ISBN 0-7099-3618-4

Printed and bound in Great Britain by
Biddles Ltd, Guildford and King's Lynn

CONTENTS

INTRODUCTION

Geoffrey Walford

Since its inception, the British state educational
system has been constantly changing - there has
never been a time of stability and consensus.
Throughout its development, the educational system
has played a major role in the reproduction,
generation and legitimisation of inequality, such
that education has long been a highly contested
area. Change and conflict have been the natural
consequence of a system of government which allows
the irreconcilable differences that exist in the
aims for education held by the various groups
concerned with education (whether they be pressure
groups, political parties, trade-unions, ages,
ethnic groups, genders or social classes) to be
played out at the national, local and individual
school level.
    A good example of continuing change and conflict
can be seen in the structure of secondary education
since the war. The pre-war system of elementary
schools and grammar schools for the select few, was
gradually replaced as a result of the 1944 Education
Act which made secondary education a distinct stage
through which all children would pass. The
system was based on the ideas put forward in the
Norwood Report which embodied ideas of meritocracy
and separate provision for three types of pupil, who
were to be educated according to their ability to
profit from either a grammar, technical or 'modern'
type of curriculum, which would thus best fit them
for their future place in the occupational structure.
Very rapidly, however, pressures arose which were to
transform this structure to a comprehensive one.
Ball (1984) has recently well described the process
by which an alliance of different pressures, which
included insufficient grammar school places,
population expansion, doubts about the selection

1

procedures and demands for greater equality of provision and social experience (Ford, 1969), combined temporarily to achieve a gradual change in the structure of secondary educational provision. The comprehensive system was, as Hunter (1984) argues, one born of compromise, and one which would inevitably continue to be the subject of change and conflict. Recent attempts to revert to a selective system, by Local Education Authorities such as Solihull, indicate that stability has certainly not been achieved.

In a similar way, the battle between those who see education as being primarily concerned with individual self-development and fulfilment of potential, and those who see it more as serving the needs of the economy and industry by preparing pupils for future positions in the occupational structure, is also long running. Reeder (1979) has shown that, since the Industrial Revolution, there have been repeated criticisms from industrial representatives about the education system's lack of concern for industry's perceived requirements in terms of a well-skilled, motivated and disciplined workforce. These criticisms have intensified at times of economic under-performance as industry searches for a scapegoat for its failures. The last few years have seen an intensification of such pressures and debate stemming from the country's poor economic performance.

What, then, is the difference about the present situation? Is saying that the educational system is in turmoil saying anything more than that it reflects these continuing elements of conflict and change?

In answer to these questions, I would wish to argue that there are both qualitative and quantitative differences between what has occurred in the last few years and the background of continuous conflict and change. Many pressures on the schooling system have come together and generated changes based upon numerous contradictory logics, which have led to what some writers have called a 'crisis in education'. (See, for example, Hall, 1983; Barton and Walker, 1984). Whether a 'crisis' can be as long-term as the present disturbances are likely to last is a matter of semantics; what is clear is that turmoil has become a permanent part of our schooling system and is likely to continue to be so for some time to come.

It is not the purpose of this brief introduction to delineate all of the pressures which have

Introduction

brought about this resultant turmoil, but an
indication of five of the major ones may help to
contextualise the articles that follow.

1. Demographic changes.   The birth rate in
    Britain has tended to oscillate about a
    general long-term increasing trend.   At
    present, however, there is a considerable
    decline in the school age population.   In
    1983 the peak age group was 18, and in the
    three years after 1983 the secondary school
    rolls in England are expected to decline by
    about ten per cent.
2. Technological progress.   The pace of techno-
    logical progress and the 'knowledge explosion'
    has led teachers and educationalists to
    question the value of the particular selection
    of knowledge and skills that they offer.   The
    rapid dating of knowledge and the numerous
    alternative sources of knowledge through T.V.,
    video and film have led to uncertainty and
    questioning.   Moreover, the growth in video
    games, electronics and computers has produced
    a situation where adults and children are
    often members of 'different cultures'
    (Greenfield, 1984), and where skills which are
    easily acquired by children are difficult or
    even impossible for adults to grasp.
3. Unemployment.   Hughes (1984) argues that the
    'age of 16+ has become the great threshold of
    inequality'. More than one in four teenagers
    between 16 and 19 are unemployed and over 20
    per cent are unemployed in the 20-24 age
    group.   Thus, while teachers have been under
    increasing pressure to provide pupils with a
    specific set of characteristics supposedly
    required by potential employers, they, and
    their pupils, know that school leavers will
    be lucky to get any job at all.   Both groups
    have questioned further what schools seek to
    offer pupils.
4. A loss of confidence.   The gradual expansion
    of the educational system from the post-war
    reconstruction to the optimism of the 1950s
    and 1960s came to an end at the turn of that
    decade.   Ball (1984) has pinpointed 1969 as
    the year in which this optimism broke, with
    the publication of the first of the Black
    Papers by Cox and Dyson.   This series of
    papers was to bring forward doubts about
    'declining standards', 'political indoctrina-

3

tion' and 'classroom violence and pupil delinquency'. The attacks on egalitarianism and progressive teaching methods could be at first ignored or simply dismissed as the death cries of the right, but as the political climate has changed, they have become the new orthodoxy. If the 'Great Debate' launched by the last Labour Prime Minister did anything at all, it was to legitimise the ideas that the educational system had failed to live up to the trust put in it.

5. Government Policy. The fifth, and perhaps major, element in the creation of the present turmoil in schools is quite simply the ill-thought-through consequences of a variety of government policies on education. Part of this is related to Britain's poor economic performance, and the Conservative government's belief that monetarist policies based on 'rolling back the frontiers of the state' will encourage economic recovery. Under this ideology financial constraints 'are portrayed as the inevitable consequence of "market forces" and the "natural" consequence of a failure to "live within our means". Schools must therefore take a "share" of the "cuts".' (Wallace, Miller and Ginsburg, 1983). As Hughes (1984) points out, cuts in finances for education have led to near disaster already, but in the three years from 1984, the government intends to cut a further 10 per cent in real spending. This will be achieved, as have the previous cuts, through government reducing the rate support grant to local authorities and by the rigid implementation of 'rate capping'. The second aspect of government policy is in some ways in opposition to the first, for while interference by the state is to be reduced elsewhere, in education, control has become more centralised. This is particularly true over matters of the curriculum where government policy on 'the basics', 'preparation for parenthood' and 'more industrial relevance', for example, has had considerable impact.

These five major pressures for change in schools have caused a confusion of responses on the part of teachers and administrators. The resulting turmoil is there for all to see. School closures have meant redeployments and redundancies, blocked career prospects and teachers teaching subjects for

Introduction

which they have had no training. The economic
cuts have led to the decimation of the school
meals service in many areas, lack of books, equipment, specialist teaching, school journeys, visits
and clubs. Parents' associations now provide
finance for basic educational necessities which are
no longer provided free by the State and, as Sallis
(1984) points out, while some parents are able to
make these contributions, the parents of those in
most need - the poorest - cannot do so. Teachers
have also been under the pressure of greater
accountability and calls for greater assessment of
their pupils. They have conducted extensive strike
action in attempts to defend their declining salaries.
At the level of what is being taught in the classroom
there have been moves towards greater centralisation,
through a flood of documents from the DES and HMI
and the development of new examinations based on
national criteria and approved syllabi. New examinations proliferate with General Certificate of
Secondary Education, Advanced Supplementary levels,
and the Certificate for Pre-Vocational Education.
At another level, Local Education Authorities have
seen their responsibilities eaten into as the
government, through the Manpower Services Commission,
has introduced the Technical and Vocational Education
Initiative in schools, and is wresting non-advanced
further education from the colleges. In higher
education, teacher training has rapidly decreased
and many colleges closed, while Universities, Poly-
technics, and Colleges of Higher Education have
attempted to grapple with major cuts in financial
support and constantly changing government policy.
     The foregoing list merely touches upon some
of the areas where turmoil is endemic. The
following articles amplify some of these themes.
The collection does not, however, attempt a full
survey, it merely presents some results from recent
empirically based sociological studies which
indicate the extent and nature of the present long-
term confusion in education. The topic areas
studied cover a wide range of problems within
education, and the articles seek to both report the
conflict and changes and to reflect upon them.
     The first three articles are concerned with
changes in the curriculum. Lesley Smith highlights some of the contradictions in the pressures
towards preparation for parenthood education, for,
at a time when the calls for such curriculum
developments are many and varied, the subject
already saturates the curriculum and girls are

largely knowledgeable and sensitive to the needs
of infants. Firstly, she outlines the philosophical notions that have formed the basis of policy
related reports, concentrating especially on the
concept of 'cycles of deprivation' and reactions to
it. This is followed by detailed information from
a recent study of preparation for parenthood education in schools, where it is shown that pupils are
able to choose different pathways through such
teaching according to ability, gender and occupational aspirations, which result in differences in
the amount and nature of preparation for parenthood
education received. A psychological construct
approach is used to show that these different pathways coincide with different perspectives towards
parenthood and also aspirations on leaving school.
Smith argues that this curriculum development plays
a part in legitimising gender inequalities in the
workforce through reflecting an ideology which
constantly informs girls, particularly those who
leave school at sixteen, that their main function as
adults is as wives and mothers. Such schooling
domesticates rather than liberates. Working class
girls are prepared for work in the home and parenthood and, at the same time, as part of an unskilled,
cheap and insecure labour force, for work outside
the home.
      Barry Troyna looks at the educational turmoil
surrounding ethnic diversity. During the 1960s
and early 1970s the educational imperative in
this area was based on the ideology of assimilation,
and schools were expected to act as major agents of
socialisation and assimilation, and to encourage
black pupils to give up their own customs, languages,
behaviour patterns and so on. The end of the 1970s
saw the beginning of a change in the dominant policy
towards ethnic and cultural diversity. Integra-
tionism was supported and teachers were expected
to acknowledge, encourage and even celebrate ethnic
and cultural differences. The beginning of the
1980s, especially after the 'riots' of 1980 and
1981, saw more dramatic changes as race related
issues became more central and prominently discussed.
Teachers are now expected to be explicit about
inequalities, to refute racism and to work for the
elimination of racist practice.
      A growing number of LEAs have now produced
policy documents which affirm a commitment to
multicultural, multiethnic and antiracist education.
One of these is Manchester, but Troyna reports the
gap that exists between the official policy and

school-based practice. He shows that the trend towards 'racialisation' in educational policy and discourse has had little influence on what Head-teachers believe takes place in the schools, especially those with ethnically homogeneous pupil populations. To understand these findings, Troyna points to the socialisation and training of these Headteachers and argues that the assimilationist ideology, current at the time of training, became an integral element of these teachers' professional values, and their commitment to assimilationist policies has been allowed to continue almost unchallenged. Cuts in expenditure and resources together with school reorganisations have also meant that the introduction of multiculturalism has been given low priority. He argues that a strategy which specifies the political and educa-tional justification for a radical reformulation of policy, practice and professional values is now required.

The third paper, by Richard Thompson and Geoffrey Walford, looks at one attempt to reshape the curriculum to give greater industrial 'relevance'. It examines the ideological underpinnings of a particular teacher secondment scheme which was sponsored by Understanding British Industry. The formal curriculum of the scheme emphasises academic ideals of understanding and learning, but the informal curriculum is one which devalues systematic study and open debate. The authors argue that the objectives of the formal and informal curricula are in conflict, but that the scheme is structured such that, in practice, the informal curriculum objectives are more likely to be achieved than the formal ones. The scheme is unlikely to prepare secondees in such a way as to enable them to handle the complex issues involved in a fair and competent manner. It does not provide them with knowledge of sources of information available, nor give them the academic tools necessary to enable them to analyse and evaluate that informa-tion and present it to pupils. The scheme can thus be seen as part of a new 'compensatory education' programme which attacks the academic culture of teachers, and is an inadequate way of systematically training teachers for their new roles in teaching about industry and commerce.

The following chapter by Kristine Mason reports a badly needed exploratory study into the educational experience of girls and boys in rural areas. Rural education has been badly neglected by sociologists of education in spite of the drastic changes that have occurred in terms of school closures and amalgamations. What few studies there have been, have tended to concentrate on this aspect alone. Mason presents qualitative data from an ethnographic study of one village, and quantitative data from a questionnaire survey of three rural schools in different areas of the country. She argues that girls and boys are faced with very different occupational prospects in these rural areas, and that this affects their expectations from school and their responses to their schooling experience. While most of the boys could obtain work locally, usually in farming, and were content to do so, many of the girls did not wish to become farmers' wives and showed a positive preference for moving away from their homes to larger towns and cities. Girls thus valued education as a means by which they might be able to achieve their objective. Mason again argues that a greater knowledge of such differential motivations, attitudes and experiences is crucial if we are to understand the effects of school closures on pupils in rural areas.

The next chapter, by Phil Carspecken, is concerned directly with school closures - in this case the successful campaign by the local community to save Croxteth Comprehensive School in Liverpool. A dramatic decline in the number of children in the City led to 'reorganisation' and the eventual closure of the school in 1982. The school buildings were occupied by parents and sympathisers and, from September 1982, a school was run by volunteer teachers. As a result of a continued campaign and support from local unions, in May 1983, on the Labour party group gaining overall control of the local council, it was resolved that the school would reopen. After a period of semi-independence, but with LEA support, it is due to become fully LEA supported in September 1985. In the chapter, Carspecken describes the stages of the campaign and the changing goals and educational arguments used by the participants in the occupation. He discusses these changes in the context of ideas of community schooling, and outlines some of the tensions between what was seen as desirable, in terms of the curriculum and teacher-pupil relationships, and the demands of the situation and the community.

The remaining five chapters deal with aspects of the turmoil in various sections of the educational system. There are two on middle schools. In the

Introduction

chapter by Colin Marsh the way in which middle
schools in England developed as a result of administrative convenience is described.   In order to
change to a comprehensive system, with little new
finance, Local Education Authorities had to use
whatever school buildings were already available.
The idea of developing a middle tier of schooling
enabled them to achieve comprehensive reorganisation
with the least new building, yet still achieve
large sixth forms in the high schools.   Once the
decision was made, the planners and educationalists
followed Plowden and the progressive movement, and
encouraged an extension of modern primary school
practice into the middle years.   Marsh shows,
however, that the progressive primary school itself
was largely a myth and thus an unsuitable model for
middle school practice.   The reality of teaching
in the middle schools is shown to be far from the
dream that was originally proposed.   Finally,
Marsh outlines the likely future of the middle
school as, again as a result of administrative
convenience, in areas of falling school rolls it
appears that the middle school will die.   The
policy implications of the whole saga are indicated.
      In the next chapter, Gwen Wallace is concerned
with the shift that has occurred in the rhetoric
used to justify and legitimate inequalities in
wealth and income.   She argues that since the mid-
1970s there has been a move from the ideology of
'equality of opportunity' to that of 'efficiency',
and that the notion of efficiency operates to
justify financial cuts in education as being in the
'general interest'.   It also implies that there
are clear objectives which would be obtainable if
only those involved were efficient.   Wallace looks
at the ways in which changes in policy and policy
orientated rhetoric have been passed down to teachers
in the classrooms of six middle schools.   In
particular, she considers the question of pupil
evaluation and selection for differentiated curricular
experiences, the issue of testing, and the problem
of the relationship between teaching method and
pupil attainment of testable objectives.   Teachers
are shown to have an increasing emphasis on accuracy,
but, at the same time, to have considerable difficulty
reconciling the concepts of ability and test performance.
      The following chapter, by Rod Ling, is concerned
with teaching in special off-site units for disruptive
pupils.   Pressures within mainstream schools have
led to a rapid expansion in the number of units

established specially for those pupils with whom
teachers cannot cope.   Ling asks, 'How do teachers
in special units teach the unteachable?'   His
ethnographic work has centred on two units in one
LEA which he shows to have very different underlying philosophies as to how to deal with their
pupils.   He describes the experiences of pupils
at these units and shows that the two philosophies
are directly related to the backgrounds and ideologies of the two Heads of Centre.   Ling then
considers the concept of 'teacher strategy' and
describes the special strategies, which include
various forms of physical contact between staff and
pupils, that teachers in these units have developed
to 'teach the unteachable'.   He is able to identify
two distinct strategies, based on the principles
of moral or pragmatic responses, which are directly
related to the underlying philosophies of each of
the units.

The chapter by Bede Redican identifies some of
the unintended consequences of comprehensive
reorganisation.   His study is of two large
comprehensives which were both formed by the fusion
of smaller schools.   The larger size of the schools
has meant that the headteachers have delegated part
of their authority to teachers within distinct
pastoral systems.   This has led to the tendency for
two separate career patterns being perceived by
teachers.   More recently, however, there appears
to have been a slippage from pastoral and guidance
functions for pupils towards the 'supervision' of
the work of other teachers.   The extent to which
'pastoral' is now perceived as both 'supervisory' and
'dominant' and how such an unintended consequence of
early staff placement decisions has been developed
and sustained by the action of teachers in daily
episodes of situated interaction are the central
issues examined.   Redican uses the idea of structuration developed by Giddins to illustrate the ways
in which supervisory staff maintain their positions
of superiority, and shows how management strategies
are used in their daily interaction with subject
teaching staff.   He then considers the possible
effects of this on the experience of pupils in the
schools.

The final chapter, by Henry Miller and
Geoffrey Walford, indicates that turmoil permeates
all levels of the educational system.   This chapter
outlines the dramatic changes that resulted from the
decision to charge overseas students the 'full
economic fee' and major cuts in University Grants

Introduction

Committee finance announced in 1981. They give
a detailed case study of some of the effects in one
of the universities that was most badly hit - the
University of Aston in Birmingham, which lost more
than 30 per cent of its income in three years.
The story is told in terms of three time periods
and the effects on courses, academic staff and
students are indicated. The University has lost
about a third of its academic staff and students,
but has now reached financial equilibrium. Such
an 'achievement', however, has not been without its
cost in personal, social, political and financial
terms. Perhaps the most important legacy is a
greater centralisation of power in the hands of a
few top administrators and an Americanised managerial
style of 'academic' leadership.

REFERENCES

Ball, Stephen, J.   (1984) 'Comprehensives in Crisis?'
     in Stephen J. Ball (ed.) Comprehensive Schooling,
     Falmer Press, Lewes
Barton, Len and Walker, Stephen (eds.) (1984) Social
     Crisis and Educational Research, Croom Helm,
     Beckenham
Cox, C.B. and Dyson, A.E. (eds.) (1969) Fight for
     Education ; a Black Paper, Critical Quarterly
     Society, London
Ford, Julienne   (1969) Social Class and the
     Comprehensive School, Routledge and Kegan Paul,
     London
Greenfield, Patricia M.   (1984) Mind and Media,
     Fontana, London
Hall, Stuart   (1983) 'Education in crisis' in
     Ann-Marie Wolpe and James Donald (eds.)
     Is There Anyone Here from Education?, Pluto,
     London
Hughes, John   (1984) 'The inequality of impoverished
     education', Poverty, 58, 19-24
Hunter, Colin   (1984) 'The political devaluation of
     comprehensives ; What of the Future?' in
     Stephen J. Ball (ed.), Comprehensive Schooling,
     Falmer Press, Lewes
Sallis, Joan   (1984) 'The poor suffer more :
     education cuts and falling rolls', Poverty, 58,
     25-27
Wallace, Gwen; Miller, Henry and Ginsburg, Mark
     (1983) 'Teachers' responses to the cuts' in
     John Ahier and Michael Flude (eds.) Contemporary
     Education Policy, Croom Helm, Beckenham

Chapter One

THE POLITICS OF PREPARATION FOR PARENTHOOD

Lesley Smith

Children's problems, and problems in society as a
whole, are frequently perceived as being due to
lack of parental knowledge and insensitivity to
the psychological needs of infants.   The education
of young people prior to parenthood has been put
forward as a way to improve the quality of life.
    In the 1970s the call for preparation for
parenthood to take place in secondary schools
reached a peak.   The rationale for this education
was to prepare future parents for parenthood,
especially girls;   to dismantle intergenerational
cycles of poverty, poor living conditions and
associated infant mortality and morbidity;   and
to benefit children by improving psycho-social
experiences, developmental and educational status.
Preparation for parenthood has also been seen to
have various other possibilities;   it has been
advocated in order to prevent teenage pregnancy,
stem the increase in divorce and single parenthood,
and stop mothers of young children from going out
to work.   A frequent media response to worrying
social phenomena is to blame parents.   For example,
Watson (1981) associated the Toxteth, Brixton and
Southall riots with 'laxity' in parent practices
and implied that preparation for parenthood in
schools might be the answer to such problems.
    I set out to investigate some of the claims
made for preparation for parenthood by comparing
groups of working class girls in ILEA who had, and
had not, taken a two-year child development subject
in the fourth and fifth years of school (Smith 1978).
This subject had developed as part of the 1970s call
for preparation for parenthood.   The study was of
girls' attitudes towards infants and knowledge of
their psychological needs.   I found them to be
sensitive to the psychological needs of infants and

also to the (largely practical) needs of mothers which they saw as undifferentiated from the needs of their children. There was no difference between the knowledge and sensitivity of those who had, and had not, taken the subject.

The provision of preparation for parenthood cannot, at least on the findings of this small study, be justified by lack of sensitivity to infants on the part of girls. It is interesting then to explore why the call for preparation for parenthood exists.

PHILOSOPHICAL QUESTIONS IN PREPARATION FOR PARENTHOOD POLICY

During the forty years following the second world war there was sustained official interest in educating young people in British schools for their future role as parents (Smith 1985). But a shift in policy can be seen to coincide with the shift from a period of economic growth, which occurred in the 1950s and 60s in Britain, and economic contraction which followed. In the 1970s official advocacy for preparation for parenthood intensified with contradictory effect. The gradual development away from traditional and conservative assumptions to do with gender roles and family, for example, was halted and reversed, while at the same time traditional assumptions were challenged both in some official policy and in academic circles.

The first initiative of note in the 1970s was made by Sir Keith Joseph. As Secretary of State for the Social Services he addressed the Pre-School Playgroups Association in June 1972. In the text of his speech 'Cycles of Deprivation' are crystalised many traditional assumptions underlying the rationale of preparation for parenthood provision. Two DHSS documents followed in 1974 which were intended to explore or confirm Sir Keith's recommendations for parenthood education. An interesting change in philosophical stance occurs between these two documents. The Family in Society: Preparation for Parenthood (DHSS 1974a) reports consultations with educational and other organisations and communicates (a somewhat muted) support for Sir Keith's initiative. Family in Society: Dimensions of Parenthood (DHSS 1974b) expresses the perspectives of academics, who found Sir Keith's 'cycle of deprivation' hypothesis to be unfounded, and to have little explanatory power.

Assumptions in Policy

The quality of children's lives and the kinds of
people they grow into, is traditionally seen in
Britain to be the responsibility of parents,
especially mothers.   This is Sir Keith's view
also.   In his speech he hypothesises a cycle of
deprivation which reflects the extreme traditional-
ism of both Bowlby (1951) and Newsom (1948).
'Deprivation' for Sir Keith is low educational
achievement, depression and despair, into which
one may be propelled by family circumstances and
inadequate care during infancy.   According to
Sir Keith, individuals may be propelled by personal
and/or economic circumstances but he does not see
these as distinct.   Personal shortcomings are
genetic endowment or illness.   Economic deprivation
such as that associated with unemployment, low
income, overcrowding and poor environment, are by
inference seen by Sir Keith to be personal shortcomings as well.   Membership of large families,
and of the working class, is seen by Sir Keith to
put children at risk of deprivation and the results
of deprivation are reflected in emotional and
educational instability of individuals and social
problems.

In Preparation for Parenthood (1974) the
view of mothers as ultimately responsible for most
of the country's problems is somewhat diluted, and
then Dimensions of Parenthood (1974b) reports the
cycle hopothesis to be under critical scrutiny.
For example Professor Rutter identifies seven myths
to be involved in the notion including genetics
as a primary influence in child development;
inheritance of social disadvantage;   the concept
of critical periods in development;   mothers as
being more important than fathers;   and the family
(rather than society) as providing the site for
any cycle which may be imagined.   In this same
document Professor Wiseman went further, and
stressed the structure of the social system as
responsible for any cycle of deprivation which may
exist.

The Court Report (1976) consolidates this
change in assumptions with regard to responsibility
for social welfare.   Court describes '... a
holocaust ...   Children still die in our lifetime
for nineteenth century reasons' (p 6).   The
reasons he gives for this are to do with unequal
distribution of social resources and not to do with
inadequate mothering.   Violence to Children (1977)
reflects the 'cycle of deprivation' theme but does

not assume that parents are entirely responsible.
For example, abusing parents are presented not only
as victims of their own parents but also, and
largely, victims of their social and economic
circumstances.

Prior to the 1974 divide in policy women were
assumed to be natural caregivers for the child and
family. Bowlby, in his 'monotropy' hypothesis,
sees mothers and children to be united by instinctive
bonds which involve hormones and parturition. Like
Bowlby, Sir Keith assumes the existence of ecological,
biological 'critical periods' in development and he
builds upon Bowlby's influence.

> '... the capacity to develop intellectually and
> to form and to maintain emotional and social
> relationships is established so early that
> it soon becomes increasingly difficult to put
> things right. The basis of future behaviour
> patterns is laid when an infant experiences a
> rewarding relationship with his mother ...'
> (Joseph 1972, p 8)

Following this Preparation for Parenthood reports
a strong theme to arise during consultations 'that
mothers of young children in particular should
say at home' (p 64). Nature-nurture assumptions
change with the 1974 divide; whereas maternal
nature had been emphasised, now nurture takes a more
dominant place and Dimensions of Parenthood refers
to mothers and fathers as equally important in
parenthood.

Similarly, trends in assumptions to do with
gender roles change at the 1974 juncture. Sir Keith
reflects the traditional view that the female is best
adapted to the domestic sphere and the male to
protecting and providing for the family through his
paid employment. Preparation for Parenthood still
assumes traditional gender roles but Dimensions of
Parenthood does not.

Good parents are usually seen in policy to
confirm the traditional notions of responsibility
based on ascribed gender roles and white, middle
class, Eurocentric notions of successful child
development. For Sir Keith, good parents are
firm; good families are small, happy, proud,
well adjusted and Christian. However Dimensions
of Parenthood presents parenthood as more problematic. For example, good parents are those strong
enough to withstand the effects of a hostile
environment: '... the provisions which help

parents to be their emotional best need spelling
out' (p 114).

The Question of Valid Knowledge

Traditionally it is the working class girl who
undergoes preparation for parenthood and her
experiences outside school are not taken into
account.   An example is provided by The Newsom
Report (1963) which considers schooling for England's
less academic children.   Homemaking and parentcraft
are recommended by Newsom as a substantial part of
a working class girl's schooling even though he
perceives through their essays that they are well
versed in the subject.   He reports this account
written by a girl of fourteen:

> 'At half past four every morning the alarm
> clock goes off.   Then I know its time to
> get up.   I get dressed and then I go down-
> stairs into the coldness.   First of all I
> put on the kettle.   While that is boiling
> I make a fire.   I make my father's porridge
> and shout him up for work.   When he's gone
> I clean up and then get ready for school.
> After that I shout up my brother and help
> get him ready for school.   Then I call my
> mother up' (p 63).

More recently, McRobbie (1978) reports her study of
working class girls in a youth club in Birmingham,
and describes their attachment to their parents
and home.   McRobbie notes:

> 'Here they learn a whole body of "really
> useful knowledge", they become familiar with
> all the facts of pregnancy, childbirth, child
> care and domestic life through informal channels,
> and in the protective emotional atmosphere
> of the home' (p 105).

The addition of added parentcraft and homecraft
subjects in school may be irrelevant in light of
girls' own experiences of homebased education but
it may also imply invalidity of homebased knowledge.
It also takes up school time during which girls
might be taking on new skills.

Some Implications of Assumptions in Preparation for Parenthood

There had been no explicit emphasis on preparation
for parenthood until Sir Keith's 1972 initiative.

16

Policy had usually before that assumed that the
education of (especially non-academic) girls should
include domesticity as an art, or a science, or a
duty, usually as a natural extension of girls'
biology. But Sir Keith was instrumental in
bringing out three publications which, for the
first time, had preparation for parenthood as the
prime focus as an exercise in social engineering.
Apparently in light of lack of support from the
academic community Sir Keith did not continue to
press his views. The 'cycle' notion had attempted
to provide a rationale for preparation for parenthood which was based upon perceptions of society
which, although persuasive at a common-sense level,
had become unacceptable to the academic community.
Thereafter we see a return to a partnership model
of society, and preparation for parenthood is again
presented as but one of a range of measures in
social engineering.

Where preparation for parenthood is recommended
in policy it usually maximises its importance as a
force for social change and minimises its contradictory nature. By definition it puts emphasis on
personal agency and responsibility. It needs
therefore to take attention away from the complexity
of the parental role and its vulnerability to social
forces such as world-wide fluctuations in the economy,
related employment statistics and personal spending
power.

It is not that one position in relation to
philosophical intangibles can be described as right
or wrong; the importance lies in what the acceptance of these positions facilitate in the material
world. For example, Court (1976) reports that
children in Britain were dying then of economic
deprivation associated with conditions in the nineteenth century. If one believes these conditions
to be under the control of individuals then one
blames the irresponsible parent and educates the
next generation in the hope of change. If one
believes that these conditions are controlled
rather by economic structures then one would suggest
changing this or revision to social policy for
health and social services. Not only does the
acceptance of the parent as responsible divert
attention away from social accountability but it
facilitates blaming the poor for poverty.

To give another example, if one takes the
position that women are primarily responsible in
parenthood, this facilitates a perception of women
as invalid competitors in the labour market. This

may be a useful view for a government in a period of economic contraction to encourage, in the general public but in women particularly, to reserve available jobs for men.

A major contradiction in preparation for parenthood is the way in which the status of individual and cultural knowledge of parenthood and home-making is diminished. Newsom's fourteen year-old describes homemaking as it is for her, dependent upon the family's economic status, and gender roles as accepted by society. It is doubtful whether the Homemaking theme in school would have quite the same preparatory value as real experience and necessity.

The continued presentation of official traditional views with regard to parenthood and who is responsible, arguably creates, perpetuates and consolidates, women's views of themselves as improper in paid employment and imperfect at home.

PREPARATION FOR PARENTHOOD IN SECONDARY SCHOOLS

Given these trends in the call for preparation for parenthood in policy documents it is useful to consider what schools were doing during the period under observation.

Examined courses in child care have been taught in schools in London, the home counties and St. Helena, since 1944 under the supervision of the National Association for Maternal and Child Welfare. This association began in 1902, a voluntary response to the high 19th century infant mortality rates. NAMCW examined courses were taken by 158 girls in 1944 and by 1977 there were 6,352 examination candidates. Preparation for parenthood in secondary schools has primarily been associated with externally examined subjects taken by non-academic girls in their fourth and fifth school years. These subjects have been under development since the 1960s, prior to Sir Keith Joseph's involvement, and since the early 1970s examinations have been provided by some GCE boards at O level but more often provided as a CSE Mode 1 or 111. Titles vary, but reflect the content areas of child care, child development, and family studies. Also based on innovative work in the 1960s non-examined subjects have joined the parenthood curriculum. These use groupwork methods, they focus more on relationships and family life than upon child care and homemaking, and they usually occupy the tutorial period or social education curriculum. Examined courses reach the low ability girl via the option system but unexamined subjects are aimed at girls and boys of all abilities through the core curriculum.

There is evidence that Sir Keith's speech in 1972 coincided with, or initiated, a new wave of interest in preparation for parenthood. For example Cox (1976) contacted every secondary school in three counties and found that half of the 84 per cent who replied were running a course in child development of some kind, and that these were new, having been developed within the five years prior to the enquiry. Interviewing teachers concerned, Cox found that for the majority their reasons for initiating these courses were related to feelings that it was a way to avoid the transmission of experiential deficits from one generation to another:

> 'Well, I wouldn't dare to allow myself to think we weren't having some influence, otherwise what's the point of putting all this effort and enthusiasm into it? And what hope is there? To me its the only hope of our ever breaking this cycle of deprivation' (Head of Home Economics in an Education Priority Area. Cox 1976 p 63)

Sir Keith's initiatives and his 'cycle of deprivation' hypothesis had apparently made an impact in schools having a real and lasting impact upon curriculum. Schools had suddenly found themselves with many more pupils following non-academic curricula so that parenthood education was greatly facilitated by the raising of the school leaving age and by comprehensivisation in the mid 1970s. In ILEA for example CSEs in child development had been available since 1972 under London's Metropolitan Examination Board and by 1977 examinations were taken by 1,953 pupils. By 1982 there were nearly 34,000 entries for child development examinations nationally.

The Aston Research

Between 1979 and 1983 the Department of Education and Science funded research carried out from the University of Aston in Birmingham (Grafton, T., Smith, L., Vecoda, M., Whitfield, R.C., 1983) which aimed to describe the extent and content of preparation for parenthood in the secondary school curriculum. The study was carried out at four levels:

Level 1.   Postal Survey involving LEAs.
Level 2.   Postal Survey involving every secondary
            school in five LEAs.
Level 3.   Interviews in schools, one in each of
            the Level 2 authorities.
Level 4.   An attitude study of fifth formers in
            one school.

Level 1.   At a first level the DES project collab-
orated with the National Children's Bureau in
circulating all Local Education Authorities in
England to enquire about preparation for parenthood
in the curricula of their schools. 71 of these
Authorities responded and 42 of these mentioned
child care courses, usually Mode 1 or 111. It was
clear that authorities were, in the main, enthusiastic about preparation for parenthood across the
curriculum although no responding Authority reported
a formal policy for its inclusion in schools.

Level 2.   A second level of study surveyed all
secondary schools in five authorities. These were
chosen on the basis of their representing the country
demographically. At this second level 217 schools
responded, identifying a total of 930 different
subjects hosting preparation for parenthood to a
greater or less extent. The maximum number of
subjects in the parenthood curriculum were hosted
by Social and Health Education. It was found
also in: Home Economics, Child Care, Biology,
Religious Education, Group and Tutorial Work, Home
or Business Maths, General Studies, Needlework or
Design, English, Remedial Studies.

Level 3.   At this third level the Aston study
looked in depth at preparation for parenthood in the
curriculum of five schools, one of each of the five
authorities surveyed. At this level, all of the
teachers in the schools were asked whether preparation for parenthood occurred as a formal or
informal part of their teaching. A total of 95
different subjects, and over 100 teachers with an
aim to prepare their pupils for parenthood, were
located in the five schools. All five schools
included child care as an optional, examined subject
taken by girls in the lower ability group. Additionally a range of subjects provided preparation
for parenthood, occupying the same curricula revealed
at level 2.
     Level 3 allowed a greater depth of study and
teachers were asked to identify the parenthood

topics that were included in their teaching. In some schools as many as 50 per cent of teachers may be including preparation for parenthood as part of their teaching. In Level 3 it was a girls' school for which this was so. Syllabus topics were identified as relevant to, and preparation for, parenthood. They covered a wide range and were divided into the following categories (listed in order of level of involvement): Aspects of Society, The Home, Health and Hygiene, Child Development, The Family, Human Physiology, Emotions and Problems, Child Care, Personal Relationships, Pregnancy and Birth, Sex and Sexuality, Family Planning. Some teachers expressed difficulties when focussing upon sexual relationships, parenthood, marriage and family life while teaching. A report focussing upon this issue explained how these aspects of preparation for parenthood concerned the realms of the personal, but also reflected prevalent notions in society. The sometimes contrasting real feelings of teachers created a dilemma for them as reported by Grafton, Vegoda, Smith and Whitfield (1982). This publication points to teachers' dilemmas as they reflect contradictions in society and in education, as they juggle their real life experience and feelings; moral issues associated with the role of teachers in society, and emancipatory influences from the feminist movement. McRobbie (1978) suggests that schools offer teachers a possibility of introducing feminist critiques, but few teachers we spoke to seemed to take this view. For example, most teachers associated parenthood with marriage and, even if they personally would contemplate parenthood outside marriage, few would express such a view to their pupils. An English teacher said, for example, that in discussing relationships with pupils one runs the risk of being considered 'permissive'...

> 'I think people ought to be political ... at the same time you have to be very careful not to impose your values ... I think what we need to do is give children a balanced view, that is what I think education is about'.

It is difficult to estimate how often a 'balanced view' would include feminist perspectives or those which are labelled 'permissive'.

Gender and Preparation for Parenthood
During the DES research, teachers involved in

parenthood education were asked how many pupils exposed to this teaching were male, and how many were female. Teachers did not always respond with actual numbers but it was obvious that in the main it was girls who were involved. Where a subject with parenthood content has been compulsory in the lower school (for example when domestic science had been taught as part of the lower school core) then boys tended to drop it when they could unless it was associated with qualifications for a career. In the upper school only the environment subjects, which included topics relevant to preparation for parenthood, were more popular with boys than with girls.

The following were usually compulsory and so reached both sexes: R.E., General Studies, Group and Tutorial Work, English, Social and Health Education. But when preparation for parenthood occurred in an optional subject, then the subject tended to attract more girls than boys. Girls outnumbered boys in Sociology and Biology - and in Human Biology less than 25 per cent of pupils were boys. In the main it was female teachers who were concerned to prepare their pupils for parenthood and it was clear that they gave it more time. Few male teachers, and few boys, were interested in the subjects with high preparation for parenthood content such as child development, domestic science, needlework, family finance.

In schools there was a consensus that boys as well as girls, and pupils of all abilities, would benefit from preparation for parenthood and positive discrimination was apparent in certain schools via Group and Tutorial Work or Social and Health Education. But there was resistance from the boys themselves, from some teachers (for example tutors reluctantly involved in group work) and from some structural influence in the school organisation.

Part of Level 3 research was a case study of curriculum choice in one school and it revealed the presence of choice at one level but a certain lack of freedom of choice at another. Curriculum structure in the school appears to facilitate free choice but in effect girls and boys take different routes through the curriculum so that their schooling reflects traditional gender roles rather than current education ideals. A report of the case study concludes:

'Given this, ironically, the introduction of
a subject intended to improve familiar

relations within a progressive and liberal
option choice system may actually have the
consequence of reinforcing traditional
gender stereotypes'.
(Grafton, et al., 1983)

It is clear from this national survey that
preparation for parenthood had come to saturate
the secondary school curriculum by the end of the
1970s and schools were selectively preparing girls
for parenthood.

PUPILS' PERSPECTIVES OF GOOD PARENTHOOD

Level 4 of the Aston research was summarised in
'School Based Preparation for Parenthood and
Attitudes of Pupils to Adult Life, the Family and
Parenthood' (Smith, et al., 1982). It was based
on the study identified on the first page of this
chapter (Smith 1978) with significant changes. In
the earlier study I had taken three groups of
twenty-two working-class girls, matched for designated ability, age, ethnicity and experience with
younger children. One group had taken a two-year
child development subject. The other two groups
had not taken such a course: the second group
because they had not opted for it although it had
been available; the third group because a child
development subject had not been available. The
girls had responded to questions in a booklet which
asked them first to imagine themselves as parents.
In this imaginative role girls wrote responses to
questions such as 'What sorts of problem situation
do you think might arise involving you and your
baby?' 'Who would you turn to in these situations?'
and 'What qualities would you like to have as an
ideal mother?' Answers to these kinds of questions
were analysed for their sensitivity to the psychological needs of infants. No significant difference
was found between the three groups: all of the
girls demonstrated a high degree of understanding.
One reason considered for the finding that the child
development subject seemed to provide no great
insights relevant to parenthood, was that child care
practices suggested by child development teachers
may have been inappropriate to some girls in light
of their own cultural experiences. For this reason
one of the recommendations of the study was comparative research into parenthood constructs of both
middle and working class pupils.
Since Levels 1 to 3 of the Aston research had

revealed that preparation for parenthood saturates
the curriculum, we found it preferable in the new
study to identify those different pathways that
pupils might take through the curriculum in one
school, noting high and low parenthood content.
This notion of curriculum pathway arose in light
of the need to explore pupils' attitudes, not in
relation to the provision of one subject (as in the
1978 study) but in relation to different combinations
of courses identified as including preparation for
parenthood to a greater or lesser extent. This
also facilitated a comparative study of the perspectives of male and female pupils as well as those
of pupils with different economic aspirations.

Pathways
Six different pathways in the school's fifth form
were identified on the basis of gender and relative
proportion of preparation for parenthood.

(1) The highest proportion of parenthood topics
     was experienced by a form of girls who were
     described by their teachers as being of middle
     to low ability. They took a core Social
     Education subject, an examined child care
     subject and two or more of the following
     (all found to be high in preparation for
     parenthood topics): Life Science, Human
     Biology, Biology, Home Economics, Religious
     Education, Needlework.
(2) A middling proportion of preparation for
     parenthood was experienced by girls in the
     same ability group who took the same mix of
     subjects, with the exception of the child
     care subject.
(3) One group of highly academic girls experienced
     no preparation for parenthood at all in the
     fifth form, because they were all withdrawn
     from core Social Education to attend a period
     on Classical Studies.

Three groups experienced a relatively low proportion
of preparation for parenthood:

(4) high, or high to middle ability girls, who
     only took the core Social Education subject,
(5) a group of high ability boys (core Social
     Education only),
(6) middle and low ability boys (core Social
     Education only).

The Politics of Preparation for Parenthood

This in-depth study revealed six different curriculum
pathways in relation to preparation for parenthood.
Clearly, again, it was girls designated of low to
middle ability who follow the high parenthood pathway.   Academic girls, and boys of all abilities,
experienced a minimum amount of preparation for
parenthood.   Highly academic girls avoided it
altogether in the fifth form, receiving less than
any of the boys.

Level Four Research
Method.   Sixty pupils were involved in the study.
They were drawn from a fifth form of 250 in a
secondary comprehensive school in a close-knit, all
white community, in the north of England.   The
60 pupils involved in the research included
representatives from all six pathways.   During the
same timetabled period they completed questions in
a booklet which asked them to imagine that they
were first a good teacher and then a good parent.
Questions were designed to explore what topics
they thought would be most helpful for young people
entering adult life, in general, as well as to
explore their perspectives toward parenthood.
Questions explored perceptions of good and bad
parenthood, reasons for working or not working
during parenthood, family structure, and knowledge
seen as relevant to young males and females.
As with the 1978 study, Level 4 research into
pupils' perspectives was grounded in Personal
Construct Theory (Kelly 1955).   The unit of analysis
is the psychological 'construct' which facilitates
the way we make sense of and interpret the world.
Kelly suggests that each individual builds up a
construct system in light of experience and uses
the system as a basis for understanding and to
predict future events.   The construct system is
flexible in the light of experience but it also
influences the way in which each new event is seen.
Kelly gives various methods to elicit constructs
so that they are available for inspection.   The
method used in both the 1978 research and the Aston
Level 4 study is a modification of the Situational
Resources Repertory Test (Kelly 1955: 313).   In
both studies the construct was defined as the meaning nucleus of statements written in response to
questions in booklets.   Constructs were isolated
from the grammatical context in responses and so
were available for quantitative, statistical
analysis.   Identifying constructs in this way also
facilitates a qualitative analysis

because quite different constructs are identifiable
and can be seen when used by different groups.
Perspectives. Results of Level 4 research suggest
that different parenthood education pathways
coincide with different perspectives toward parenthood, with gender, and also with aspirations upon
leaving school. Pupils in different pathways
were divided according to gender and ability and
according to their choice of subject in relation
to the work they hoped to do upon leaving school.

Group (1) above were those who had experienced
a great deal of preparation for parenthood. Their
choice of subjects, and their stated work aspirations,
suggested that paid employment was less in their minds
than marriage, parenthood and domesticity. For
convenience this group was labelled the 'Counter
Clerks'. From their choice of subjects, and job
aspirations, it appeared that these girls were not
preparing seriously for paid employment.

Group (2) were girls of the same ability group
(low and middle) who prepared themselves both for
homemaking and employment, taking commercial
subjects as well as parenthood ones. The 'Office
Clerks', as these were labelled, apparently expected
to be employed, albeit not for long, before marriage.

Group (3) were highly academic girls who
experienced no preparation for parenthood at all.
They expected to enter professions which required
long training and were labelled the 'Doctors'.
Parenthood hardly occurred yet on their horizon.

Group (4) girls experienced core Social
Education only; they were headed for the professions
which required less training than the 'Doctors' and
were labelled prospective 'Teachers'.

Boys' groups (5) and (6) also experienced
preparation for parenthood in core Social Education
only. (5) were looking ahead to the professions
(the 'Lawyers') and (6) to skilled craft work (the
'Builders').

Individuals had more, or less, to contribute
in their responses. The average number of constructs
over all was 33, ranging from 60 from a prospective
Teacher to 15 from a Builder. Individual construct
scores were related to different pupil characteristics during an analysis of variance. The following class-related characteristics were considered
and proved significant for boys, but not for girls:
school subjects taken, ability, school leaving age,
preferred occupation. Results of the statistical
analysis suggest that, although individual girls
gave different numbers of constructs, this was not

associated with any of the class-related factors
considered - although with boys it was. This is
an indication that quite different social forces
are in operation for boys and girls and highlights
the significance of gender differences in parenthood.

When asked which topics in school would be
most useful to them in adult life, pupils provided
constructs which referred both to established
subjects in the school and to individual topics
within subjects. Sixty per cent of subjects
mentioned were included in the school's broad
definition of preparation for parenthood. Careers,
part of social education, was the most common
choice as a topic useful for adult life. Home
economics and English were also noticeable amongst
the range mentioned.

All topics mentioned had been identified by
teachers as aspects of preparation for parenthood
in the school and money-management and independent
living were topics most often mentioned. Upon
being asked to identify those topics which would
be most useful for adult life, pupils with the
exception of Counter Clerks, emphasised the fringe
areas more closely related to the economy and
autonomous living. Counter Clerks were the only
group taking the subject specifically designed to
prepare them for parenthood; this was reflected
in their responses because only they tended to
include child care and domestic topics.

Among the boys, the Lawyers (the more academic
boys) felt they should know about the economy and
about relationships. The Builders felt it would
be useful to concentrate on careers and maths.

Pupils were asked to identify similarities
and differences in the educational needs of girls
and boys for adult life. Only 36 per cent of
pupils as a whole seemed to assume equality of
gender roles and mentioned the same topics as
useful for boys as well as girls. 34 per cent
suggested that certain topics would be equally
useful for both boys and girls but gave different
reasons: for example, 'knowing about employment'
would be useful for both sexes, but only useful for
girls if they didn't marry. 30 per cent perceived
needs of girls and boys to be quite different:
for example three girls (two prospective Teachers
and one Office Clerk) wrote that boys would find it
useful to know how best to spend their wages and
how to save, while girls would find it useful to
know how to economise and how to do housework.

A higher proportion (63 per cent) of boys mentioned topics of relevance to parenthood as useful, more so than girls (51 per cent) but when such topics were included by either gender they were usually seen to be topics useful for girls, not boys.

Differences in perspectives were apparent between girls' groups. Counter Clerks revealed strikingly traditional views with regard to educational needs of boys and girls for adult life. No-one in this group assumed identical needs, and different needs were seen as sex-specific, e.g. plugs, taxes and rates for boys, and cooking, needlework, birth and parenthood for girls. This was in contrast with a closely related (in all but preparation for parenthood) group, the Office Clerks, of whom 37 per cent assumed identical needs. Office Clerks were much more emancipated. Only one of the Doctors included topics relevant to parenthood and all Doctors assumed educational needs of boys and girls to be the same. Counter Clerks were the only group taking Child Care and the Family; their traditional views with regard to different educational needs of boys and girls may have led them to opt for that subject; if so, then the subject had not enabled them to take up alternative views.

Pupils were asked to describe their own family background as well as imagine with whom they would live when they themselves became parents. There was no difference between the groups with regard to factual or anticipated circumstances. In their real lives 83 per cent of the 60 pupils were living in nuclear family with both original parents. Five per cent lived in extended family groups with their parents. Twelve per cent were in single parent or reconstituted families. The result reflects the unusually stable and close-knit community the school served. With regard to family structure 90 per cent assumed they would live in nuclear family when they were married and three per cent assumed an extended family (seven per cent misinterpreted this aspect of the task). In their imaginary lives as parents 98 per cent of pupils assumed they would be married; the remainder felt that they could become parents outside marriage.

When asked about the qualities of good and bad parents pupils had most to say. They all prioritised love, care and affection but after that there were distinct between-group differences. Parental behaviour was generally categorised as either nurturant or neglectful. Builders' and Lawyers' attitudes expressed traditional male gender orientations toward parenthood. Lawyers were most forthcoming especially with regard to neglect. They seemed to be able more easily to identify how one should not behave in relation to children: one should not abandon one's parental responsibility, nor neglect one's wife or child, nor become violent. Builders tended to portray bad fathers as those who go out with the boys every night, lose their temper, or beat their wives and children. With regard to positive aspects of parenthood also, perspectives between Lawyers and Builders were similar; both Builders and Lawyers stressed the mother's need for affection, and the child's need for tolerance and understanding, as aspects of good parenthood.

Doctors and prospective Teachers had more than the others to say about good and bad parenthood; responses emphasised the emotional and psychological needs of children, including the need to nurture cognitive development, positive and negative aspects of discipline, and the commitment and responsibility required of parents.

Counter Clerks had a little more to say about the qualities of good and bad parents than Office Clerks but attitudes between these groups toward good and bad parenthood were similar. Counter Clerks, more so than Office Clerks, mentioned the physical needs of children, and the necessity that mothers should stay with their children. They prioritised maternal roles of keeping house, cooking meals and delivering and picking a child up from school.

Replies contributed in response to questions about good and bad parenthood revealed clearly the differences between groups with regard to gender role assumptions. Both class and gender differences were apparent. Both groups of boys saw good fathers as responsible providers and nurturers of all the family. All the girls concentrated on children's needs, but Doctors and Teachers concentrated more on psychological aspects of nurturance and cognitive development while Counter and Office Clerks emphasised traditional female responsibility for physical child care and homemaking.

Both class and gender differences were apparent with regard to life changes expected to accompany the transition to parenthood. Although 68 per cent of Builders thought they would no longer be able to do exactly as they would like to, it was girls

rather than boys who foresaw most restrictions on
their freedom.   Lawyers, least of any group,
expected restrictions, although they did expect
added responsibility.   Among the boys, Builders
differed from Lawyers little, although the latter
were slightly more worried about the economy and
its effects on them as parents.

Among the girls the Counter Clerks recorded
more on the theme of changes to life style than
other groups;   they worried about lack of money but
more so about problematic relationships with their
husbands, about sleepless nights and social
isolation.   Prospective Teachers were concerned
with discipline and control and also, but to a
lesser extent, with marital relationships.
Doctors, more than others, expected to gain in
maturity as a result of the responsibilities of
parenthood, but also foresaw restrictions on their
freedom to work.

Commitment and satisfaction to be gained from
the experience of parenthood was predicted by
Teachers as well as by Office and Counter Clerks.
Upon becoming parents they expected a consolidation
of a bond with their husbands, a fuller and happier
life, and something special to love and live for.
Among these groups the Office Clerks were down to
earth about the work and fatigue which they expected would accompany these more positive aspects of
parenthood.

Adjustment to parenthood was a problem cited
by everyone.   All of the boys expected economic
problems and problems to do with physical 'handling'
of a child, and all the girls demonstrated some
concern that they might not have the necessary
characteristics to look after a child properly.

To elicit feelings about parents in employment
pupils were asked why they worked in their imaginary
role as parents and then why they did not work.
For the boys,reasons for not working were usually
because of the lack of work available (although a
few Lawyers added that they might be needed to look
after the child).   Girls obviously believed it
was better to stay at home but they recognised they
might have to go out to work if family economics
so demanded.   Doctors indicated that work would
remain their prime consideration for some time to
come;   for them this was hardly a relevant question.
Prospective Teachers indicated that they would try
to balance career and motherhood while taking the
primary responsibility for the home.   For the
Counter Clerks and Office Clerks motherhood would

dominate paid work while it was economically
possible.   Reasons were rarely given for this
traditional stance.   Non-academic girls and boys
in particular seemed to accept traditional gender
roles without question: boys would be the bread-
winners and girls the homemakers.   Office Clerks,
prospective Teachers and Lawyers supposed some
sharing in domestic tasks while the Counter Clerks
saw women as self-sacrificing, nurturant, and wholly
responsible for home and family.

Girls' perspectives.   From this analysis of
psychological constructs it is apparent that these
girls, with the exception of the more academic,
subscribe to traditional notions of female responsibility in parenting and traditional gender roles.
They are, however, not in the least ignorant of
the practicalities of parenthood, nor are they
insensitive to the psychological needs of infants
and children.   The girls most consistently
preparing themselves for parenthood communicated
expectations of strife in the home.   They
concentrated on children's physical needs above
their psychological or cognitive needs.   Cognitive
development was seen as a priority concern for
good parents by prospective Teachers and Doctors -
the girls who had experienced least preparation
for parenthood amongst the girls' groups.

Boys' perspectives.   There was less difference
between the boys' groups.   They both assumed
traditional male gender roles and predicted little
real change in their life styles once they became
parents.   Both boys' groups expected their major
contribution to be a financial one, although they
would also provide emotional support for their
wives.   The Builders especially high-lighted non-
violence as an important characteristic of good
parenthood.

It must be remembered that this Level 4 research
was carried out in one school only, in a stable
and perhaps atypical community.   Nevertheless, the
study high-lights the importance of looking at the
implications of pupils' gender and class for
educational programmes.

POLICY, PRACTICE, PERSPECTIVES AND POLITICS

The contradictions of preparation for parenthood
are several: (1) the assumption that major social,
economic and demographic phenomena (e.g. rates of
birth and perinatal mortality; poverty and employment patterns; rates of marriage and divorce) are

the responsibility of individuals, many of whom
find themselves unable to control these very
phenomena; (2) while implying that females as
mothers have the primary responsibility for the
quality of life, their personal and cultural
experiences are made to appear to them to be
without value; (3) in calling for preparation for
parenthood in order to engineer a better world
(while this initiative is patently non-viable)
policy appears to have the well-being of the
general populace in mind but the initiative may be
merely rhetorical; (4) similarly, changes toward
women's emancipation are apparently approved at one
level but at another level approval seems merely
to be lip service.

The first part of the answer to my question
'why does the call for preparation for parenthood
exist' seems to be that it provides a rhetoric
which 'finds resonance' with people's experience
(Kellner 1978). For example, Sir Keith Joseph's
'cycle of deprivation' notion is appealing at a
common-sense level; it finds resonance with
teachers' experiences and has provided impetus to
develop relevant parenthood-related curricula.

Research suggests the following influences to
be at work (but not unhindered). In policy and in
schools there is an emphasis on traditional gender
stereotypes in parenting based on and supported
by biological assumptions. Remembering the brief
shift in policy toward a view of women as valid
competitors in the labour market, expressed in the
Crowther report (1959) when the economy needed
more labour, views about women do seem to change
with economic needs. Working class girls (those
who are more likely to be exposed to parenthood
education) seem more especially to subscribe to
traditional views of femininity. Femininity
allows a girl to survive her current and prospective
'unexciting life' - using McRobbie's expression -
but it also locks her into it (McRobbie 1978 : 108).
This is an important point because girls necessarily
give their consent, in a way, to their lives, and
consent needs to be won ideologically.

It is basic to the perpetuation of the economic
system that inequalities of power and privilege
are seen to be legitimate and that the cost of the
labour required to support it does not rise to
reduce profits below a level acceptable to those
in control. As Dale (1981:5) argues:

'... the state in capitalist societies is

confronted by three basic problems, those of
facilitating the process of capital accumula-
tion, ensuring a context favourable to that
process and providing legitimation for the
process, and that the solution of these
problems is centred in the operation of all
state apparatuses, including the education
state apparatus.'

Dale goes on to say that these three problems are
parallel throughout the education system with many
problems facing teachers in classrooms traceable
'back to contradictions engendered by the attempt
to solve two or more of the problems simultaneously'
(p 35). He adds '... it is quite crucial to
recognise that their mutually contradictory
implications are the dynamic forces of the education
system' (p 36).

Contradictions experienced by teachers while
teaching preparation for parenthood were clearly
expressed during Aston Level 3 research. Many
teachers find themselves in a dilemma when they
touch upon the personal sphere: should they express
the contradictions they feel? For example, this
view was expressed by a biologist head of careers:

'I wouldn't try to put my personal view over
... I would teach it from the point of view
of what is generally accepted in society.'

This teacher is in a dilemma because her personal
view is not what is generally accepted in society.
She might also at times feel that the generally
accepted view is not in the real interests of her
pupils. Perhaps this is communicated in non-
specific ways - by gestures, reticences, encourage-
ments and so on. But what will be selected from
the breadth and variety of explicit and implicit
school communications, is likely to be what pupils
see as relevant, and what is real in accordance
with their own experiences.

Newsom's statements in 1948 could serve as
a summary for some aspects of the Aston Level 4
findings. He says:

'... for the vast majority of women, the
business of homemaking and the early nurture
of children is a dominant theme in their lives,
while for men the equivalent dominant is to
earn enough to support their wives and families.' (p 12), and

> 'Girls leaving school ... regard their job
> as temporary, as a preliminary period between
> finishing education and getting married'
> (p 36).

In 40 years of schooling little seems to have
changed in terms of working class assumptions
despite the growth in the women's movement, the
Sex Discrimination Act of 1975, and lip service
paid to it in official education documents published
since then.

Another of Newsom's statements carried a clue
as to why this may be so. He says the guiding
principle in planning a curriculum for a girl who
leaves full-time education at 15 or 16 should
enable her to 'endure the frustrations of her
temporary work while at the same time to prepare
her for marriage '(p 120). Scott (1980) more
recently perceives schools as helping to produce
the consciousness necessary to accept this situation.

There was a growing demand for part-time
female labour all through the period under observation here, more especially in clerical and
unskilled manual occupation. Seventy per cent of
women who were leaving school when Newsom was
writing are now in the labour force. In 1980
54 per cent of mothers with dependent children
were working either full or part-time (OPCS 1981:10).
Rees (1983) identifies the most serious obstacle
to girls' aspirations toward serious work to be the
dominant ideology 'which constantly informs girls,
particularly early school leavers, that their main
function as adults is as wives and mothers' (p 19).
I suggest that girls' acquiescence is vital to the
economy.

Johnson (1979) describes ideology as involved
in 'the production of consciousness - ideas,
feelings, desires, moral preferences (or) forms
or subjectivity'. Kellner (1978) suggests that
one should 'perceive the contradictions and tensions
as well as efforts to harmonious and mutual
reinforcements within the field of ideology'.
Ideologies of the dominant culture seek to mask
class domination, antagonistic class relations,
and exploitation.

Girls contribute to their own exploitation.
McRobbie's youth club girls responded similarly to
Level 4 school girls with 'an ultimate if not
wholesale endorsement of the traditional female
role and of femininity, simply because to the girls
these seemed to be "natural".' (p 97). Similarly,

34

working class girls in the youth club and in school did not expect much romance from marriage in the long run. Marriage for them seems to be a necessity both in terms of personal status, a secure basis for sexual expression, and economic survival. Femininity and romance may be an essential element during the transition to marriage, obscuring the accompanying transition to the reserve army of labour.

Young and Whitty (1977 : 1) suggest that schooling in general may be more a process of domestication than liberation. Research that has been drawn upon in this chapter suggests that preparation for parenthood in particular domesticates working class girls for work both in the home and temporary work outside. Paid jobs have become a necessity for women, even though they might prefer not to work outside the home, but some girls do not prepare for it, nor do they see themselves as valid competitors on the labour market. They prepare for parenthood and in so doing also prepare to meet the needs of the economy which depends upon compliant, unskilled, cheap and insecure labour.

REFERENCES

Bowlby, J. (1951) Maternal Care and Mental Health
     W H O, Geneva
Cox, M.H. (1976) 'The teaching of child development
     in secondary schools: a preliminary study'
     Unpublished Master's thesis, University of
     Nottingham
The Court Report (1976) Fit for the Future, Report
     of the Committee on Child Health Services,
     HMSO, London
The Crowther Report (1959). A report of the
     Central Advisory Council for England, HMSO,
     London
Dale, R. (1931) The State and Education: Some
     Theoretical Approaches, Open University Course
     E353, Open University Press, Milton Keynes
DHSS (1974a) The Family in Society: Preparation
     for Parenthood, HMSO, London
DHSS (1974b) The Family in Society: Dimensions
     of Parenthood, HMSO, London
Grafton, T., Miller, H.D.R., Smith, L., Vegoda, M.
     and Whitfield, R.C. (1983) 'Gender and
     curriculum choice : A case study', in
     M. Hammersley and A. Hargreaves (eds.)
     Curriculum Practice: Some Sociological

Case Studies, Falmer, Lewes

Grafton, T., Smith, L., Vegoda, M. and Whitfield, R.C., (1983) _Preparation for Parenthood in the Secondary School Curriculum_, A study carried out for the Department of Education and Science, Department of Educational Enquiry, University of Aston in Birmingham

Grafton, T., Vegoda, M., Smith, L. and Whitfield, R. (1982) 'Getting personal. The teachers' dilemma' _International Journal of Sociology and Social Policy_, 2, (3)

Johnson, R. (1979) 'Three problematics: elements of a theory of working class culture' in Clarke, J. (ed.) _Working Class Culture: Studies in history and theory_, Hutchinson, London

Sir Keith Joseph (1972) 'Cycles of Deprivation' in _The Importance of Playgroups in Education and the Social Services_, Conference proceedings, PPA, London

Kellner, D. (1978) 'Ideology, Marxism and advanced capitalism' _Socialist Review_, 42

Kelly, G. (1955) _A Psychology of Personal Constructs_ Volumes 1 & 2, Norton

McRobbie, A. (1978) 'Working class girls and the culture of femininity' in Centre for Contemporary Cultural Studies (eds.) _Women Take Issue_, Hutchinson, London

Newsom, J. (1948) _Education of Girls_, Faber & Faber, London

The Newsom Report (1963) A report of the Central Advisory Council for Education (England), _Half our Future_, HMSO, London

The Norwood Report (1943) _Curriculum and Examinations in Secondary Schools_, HMSO, London

OPCS Monitor (June 1981)

Rees, T. (1983)'Educating Girls for Women's Work' _Journal of Community Education_, 2, (3)

Rogers, R. (1980) _Crowther to Warnock_, Heinemann, London

Scott, M. (1980) 'Teach her a lesson - the sexist curriculum in patriarchal education' in D. Spender and E. Sarah (eds.) _Learning to Lose_, The Women's Press, London

Smith, L. (1978) _The Attitudes of Adolescents to Child Development: Does Education Make a Difference?_ Unpublished report submitted in partial fulfilment of the requirements for the Master's Degree in Child Development, University of London

Smith, L. (1985) 'The economy and parenthood education' Journal of Community Education, 4, (1)

Smith, L., Vegoda, M., Grafton, T. and Whitfield, R.C. (1982) School-Based Preparation for Parenthood and the Attitudes of Pupils to Adult Life, the Family, and Parenthood, unpublished paper presented to the Tenth International Congress of the International Association for Child and Adolescent Psychiatry and Allied Professions, Dublin

Watson, P. (1981) 'Why so many children take to the streets' The Times, July 11

Violence to Children (1977) First Report of the Parliamentary Select Committee, HMSO, London

Young, M. and Whitty, G. (1977) (eds.) Society, State and Schooling, Falmer, Lewes

Chapter Two

THE 'RACIALISATION' OF CONTEMPORARY EDUCATION
POLICY: ITS ORIGINS, NATURE AND IMPACT IN A PERIOD
OF CONTRACTION

Barry Troyna

TOWARDS THE 'RACIALISATION' OF CONTEMPORARY
EDUCATIONAL POLICY

Looking back on the 1960s and 1970s[1] it is possible
to conclude that the educational debate about black
pupils (i.e. those of Afro-Caribbean and South
Asian origin) was not only structured in racially
inexplicit categories but was deliberately and
purposely 'deracialised'. As Frank Reeves suggests,
deracialisation often takes the form of persons
consciously speaking 'to their audiences about
racial matters while avoiding the overt deployment
of racial descriptions, evaluations and pres-
criptions' (1983, p.4). The educational debate at
this time provides a useful exemplar of this process at work as policy makers tended to diminish
and defuse the significance of race and embedded
relevant initiatives and interventions in more
broadly-based programmes (and discourse). The
perceived 'special educational needs' of these
pupils, most of whom attended inner city schools,
were tackled as part and parcel of the more general
policies aimed at all pupils in those residential
and educational contexts. In this scenario, racism
was not considered a sufficiently significant
determinant of educational progress to require
specific policy intervention. Instead, as David
Kirp has pointed out, the aim of policy was to do
good by stealth; the rationale: to ensure that
there was no 'white backlash' from parents who
might otherwise feel that black immigrant pupils
were receiving preferment over their own children
with regard to the allocation of resources. Kirp
sums up the approach and its logic in these terms:
'... one helps non-whites by not favouring them
explicitly. The benefits to minorities from such
an approach are thought to be real if invisible -

38

or better, real because invisible' (1979, p. 61).[2]
Of course, neither this policy approach nor
the ideological rationale on which it was predicated
can be disengaged from the prevailing ideological
and policy approach to the issues of immigration
and race relations in this period. The imperative
in all spheres of social policy on race was assimilation; in educational matters this demanded that
ethnic minority pupils be inculcated with the
values, beliefs and language of a 'British way of
life', whatever that was. As the research of
Jenny Williams (1967) and H.E.R. Townsend and
Elaine Brittan (1972) indicated, schools constituted important socialising, anglicising and inte-
grating agencies within which black pupils were
actively encouraged to give up their different
customs, languages, ways of behaviour and so on,
because all were seen to have the potential to
inhibit assimilation.

However, as the 1970s drew to a close, it
was recognised belatedly that ethnic and cultural
diversity was not inevitably dysfunctional to the
educative process and that rather than suppressing
such differences teachers should be encouraged to
acknowledge and celebrate their significance. Even
so, this 'integrationist' approach, as it is
commonly termed, signalled only minor changes from
those advanced by assimilationist ideas. As I have
suggested elsewhere: 'The difference was that
while assimilationists had argued that the values
and assumptions of the majority culture could only
be maintained if minority cultural differences
were suppressed, integrationists insisted that this
end could best be ensured by minimal recognition of
these differences, that is "unity through diversity" (Troyna, 1982, p. 135). Nor did 'race'
feature any more prominently on national or local
government educational policy agendas during this
period. In fact, as Sally Tomlinson has noted,
between 1973-1981 a number of interested parties
submitted a total of 228 recommendations to
national and local governments for clear and
explicit policies on this matter, none of which was
successful (1981, p. 150).

The last couple of years has seen a per-
ceptible shift in thinking and policy-making, however. There has been some evidence of a 'racialisation' in education, as well as other spheres of
social policy (Young, 1984). What I mean by this
is that, in contrast to the inexplicit, 'doing good
by stealth' approach, there is currently a growing

tendency to accord race-related issues a more
central and prominent role on the policy agenda of
local government. As Reeves has argued:

> 'Racialisation', in this sense, then, has to
> do not with groups increasingly subscribing
> to racism in a negative inegalitarian sense
> but to their growing awareness of, and
> indignation at, racial injustice. Racial
> evaluation and prescription is directed at
> refuting racism and eliminating racialist
> practice (1983, p. 175).

Pressure from civil liberties and black groups,
changes in the political complexion of certain local
authorities and the impact of the 1976 Race Relations Act (especially Section 71) have all played
a part in facilitating this development. However,
it is undoubtedly the case that the occurrence of
violent confrontation on the streets of Brixon,
St. Paul's, Toxteth and elsewhere in 1980 and 1981,
and the concern to prevent their recurrence has
played the most significant role in this context.
The 'riots' constituted the major turning point on
race and in this perspective, education was identified as an area in which blacks, particularly those
of Afro-Caribbean origin, were 'disadvantaged'. In
his report on the disturbances, Lord Scarman urged
the need for the provision of more 'suitable educational ... opportunities' for blacks as a means
of securing 'social stability'. He also endorsed
a view which had previously been articulated in a
report of the Select Committee on Race Relations
and Immigration; namely, that ' ... a failure to
act, now the facts are generally known, will cause
widespread disappointment and ultimately unrest
among the ethnic minority groups of our society'
(1981, p. 106). Of course, warnings of this
nature were not new. As long ago as 1969 a Select
Committee report on The Problems of Coloured School
Leavers heavily stressed the role of education in
averting an impending (racial) conflict; subsequent
reports from the Select Committee (1973), Community
Relations Commission (1974) and the DES (1980) had
all argued substantially along these same lines
(Troyna, 1984a, pp. 79-82).
     All of this suggests that the re-appraisal of
'race' in educational policy has been prompted
largely by political, rather than educational,
imperatives. But this is not entirely without
precedent. Ken Jones (1983, p. 19) has referred to

other, earlier educational initiatives in the UK
which have had a purely functional political basis.
Similarly, as James Banks (1981) and Geneva Gay
(1983) indicate, many of the initiatives in multicultural education in the USA arose in response to
political pressures and events rather than from
pedagogical foresight. As I will argue later in
this chapter, the political source of multicultural
initiatives in the UK has important implications
for the way in which the new orthodoxy of multi-
cultural/antiracist education is perceived and for
its institutionalisation (or lack of it) in contemporary educational settings.

Before this, however, it is important to spell
out more precisely the extent to which educational
policy has become 'racialised' and what form this
process has assumed. Here, it is salutary to point
out, first of all, that the DES has retained a
hesitant and ambiguous stance on this issue for
reasons which Andrew Dorn and I have discussed
(1982). The main flurry of activity has taken
place at LEA level where, since the 1980/1981 street
disturbances, a growing number of Authorities have
produced policy documents or statements of principle which affirm a commitment to multicultural,
multiethnic or antiracist education. For some time
the Inner London Education Authority (ILEA) stood
alone in possessing a formal document on this
issue having produced its policy in 1977. And
before the 1981 disturbances only Manchester Education Committee had followed ILEA down this path.
Since then, something like 20 LEAs, including a
small number of non-metropolitan counties, have
officially endorsed multiculturalism/antiracism.
There are also a large number of LEAs which are
pursuing explicit policies and which have developed
extensive practices and arrangements in this area
but, as yet, do not have written documents. The
number of specialist staff appointed to orchestrate
Authority initiatives and facilitate the diffusion
of multicultural/antiracist perspectives in schools,
colleges and County Halls themselves has also increased prodigiously. In Birmingham, for example,
the Multicultural Support Service comprises over
120 teachers. In Berkshire, a similar number is
employed to work on issues concerned with racial
equality. Now, although the vast majority (if not
all) of these appointments are funded principally
by central government - through Section 11 of the
Local Government Act 1966 - it would be wrong to
assume that race relations policies have made no

41

impact on LEAs' mainstream expenditure programmes. The ILEA, for instance, is committed to providing 'a substantial proportion' of its budget for in-service education courses and secondments to multi-ethnic and antiracist initiatives.

It is far easier to provide a descriptive profile of the various initiatives taken in the name of multicultural/antiracist education than it is either to specify the principles and predicates on which these are based or to pinpoint the objectives to which they are geared. As I have already suggested, the trend towards a 'racialisation' of educational policy emerged largely as a response to the 1980/81 disturbances and constitutes, therefore, a deliberate move towards the amelioration of some of the factors which precipitated those disturbances. To this extent multicultural/antiracist education engages, to a greater or lesser degree, with notions of equality of opportunity in education. According to this argument, the assimilationist/integrationist perspectives, which rested on the view that educationists should adopt a 'colour blind' approach to ethnic and cultural differences, denied systematically equality of opportunity for black pupils. Those who were committed to an assimilationist perspective and who adopted the modes of operation it impelled, turned a blind eye to the ethnocentric and racist images portrayed in textbook and other teaching materials; ignored the special educational needs of black pupils (with the conspicuous exception of language provision for non-English speaking youngsters from South Asia); disparaged the ethnic and cultural identities of pupils and through adherence to other various and routine administrative, pedagogic and curricular procedures allowed racism to operate with impunity in the educational system.

Now, if we accept the argument that multicultural/antiracist education represents a corrective to the assimilationist stance, a re-appraisal of routine practices and procedures to ensure, amongst other things, that all pupils have equal access to educational opportunities and are not differentially treated on a <u>racial</u> basis in their pursuit of these opportunities, then one thing is clear. This trend towards the provision of equality of opportunity contrasts sharply with other strands of the state's ideological and policy stance on both race and educational issues. In other words, it invalidates the claims of those who continue to see the state as a monolithic entity

which has a set of uniform needs and interests. As
Gideon Ben-Tovim and John Gabriel have suggested,
a more accurate picture would reveal 'a highly
contradictory set of developments at both national
and local state levels' (1984, p. 16). For instance, the move towards equalising educational
opportunities for blacks - thereby acknowledging
that, hitherto, they have not enjoyed this 'right' -
comes at a time when other elements of the state's
policy in race relations have effectively imposed
second class citizenship on blacks: restrictive
immigration laws, passport checking, police
surveillance of 'suspected' illegal immigrants and
other invidicus forms of internal controls have all
increased dramatically in recent years and served
to undermine the welfare and civil liberties con-
ventionally accorded other UK citizens (Cashmore
and Troyna, 1983).

In education, it is possible to identify
similar contradictions and ironies. The promotion
of antiracist education as a strategy for facilitating equality of opportunity for blacks is taking
place at a time when, as Ken Jones and others have
pointed out, the principal of equal opportunity
has been dislodged 'from its place as the central
reference point of educational strategy' (1983, p.
68). More compelling concerns for educational
policy-makers at national and local state level
have been matters such as 'national needs', educational standards, professional accountability and
so on. And the contradictions and ironies do not
end there. The aggrandisement of multicultural/
antiracist services and provision is occurring
against the backcloth of turmoil and uncertainty
generated by falling rolls, threats of redundancy,
the closure and re-organisation of schools, minimal
recruitment from initial training and other
'regressive educational offensives' to use Stuart
Hall's phrase (1983, p. 2). A cursory glance at
developments in Birmingham serves to demonstrate
this contradiction. Between 1982-84 the then
Conservative Council decided to increase resources
for multicultural/antiracist education. This contrasted with its general educational policy which
had seen the budget reduced savagely, the decision
to close some comprehensive schools and a worsening
of pupil-teacher ratios, despite falling rolls.

What are we to make of these developments, in
general, and the emergence of 'racialised' LEA
policy statements particularly? The overtly cynical
and/or deterministic marxian interpretation of

these policies would not seriously conceive of
these policies as change-agents: the policies
would be seen purely and simply as gestural, knee-
jerk reflexes to the 1980/81 disturbances. As such,
it could be pointed out that the policies tend to
be (deliberately) couched in what Murray Edelman
(1977) refers to as 'symbolic political language';
that is to say, phrases such as equality of opportunity are selected largely because of their
rhetorical power and their susceptibility to various meanings and intentions. Proponents of this
view, then, would say that the intention is to give
the impression to blacks and campaigning organisations that ameliorative action is being taken to
ensure that pupils of Afro-Caribbean and South
Asian pupils are not short-changed in their schooling. But, in reality, nothing is being changed and
the form of sloganising which is characteristic of
these policies simply obfuscates the main issues
and diverts attention away from the fundamental and
structural bases of inequality in capitalist society. This is precisely the argument advanced by
Brian Bullivant who emphasises the point that the
adoption of short-hand ideologies, such as equality
of opportunity,

> ... may maximize one advantage for those in
> control of education, namely, a reduction of
> guilt, but it does not escape the obvious
> charge that educational solutions by them-
> selves cannot bring about changes in the
> structure and strategies of social closure in
> society that result in massive inequalities
> and discrimination for those excluded on
> grounds of race, ethnicity and social class
> (1984, p. 110).

This view of the reformist measures taken in
support of multicultural/antiracist education
should not be discounted entirely. After all,
multiculturalism is an educational orthodoxy which
draws its life blood from the belief that schools
have the power not only to improve substantially
the academic achievement of non-white pupils but
also the potential to increase their life chances.
Despite the highly questionable status of these
assumptions they have been adopted, to a greater or
lesser extent, as the central propositions and
principles of LEA policy statements.
    Nevertheless, although many of the declared
aims of these policies and related initiatives are

open to critical scrutiny and are based on what
might be termed as a 'wishful thinking' approach,
it would be wrong to dismiss them entirely out of
hand. To do so might well presage a return to the
'colour blind' stance favoured, as we have seen, by
the majority of educationists until very recently.
As Bullivant has pointed out in his earlier book,
at the very least, critical educational sociologists (or as he puts it, 'counter-ideologists')
should insist that 'ideologists define their terms
and adopt theoretically respectable concepts if
they want to be taken seriously and have their
views accepted' (1981, p. 13). His prescriptive
advice is important and timely and in my other work
I have deliberately focussed attention on scrutin-
ising the rhetoric and conventional wisdom of
multicultural education as it is displayed in national and local government documents and statements
(see Troyna, 1983; 1984b; Troyna and Ball, 1983;
1984 and 1985). None of these interventions, however, has denied the fact that there are a number of
LEAs which are committed politically to legitimating
multiculturalism/antiracism as a principle and mode
of practice in their educational provision. And in
this scenario, LEA policy statements are generally
accorded a significant role in the diffusion and
institutionalisation of this educational orthodoxy.
They are endowed with the responsibility of height-
ening teachers' awareness of the pervasiveness of
racial inequality in education and are intended to
provide an institutional base and support for
corrective antiracist action.

I have already indicated that this development
is in contradistinction to broader political trends
in education and in the rest of this chapter I want
to elaborate this argument by pinpointing some of
the factors which currently militate against the
likelihood of multiculturalism/antiracism obtaining
a strong foothold in schools. In effect, I want to
highlight the difficulties which many practitioners
confront in their attempt to engage directly with
the notion(s) of multicultural/antiracist innovations in the current political and economic climate.
The empirical data which I will adduce to illustrate
and sustain my arguments derive from ongoing research in Manchester schools. The aim of the research is to examine the complex relationship between LEA policies and school based practices in
multicultural/antiracist education. Now it may be
that some of the difficulties experienced in
Manchester are not shared by teachers in other

parts of the country. The disruption caused by the
re-organisation of the secondary sector in that
Authority is an obvious case in point. Nevertheless, any such differences, especially in relation
to their impact on the day-to-day events in the
school, are likely to be in degree rather than
kind. After all, as Walter Roy has observed:

> At the beginning of the 1980s, the teaching
> profession has to work in an increasingly
> hostile environment. Successive cuts in
> educational expenditure, imposed by govern-
> ments and local authorities, coinciding with
> falling rolls, have produced a scarcity of
> jobs, both in primary and secondary schools,
> and mounting teacher unemployment. Those who
> have jobs feel less and less secure; conditions
> of service are worsening and prospects for
> promotion seem poor (1983, p. 1).

Other contributions in this volume demonstrate the
pertinence and veracity of Roy's observation.

'WE'RE ALL MUNCUNIANS AREN'T WE': MULTICULTURAL POLICIES IN ACTION

In June 1980, Manchester Education Committee approved the Chief Education Officer's policy statement, Education for a Multicultural Society and
subsequently circulated it to the heads and principals of all local education institutions.
Briefly, the statement alerted LEA employees to the
culturally varied nature of British society, a
demographic feature which also characterised
Manchester. In response to this fact, teachers
were encouraged to respond positively to the policy
statement and to base their practices and approaches on cultural pluralist grounds. What is
more, this policy was designed deliberately to
implicate all local schools, not simply those in
the inner areas of Manchester or which contained
an ethnically mixed pupil population. This last
point is significant because throughout the 1960s
and 1970s, multicultural (or multiracial) education tended to be discussed, if at all, as a
compensatory education initiative; a synonym for
the treatment of the special educational needs of
black pupils. Manchester's policy, however,
signified a move away from this narrow definition
and endorsed multiculturalism as an orthodoxy which
should permeate all educational institutions.

Wendy Ball and I have published the main results of this first phase of our research in Manchester schools and sixth form colleges elsewhere (1983; 1984). Briefly put, we had secured the support of local professional officers, elected members and representatives of the teacher unions to initiate a programme of research into the impact of the LEA's multicultural education policy on the consciousness and routine practices and procedures of headteachers and their senior members of staff. The first phase of the programme was carried out in 1983 and comprised interviews with 71 local headteachers in a variety of schools: secondary and primary; county and voluntary; inner city/ outer city and so on. The interviews crystallised around issues related to the heads' views of the Authority's policy and their personal and institutional responses to its main recommendations and principles. Had they, for instance, used any of the services and facilities provided by the LEA for the development of multicultural education? Did they intend to produce an anti-racist school policy or elect a member of staff to assume responsibility for multicultural matters in the school? Did they encourage members of staff to attend in-service courses in multicultural education? These and a range of similar questions figured prominently on the interview schedule and during our discussions with individual headteachers (which lasted anywhere between 30 minutes and three hours) we were able to build up a fairly precise profile of the extent to which the head had engaged with the LEA's policy statement and recommendations.

Our statistical analysis of the data was complemented by a wealth of qualitative material and showed that the Authority's policy and related initiatives had made a patchy and limited impact amongst these heads (who comprised, incidentally, 36 per cent of all local heads and principals). In all, 24 headteachers freely admitted that they had not gone out of their ways to encourage their staff to develop multicultural perspectives in their teaching; nor could they say that their schools were involved in multicultural education. These heads were all in schools in largely ethnically homogeneous areas of the Authority and they continued to conceive of multiculturalism as a 'device' for use only with black pupils. In the words of one head: 'There are few ethnic minority pupils here so we tend not to get involved'. According to another: 'If we got an influx of ethnic groups (sic) our attitude would change.'

It could be contended that the views of head-teachers are not necessarily an accurate indication of what goes on in the school; that developments along multicultural/antiracist lines might well be proceeding without the knowledge or formal endorse-ment of these headteachers. In one or two schools this may be the case. However, as other analyses of how innovations are introduced and managed in schools have shown '... it is usually the head-teacher who takes the initiative in introducing innovations into the school, and even where this is not the case his (sic) support is necessary for any innovation proposed by a member of staff' (Nicholls, 1983, p. 39). The headteacher then, defines the internal organisation, management and general ethos of the school; s/he is the pivot and focus of the school and in the absence of the head's support innovations can, at best, only proceed in an ad hoc manner, with little procedural, administrative or curricular consistency. As Manchester's working party on multicultural education in the secondary school curriculum recognised: 'If a policy is to stand any chance of success in a school, it must have the approval of the headteacher ... (1982, p. 70).

Our research, then, would seem to provide a fairly accurate indication of the impact (or lack of it) of Manchester's policy. At the risk of oversimplification, it would seem that the trend towards 'racialisation' in educational policy and discourse has had little influence on what takes place in a number of schools, especially those with ethnically homogeneous pupil populations. In those settings, headteachers often, if not always, dis-avowed any responsibility for the integration of multiculturalism into the practices and arrange-ments of their schools. Multicultural education continued to be defined as and confined to a pres-cription for reform in ethnically mixed schools, despite the LEA's policy intervention and 'pro-testations' for the contrary. How, then, do we account for a pattern of responses which, to all intents and purposes, corresponds with the findings of a similar survey carried out ten years ago, during the phase of 'racial inexplicitness' in education (Townsend and Brittan, 1972)?

Other researchers and commentators on this issue have focussed on racism embedded within the teaching profession as the central operative var-iable in differential responses to multicultural education (see Troyna 1984c for discussion). There is certainly considerable evidence to suggest that some teachers are opposed to multicultural education, purely and simply on racist grounds (see Schools Council, 1978; Brittan, 1976 for example). Our research, however, did not engage directly with attempts to explicate such attitudes from headteachers or to subject their views systematically to conventional modes of attitude measurement. Nevertheless, it seems likely that at least some of the heads we spoke to were racist if only because as the Rampton Committee pointed out: 'Since a profession of nearly half a million people must to a great extent reflect the attitudes of society at large there must inevitably be some teachers who hold explicitly racist views' (1981, p. 12). What we did find in the course of our discussions was a tendency for some heads to articulate less overtly hostile views based, nonetheless, on racist assumptions. Consider the view of one headteacher who insisted that multiculturalism was a divisive ideology and that, 'We're all Mancunians aren't we?' or another who told us that one of the main aims of education should be to ensure that 'all people are integrated into one whole society' and that multiculturalism should be discouraged because it was anathema to this ideal. As I pointed out earlier, sentiments such as these, based on a 'colour blind' perspective which is seemingly innocuous, even benign, actually reflect a racist definition of reality. Further, they prompt actions and practices which discriminate against black pupils. Reeves makes a similar point when he writes: 'The stubborn refusal to see the way a social system operates on racial lines may support and maintain racially discriminatory practices' (1983, p. 175). What Reeves and I are saying here is that 'colour blind' approaches in education constitute a classic example of institutionalised forms of racism, in the way the concept is defined by A.K. Spears (1978).

Attitudes, then, constitute one of the factors inhibiting the penetration of multiculturalism into schools and negative racial attitudes were certainly most common amongst the 24 'non-involved' heads in our sample. But perhaps this is not entirely surprising when seen in relation to the personal biographies of these heads (and many of their colleagues, I suspect). To begin with, they trained as teachers and spent their formative years in the profession when race matters were discussed

rarely and, even then, in assimilationist terms.
That is, teachers were actively encouraged by the
DES, LEAs and their teacher unions to diminish the
significance of ethnic and cultural differences in
their classrooms. In effect, the assimilationist
ideology became an integral element of teachers'
professional values. What is more, the vast majority of these heads have taught in ethnically
homogeneous schools, settings where, as I mentioned
before, multicultural education was thought to have
little relevance until very recently. As such,
their contact with philosophies on multicultural
education has remained partial and indirect and
their commitment to assimilation allowed to continue, almost unchallenged.

Against this background, then, it is unlikely
that they would respond enthusiastically or
immediately to recommendations for action based on
multicultural grounds. Simply put, it is a philosophy which contradicts some of their deeply en-
trenched professional values. Ken Young and Naomi
Connelly specify the dilemma facing these teachers
in substantially the same terms:

> ... since the late 1970s, the concept of
> cultural pluralism has accumulated more
> support, and assimilationist policies have
> been viewed as a threat to a desirable
> diversity of cultures. Thus, more recently,
> it has been argued that schools should go
> some way to reinforce some of the very char-
> acteristics that in the past they had sought
> to chance (1981, p. 122).

The suggestion then is that the opposition to
multicultural/antiracist education may have less to
do with the innate political conservatism and
racism of these heads than with deeply embedded
professional values. The view of one headteacher
who reckoned that non-white groups 'are maintaining
differences and making demands which are harmful'
exemplifies the discrepancy which is more generally
perceived between assimilation and cultural pluralism. The same head went on to insist, 'I'm for
integration' therefore implying that the cultural
pluralist approach favoured by the LEA was contrary
to this goal.

In all, this discussion shows that attitudes
on race do constitute a fairly formidable barrier
to the penetration of multicultural/antiracist
dimensions into school. At the same time, racial

attitudes do not explain the pattern of responses entirely. Multicultural education is an innovatory educational philosophy which, though difficult to define in a way which would attract consensual agreement, nevertheless signifies to most educationists a systematic reformulation and reappraisal of what takes place procedurally in schools. Now, even in favourable political and economic circumstances, the maintenance of curricular and pedagogic procedures is the dominant activity in schools. Innovation, on the other hand, generally has to wait for what Ken Shaw calls 'a happy conjunction of surplus resources, internal initiative and a strong external stimulus in the form of a problem to be solved' (Shaw, 1977, p. 46). This 'happy conjunction' is certainly not an apt description of what is happening in schools today. What is more, those in ethnically homogeneous schools simply do not perceive multiculturalism as an apposite philosophy or set of practices. As we have seen, its conception as an educational approach to black pupils continues to prevail in the eyes of a sizeable number of teachers; therefore, in all white schools the 'strong external stimulus in the form of a problem to be solved' (i.e. black pupils) simply does not exist. Put bluntly, there is no discernable incentive to adopt, let alone prioritise, multicultural education in these schools.

This tendency to accord multiculturalism low priority (especially in ethnically homogeneous settings) is of course underlined, even justified, by other factors, especially the cutback on expenditure and resources. As the HMI report on the effects of LEA expenditure policies on schools in 1982 acknowledged: 'The professional commitment and resourcefulness of teachers' continues to be stretched simply by 'the efforts needed to maintain the status quo ...' (1983, p. 13). This is particularly the case in Manchester where the disruptive effects of re-organisation of secondary schools - and the protracted discussions between the LEA and DES over the scheme - continue to be felt (see Fiske, 1982; Whitworth, 1983). Re-organisation naturally involved the closure of some schools, amalgamation of others, the redeployment of staff, voluntary redundancies and so on. As part of our study we also found that few of the headteachers we spoke with had any lengthy experience of the role and that even fewer had been heads of their present school for more than three years.[3] In effect, then, these headteachers were relatively inexperienced in the role and were having to come to grips with the management of an unfamiliar school and staff. It is against this background of instability, limited resources, inexperience and worsening employment conditions that the partial impact of the Authority's policy on schools has to be placed. As Len Barton and Stephen Walker observe, headteachers and their staff are being encouraged to develop innovatory policies and practices along multicultural lines at a time when they are also being required to cope with the management of a system in contraction: '... cutbacks, higher teacher-pupil ratios, lack of equipment and an extension in their teaching role' (1983, p. 7). In the words of one head, teaching staff are currently 'on the edge of incompetence'. That is to say, the professional competence and effectiveness of teachers is being seriously threatened by the diminution of resources, a worsening of employment conditions and the problems generally engendered by Thatcherite education policies.

FROM 'EVANGELICAL' TO POLITICAL AND EDUCATIONAL APPROACHES TO MULTICULTURALISM

> Multicultural education is like virtue; everyone's in favour of it (LEA adviser)

> I get the impression that it is because of recent events such as the riots that multicultural education has been forced on us for political reasons (Secondary headteacher).

Perhaps above all else, the 1980 and 1981 civil disturbances signified an unwillingness by those designated as racial minorities to passively accept and tolerate their subordination and oppression in the UK. They demonstrated, not for the first time, that although equality of opportunity was enshrined as an article of faith in the UK's post-war welfare state, it remains a sham: an almost totally unrealisable goal.

The response from national and local government to the disturbances and the conditions which precipitated their eruption has been slow and largely ineffectual. Lord Scarman had recommended 'urgent action' by government to ensure that the events in Brixton, Bristol, Toxteth and elsewhere were not repeated. But, as John Benyon has commented, three years on there is scant evidence of such 'urgent action' either to improve the quality of life in the inner cities or to ameliorate the pervasiveness of racial disadvantage and discrimination (1984, p. 234). Even in education, a sphere of social policy which has tended to respond more vigorously to the fact of racial inequality than many others, it is important not to over-estimate developments. The DES, as I said earlier, has done little to promote the notion of anti-racist education; the overwhelming majority of LEAs do not have either formal policies or advisers on multicultural/antiracist education and black people are still largely excluded from positions of authority and power in the education system. Moreover, the evidence adduced from the study in Manchester has shown that, even in Authorities which have formally accorded race matters a relatively high profile in their policy approaches, the issues surrounding antiracist education continue to be selectively and differentially considered in local schools. To put it bluntly, such policies have failed perceptibly in their role as catalysts of change; those in ethnically homogeneous schools continue to go about their business as usual and seem impervious to persuasion.

So far in this chapter I have concentrated on those factors found on the 'chalk face' which have conspired to prevent a more positive and uniform reaction to the LEA's policy. An alternative, or complementary, critique might focus on the style of intervention; along these lines it could be argued that a laissez-faire approach which devolved ultimate responsibility for initiatives and action to individual heads and their staff was always bound to fail. What is needed, in other words, is a coherent plan for implementation which would comprise some form of monitoring procedure. Indeed, one or two LEAs are currently adopting this approach and have informed local heads that discernible evidence of antiracist education in their schools is required, in the form of formal school policies. Now, I have severe reservations about this approach especially at a time when there are moves toward centralism and the accountability movement in education is on the rise (Troyna and Ball, 1985).

The discrepancy between multicultural/antiracist policy and practice seems to me to derive less from styles of policy intervention than from

the need to convince educationists of the educational and political value, necessity and efficacy
of this new orthodoxy. As we have seen, current
circumstances are not conducive to educational
innovation and even if they were it would be
completely utopian, as Richard Hatcher and Jane
Shallice remark, to expect multicultural/antiracist
education 'to steadily spread through the school
system by the normal process of curriculum innovation' (1983, p. 15). Such processes are
naturally important and I have suggested elsewhere
that their significance in the sphere of multi-
cultural/antiracist education have not been
adequately considered (Troyna, 1984c). But, it is
also important to specify in clear and precise
terms the rationale for and objectives of multi-
cultural/antiracist education. Perhaps the barrier
to change is not as daunting as many people tend to
believe. The majority in a national sample of
teachers recently stated that they wanted a stand
taken against racist attitudes in the classroom
(TES, 27 May 1983) and in Manchester over 90 per
cent of the headteachers interviewed said they were
in favour of the Authority's policy on multicultural education. These data suggest that multi-
cultural/antiracist education has not been rejected
entirely by those on the 'chalk face'. What they
do indicate is the success achieved by those who
have routinely promoted multicultural education as
'a good thing'; a 'gospel of educational salvation'.
This 'evangelical approach' to multicultural
education, as Dorn calls it (1983, p. 5), now needs
to be superceded by a strategy which specifies the
political and educational justification for a
radical reformulation of policy, practice and professional values. I have shown in this chapter
that conditions are not conducive to such radical
departures from existing practice; that the maintenance of such practices constitutes the overwhelming activity in a period of contraction. Nor
do the vicious attacks on the new orthodoxy from
members of the New Right, such as Anthony Flew
(1984),facilitate the struggle. For these reasons
a change in strategy and argument by anti-racists
is imperative if this new orthodoxy is to secure a
permanent and permeating grip in the UK's education
system. To be sure, even a reappraisal of strategy
will be insufficient to change radically the in-
iquities and inequalities which characterise and
pervade the society. Such tasks are simply beyond
the power of education. Nevertheless, without

this reformulated strategy the structures and practices which perpetuate and legitimate racial inequality in education will remain intact and continue to operate with impunity. As anti-racist educationists, then, this is where our struggle must begin.

Acknowledgements
Wendy Ball, John Solomos and Geoffrey Walford all commented on an earlier draft of this chapter and many of the points they raised have been included in this final version. What remains, however, is entirely my own responsibility.

NOTES

1.   A table outlining the major educational policy responses to the presence of black pupils in British schools (1962-1980) appears in Troyna (1982, pp. 140-141).
2.   See Dorn and Troyna (1982) for a critique of Kirp's appraisal of the 'racially inexplicit' policy approach.
3.   In the sample of headteachers, 42 (60 per cent) had held the position for less than five years and 46 (65.7 per cent) had been head of their present school for less than three years.

REFERENCES

Banks, J. (1981) Multiethnic Education: Theory and Practice, Allyn and Bacon, Boston
Barton, L. and Walker, S. (1983) 'Introduction' in L. Barton and S. Walker (eds.), Race, Class and Education, Croom Helm, Beckenham, pp. 1-9.
Ben-Tovim, G. and Gabriel, J. (1984) Marxist Approaches to Race Relations. Paper presented to the conference on Theories of Ethnic and Race Relations, St. Catherine's College, Oxford (March)
Benyon, J. (1984) 'Scarman and after' in J. Benyon (ed.), Scarman and After: Essays Reflecting on Lord Scarman's Report, The Riots and Their Aftermath, Pergamon Press, Oxford, pp. 233-243
Bullivant, B. (1981) The Pluralist Dilemma in Education, Allen and Unwin, Sydney
Bullivant, B. (1984) Pluralism: Cultural Maintenance and Evolution, Multilingual Matters Ltd., Clevedon

Cashmore, E.E. and Troyna, B. (1983) Introduction to Race Relations, Routledge and Kegan Paul, London

Committee of Inquiry into the Education of Children from Ethnic Minority Groups (Rampton Committee, (1981) West Indian Children in Our Schools, (Interim Report), HMSO, London, Cmnd. 8273

Department of Education and Science (1983) Report by Her Majesty's Inspectors on the Effects of Local Authority Expenditure Policies on the Education Service in England - 1982, HMSO, London

Dorn, A. (1983) 'LEA policies on multiracial education', Multiethnic Education Review, Vol. 2, No. 2. pp. 3-5

Dorn, A. and Troyna, B. (1982) 'Multiracial education and the politics of decision making', Oxford Review of Education, Vol. 8, No. 2, pp. 175-185

Edelman, M. (1977) Political Language: Words that Succeed and Policies that Fail, Academic Press, New York

Fiske, D. (1982) Reorganisation of Secondary Education in Manchester, University of London Institute of Education, Bedford Way Papers 9, London

Flew, A. (1984) Education, Race and Revolution, Centre for Policy Studies, London

Gay, G. (1983) 'Multiethnic education: historical developments and future prospects', Phi Delta Kappan, Vol. 64, No. 8, pp. 560-563

Hall, S. (1983) 'Education in Crisis' in A.M. Wolpe and J. Donald (eds.), Is There Anyone Here from Education? Pluto Press, London, pp. 2-10

Hatcher, R. and Shallice, J. (1983) 'The politics of anti-racist education', Multiracial Education, Vol. 12, No. 1, pp. 3-21

Jones, K. (1983) Beyond Progressive Education, Macmillan, London

Kirp, D. (1979) Doing Good by Doing Little, University of California Press, London

Manchester Education Department (1982) Reviewing the Secondary Curriculum: Working Party F: Education for a Multicultural Society, Education Department, Manchester

Nicholls, A. (1983) Managing Educational Innovations, Allen and Unwin, London

Reeves, F. (1983) British Racial Discourse: A Study of British Political Discourse About

Race and Race-Related Matters, Cambridge
University Press, Cambridge

Roy, W. (1983) Teaching under Attack, Croom Helm,
Beckenham

Scarman, Lord (1981) The Brixton Disorders 10-12
April 1981, HMSO, London, Cmnd. 8427

Select Committee on Race Relations and Immigration
(1969) The Problems of Coloured School
Leavers, HMSO, London

Shaw, K. (1978) 'Managing the curriculum in con-
traction' in C. Richards (ed.), Power and the
Curriculum: Issues in Curriculum Studies,
Nafferton Books, Driffield, pp. 40-50

Spears, A.K. (1978) 'Institutional racism and the
education of blacks', Anthropology and Education Quarterly, Vol. 9, No. 2, pp. 127-136

Tomlinson, S. (1981) 'Inexplicit policies in race
and education', Educational Policy Bulletin,
Vol. 9, No. 2, pp. 149-166

Townsend, H.E.R. and Brittan, E. (1972)
Organization in Multiracial Schools, N.F.E.R.,
Slough

Troyna, B. (1982) 'The ideological and policy
response to black pupils in British schools'
in A. Hartnett (ed.), The Social Sciences in
Educational Studies, Heinemann Educational
Books, London, pp. 127-143 (Paperback
edition 1984)

Troyna, B. (1984a) 'Multicultural education:
emancipation or containment?' in L. Barton
and S. Walker (eds.), Social Crisis and
Educational Research, Croom Helm, Beckenham,
pp. 75-97

Troyna, B. (1984b) '"Policy entrepreneurs" and the
development of LEA multiethnic education
policies: a reconstruction', Educational
Management and Administration, Vol. 12 No. 3
pp. OO-OC

Troyna, B. (1984c) The Great Divide: Policies and
Practice in Multicultural Education. Paper
presented to the 10th annual conference of the
British Educational Research Association,
Lancaster University (August)

Troyna, B. and Ball, W. (1983) 'Multicultural
education policies: are they worth the paper
they're written on?' Times Educational
Supplement, 9 December, p. 23

Troyna, B. and Ball, W. (1984) 'Multicultural
education policy in practice', Runnymede Trust
Bulletin, Race and Immigration, No. 166
(April), pp. 7-15

Troyna, B. and Ball, W. (1985) 'Styles of LEA policy intervention in multicultural/anti-racist education', Educational Review, Vol. 37, No. 2

Whitworth, R. (1983) 'Falling rolls in Manchester: the authority's response', Secondary Education Journal, Vol. 13, No. 3, pp. 19-21

Williams, J. (1967) 'The younger generation' in J. Rex and R. Moore, Race, Community and Conflict, Institute of Race Relations/Oxford University Press, Oxford, pp. 230-257

Young, K. (1984) 'The challenge to local government' in J. Benyon (ed.), Scarman and After: Essays Reflecting on Lord Scarman's Report, The Riots and Their Aftermath, Pergamon Press, Oxford, pp. 220-229

Young, K. and Connelly, N. (1981) Policy and Practice in the Multiracial City, Policy Studies Institute, London

Chapter Three

TEACHERS LEARNING ABOUT INDUSTRY: THE TWO
CURRICULA AND CULTURAL DISADVANTAGE

Richard Thompson and Geoffrey Walford

In the last few years the study of industry
and commerce has become one of the few growth areas
in the school curriculum. A succession of reports
and papers from government, industry and various
educational organisations has led to considerable
financial investment in the area from both Local
Education Authorities and industry which, in turn,
has led to a boom in school-industry liaison
schemes and major additions of 'industrially related' material to the curriculum.
There is now a large number of separate
organisations working in their own, sometimes dis-
parate, ways to maintain and enlarge the foothold
that has been gained within schools. The CRAC
Insight Programme, for example, aims to increase
understanding of the demands of management through
business games and role play, while Young Enterprise encourages the formation of real productive
companies in which groups of teenagers design,
manufacture and sell products or supply services.
Many Local Education Authorities now have their own
School-Industry Liaison Officers, who are able to
work within a growing national network of SATROs
(Science and Technology Regional Organisations).
In some areas, the curriculum now includes periods
of work experience in manufacturing industry or
commerce (Watts, 1983). Two of the largest and
most influential bodies involved in encouraging
education-industry liaison are the Schools Council
Industry Project (SCIP) (Jamieson and Lightfoot,
1982) which has the backing of both the CBI and the
TUC, and the Understanding British Industry project
(UBI) which is backed by the CBI and which is the
subject of detailed study in this chapter.
At first sight there would seem to be a severe
contradiction between the growth of courses and

schemes designed to better equip young people for work, and the facts of growing youth and adult unemployment. It might be expected that there would be growth in leisure education rather than in that designed for non-existent work. Contradiction there certainly is, yet Reeder (1979) has indicated that the development of industry courses is not unexpected at times of economic recession. He shows that the debate about the nature and extent of the relationship between education and industry is not new and that since the Industrial Revolution there have been repeated criticisms from industrial representatives about the educational system's lack of concern for industry's perceived requirements in terms of a skilled, motivated and well-disciplined workforce. Further, such criticisms have intensified during periods when Britain has been economically out-performed by competing countries and when it has also been undergoing structural change. Reeder argues that it was thus to be expected that the present deepening economic recession and massive changes in the nature of work due to changing technology, would lead to renewed pressure from industry on education and greater questioning of the nature and purpose of education.

James Callaghan's Ruskin College speech of 1976, which launched the 'Great Debate' on education, must be seen as a key event. While some have argued that, in terms of opening a debate as such, the speech was more rhetoric than reality (see for example Salter and Tapper (1981), Ginsburg, Meyenn and Miller (1979)), it was certainly used as a legitimisation for the present highly active phase in the development of education-industry initiatives. Since that speech in 1976 it has become acceptable to cast a large amount of the blame for Britain's poor economic performance on to the schools, which are seen as having an excessively academic curriculum and not providing pupils with the basic skills that are required by industry and commerce. In the words of Sir John Methven, Director General of the Confederation of British Industries:

> The fact remains that after one of the longest periods of compulsory education in Europe many young people seem ill equipped for almost any kind of employment and woefully ignorant about the basic facts. (Methven, 1976).

These comments were echoed in the report Curriculum
11-16:

> The curriculum of the school must reflect the
> needs of this new industrial Britain ... only
> a minority of schools convey adequately to
> their pupils the fact that ours is an
> industrial society - a mixed economy, that we
> depend upon industry to create wealth, without
> which our social services, education and arts
> could not flourish. (DES, 1977)

And, as Cathcart and Esland (1983) relate, 'in
spite of the deepening recession after 1979 and the
collapse of the youth labour market, this message
continues to prevail'. For example, the Director
General of the National Economic Development
Council has recently reinforced his belief that:

> There is a widespread concern in industry that
> the educational system does not provide a
> general training which adequately prepares
> young people for work. This is strengthened
> by the apparently low priority which education
> accords industry through its curricula,
> emphasis on academic attainment, and very
> limited awareness of, or links with, industry.
> (NEDC, 1982)

It might be argued that this last comment was, by
1982, somewhat unjustified. For by then industry
had begun to boom as a growth area in schools. The
increase in the number of special link schemes
between education and industry, for example, had
been so dramatic that a special report had been
commissioned by the DES to enquire into the schemes
currently in operation and to make recommendations
as to how their work could be more effectively coordinated (Cooper, 1981).
    Whilst agreeing with Reeder (1979) about the
recurring nature of increased concern for greater
education-industry links, Wood (1983) argues that
the education and industry debate has now moved
into a distinctive new phase which has major
differences from any similar period. He argues
that the present economic recession, with the worst
youth unemployment levels since the 1930s, has had
a major part to play in creating an atmosphere in
which traditional values and procedures can be
questioned. For those in employment, the unprecedented rate of technical change, causing

traditional skills to become obsolete and forcing rapid social change, has had a similar effect. The pressures for change within schools have increased considerably and criticisms of curriculum content and methods of teaching have become both more specific and more orchestrated. But of greater importance is the fact that, in the last few years, those pushing for change have been able to establish organisational bases and that there is now a political demand for change.

In this chapter we look in detail at one scheme sponsored by Understanding British Industry which was designed to encourage teaching about industry and commerce in schools by way of year-long secondments for selected teachers. We examine the ideological underpinnings of the scheme, and the ways in which those ideological messages were transmitted to teachers who took part in the scheme. First, however, it is necessary to outline the nature of the specific scheme and its sponsoring body, UBI.

THE UNDERSTANDING BRITISH INDUSTRY SCHEME

In 1976 the Confederation of British Industry (CBI) established the CBI Educational Foundation, which is a company limited by guarantee and a registered charity. The Foundation, in 1977, set up the Understanding British Industry project (UBI) which had the overall objective of providing closer links between education and industry. The project has a particular emphasis on teachers and pupils in the 13 to 16 age group and aims to help them 'to become more aware of the part which industry and commerce play in the social and economic life of the United Kingdom' (UBI, 1978).

Although UBI has a Headquarters and Resources Centre at Oxford, the emphasis has been on 'bridge building' between education and industry, which has meant that the majority of resources, both human and material, have been devoted to work at the local level. Nine Regions had been established by 1983, each with its own Regional Liaison Officer and, in association with Local Education Authorities, a network of Satellite Resource Centres had been provided.

Understanding British Industry is not a curriculum development project in the accepted sense. While it does aim to encourage teaching about industry and commerce within and throughout the school curriculum, it does not aim to produce

curriculum materials or directly initiate specific
curriculum changes itself. Nor is it concerned
with industrial careers recruitment. Instead, it
aims to encourage curriculum development through
working closely with teachers, schools, Local
Education Authorities and the many other interested bodies. The emphasis is on influencing the
school curriculum through influencing school
teachers, and a major aspect of this policy has
come to be the encouragement of in-service training
for teachers about industry. It was perceived that
even where schools and LEAs were keen to develop an
industrial component to the curriculum, this was
difficult because, as the Director of UBI put it,
'Few teachers are secure enough in their knowledge
of industry and commerce to be able to teach it
effectively' (Nisbet, 1979). UBI has thus worked
on the assumption that there should be an expansion of secondment schemes for teachers into
industry, and that these enable teachers to deepen
their experience and knowledge of industry through
direct involvement.

Teacher secondment schemes into industry are
not, in themselves, new. There is now a range of
different schemes which have been in operation for
many years. In 1980/81, for example, some 960
teachers took part in industrial secondments of
some form (UBI, 1982). However, practically all of
these secondments were for very short periods,
typically only a week or so, and were aimed at the
normal classroom teacher. The UBI scheme, on the
other hand, is atypical in that it is aimed at
senior status teachers and lasts an entire year.

This article results from an evaluation of the
early stages of the secondment scheme, which was
conducted from September 1981 to April 1983. The
evaluation itself, which was funded by British
Petroleum through a Research Fellowship, is reported in full elsewhere (Thompson and Walford, 1983)
and dealt with fifteen year-long teacher secondments that had occurred in three West Midlands
Local Education Authorities. Essentially, it took
an illuminative approach to evaluation (Parlett and
Hamilton, 1972), and attempted to discover and
document what it was like to participate in the
scheme from the point of view of the various people
involved. Thus over 100 semi-structured interviews
were conducted with teachers, headteachers, LEA
administrative officers and advisers, representatives from each of the industries accepting a
secondee, and with the seconded teachers them-

selves. All of the schools and all of the
industries involved were visited, and, in some of
the schools, teaching associated with industry was
observed. Two schools where substantial development had occurred were chosen for intensive case
study.

While the evaluation report did identify the
scheme's most significant features and failings,
and did give a list of recommendations, it left
largely unquestioned the basic assumptions on which
the scheme rested. The evaluation and recommendations were limited to the performance of the
scheme in the light of the original aims set for
it. While some more critical comments have been
made elsewhere (Thompson, 1984), in this article
we hope to raise some wider questions about the
scheme and its possible effects on teachers and
schooling. Although the evaluation was directly
concerned with only fifteen secondments in the
West Midlands, it is of much more general interest
than this small number would suggest. For UBI has
sponsored similar schemes for schoolteacher
secondments throughout the country, all of which
have been predicated on a similar ideology of
education and industry. In addition, as UBI is one
of the major bodies working in the area of educ-
ation/industry liaison, its ideology has been
widely influential.

The secondment scheme was predicated upon two
central assumptions:
1.   That a major problem underlying teaching
      about industry is that of lack of teacher
      understanding and knowledge about industry.
2.   That dissemination of teacher understanding
      acquired through a long-term secondment is
      most effectively conveyed through the school's
      hierarchical structure. The secondment scheme
      is based upon the concept of 'influence' and
      has hence been targeted on senior members of
      a school's staff, generally of head of
      department or senior 'management' status.

Although UBI has increasingly come to recognise
that the process of incorporating the teachers'
industrial experience into the school curriculum
may be a difficult and slow process, a prime
pre-requisite of successful curriculum development was perceived to be the depth and quality of
the knowledge and experience acquired by the
teacher during the placement year. The industrial
year was therefore structured by a series of

learning objectives set out by UBI in a document used to brief teachers, LEAs, schools and host companies. These objectives may be said to represent a formal curriculum of industrial learning, and are set out clearly in UBI (1980).

The notion of the 'formal' curriculum may be set against that of what has come to be termed the 'hidden' curriculum. The formal curriculum of secondary schooling has been defined as a series of subjects, or more generally of learning experiences which are deliberately planned and structured. The 'hidden' curriculum, on the other hand, is concerned with the social and ideological messages transmitted by the school, and with the development of expectations and attitudes.

The term 'hidden' curriculum has been used to describe this curriculum which is not formally intended or planned, and whose long-term social effects may not be perceived. However, the extent to which this curriculum is hidden and unintended is perhaps open to question. Many teachers would concede that the development of attitudes as well as intellectual skills is a fundamental aspect of their work. Similarly, as we have seen, many recent documents from DES and HMI have focussed upon the importance of preparing children for adult and working roles and thereby equipping them with 'appropriate' skills and attitudes. In certain contexts the essential distinction between the two curricula of schooling is one of the degree of formality and of intent, thus formal/informal, rather than formal/hidden, may be a more useful dichotomy.

However, this basic distinction is certainly helpful in enabling us to understand the different types of learning which took place during the one-year teacher secondment scheme.

The formal industrial curriculum stressed the acquisition of knowledge, understanding and experience. The series of learning objectives established for the scheme may be appropriately summarised by the following overriding aim:

> The teachers on the scheme aim to acquire a
> better understanding of industry and commerce.
> (UBI, 1980).

The concept of industrial understanding is thus placed at the heart of placement year.

However, as the evaluation progressed, it became increasingly clear that there was an

informal curriculum which was perhaps more powerful in the minds of many of the participants than
the formal agenda. This agenda did not find
expression in the official objectives for the
scheme. At its centre was the question of teacher
attitude towards industry.

Reviewing the general field of school/industry
liaison work, Bell (1981) has argued that this
activity is based upon the largely accepted
assumption that teacher attitude towards industry
varies between the actively hostile to the mildly
unsympathetic. It became clear from the evidence
of interviews conducted with industrial personnel
responsible for the organisation of secondments in
host companies that there was in fact a broad
consensus amongst them about the allegedly negative
effects teachers had upon pupil attitudes towards
industry in general, and towards industrial careers
in particular. There was a strong feeling that
pupils, especially able ones, were diverted from
taking up an industrial career option. Teachers
were perceived to be either ignorant of or
unsympathetic towards industry and its requirements.

The following informal expectations of the
secondment scheme voiced by one industrial training manager would have commanded assent across the
whole field of industrial personnel interviewed:

> What I wanted the secondee to take back to
> school was the notion that industry offers
> opportunities at all levels and to affect
> teachers' attitudes positively towards
> industry from what I consider to be a pretty
> low base.

It is worth noting that, though this view of
teachers' attitudes was unanimously held by
industrial personnel interviewed, there is, in
fact, very little evidence for its veracity.
Jamieson and Lightfoot (1982), in their study of
attitudes, found that pupils had much more negative
attitudes than teachers, and that teachers held
more negative and equivocal attitudes on Trade
Unions than on industry.

THE FORMAL CURRICULUM OF INDUSTRIAL LEARNING

It is possible to identify two basic principles
upon which the formal curriculum was based.
1. That learning about industry is most
   effectively accomplished through experiential

learning. The teachers were allocated specific industrial tasks to perform, Learning hence took place largely through doing, rather than through observation or formal study.

2. That learning about industry can take place effectively and primarily through in-depth experience of one company.

The industrial or commercial companies involved used a variety of different structured patterns in their attempts to achieve these formal curriculum aims. In four of the fifteen secondments the teacher spent the whole of his or her year in one particular task-orientated job, with only limited periods being given to structured observation of other jobs and activities. Eight more of the teachers were again involved primarily in task orientated jobs, but were shifted during the year so that they experienced from two to four separate jobs. These teachers also spent some short time observing. The remaining three teachers experienced unique organisational patterns for their secondment. One had a highly structured year comprising fifteen different components related in detail to the UBI objectives, while the other two had a mixture of task orientated work and extended periods of observation.

DOING A JOB AND LEARNING ABOUT THE COMPANY

It was claimed that, within the limitations imposed by the organisational patterns chosen by the company, all of the teachers were treated as far as possible as 'normal' employees of the company. They were, for example, subject to the same working conditions as employees working at an equivalent grade. Consistent with this, teachers and company officials stressed that the tasks allocated were not devised to isolate the teacher from the pressures of a business environment. It was asserted that the work undertaken was selected and designed to approximate as closely as possible to 'authentic' industrial experiences. Indeed, personnel from some companies stressed that one of the objectives they had established for the secondment was that tasks of commercial worth should be accomplished by the teacher.

It must be said, of course, that in many significant ways, the industrial experience offered in fact differed from that of the normal employee.

The secondment structures outlined demonstrate this, as it was clearly the aim of industrial personnel to include a variety of 'work experience' in the programme. Several secondments were, in fact, designed to incorporate direct experience of the broad categories of work performed in the company. The remarks of one company personnel director illustrate this particular structure:

> There are basically three kinds of work done in this company: shop floor, clerical and managerial. It was our aim that (the secondee) should sample these three types. We put the stress on the first as that is where most pupils find jobs.

In a few cases, however, there were constraints internal to the company with regard to the 'work experience' roles the teachers performed. For example, in one company, there was fairly strong trades union pressure, which made it impossible to include working on the shop floor as an integral part of the experience. Managerial experience itself was also rarely made available, although the majority of the roles performed were management oriented and related.

The situation and roles of the teachers also differed in several other respects from those of the 'normal employee'. All of the teachers were, for example, involved to some extent in observation as opposed to doing. A number of teachers asserted they were privy to much information which might not have been made available to many employees. In addition, two special characteristics of practically all the secondments were cited by teachers as facilitating an understanding of the company. First, the close liaison with company personnel, especially those designated responsibility for the design and administration of the secondment. Such staff were almost always drawn from management, or education and training departments. Secondly, the freedom of access and movement accorded within the company.

When company personnel were asked whether they felt that the teachers had achieved an overall 'grasp' of the company they responded, not surprisingly, largely in the affirmative. Yet the concept of understanding implied in many of the replies was matter-of-fact and circumscribed. Understanding seemed to imply knowing how the company worked on a day-to-day basis and, perhaps significantly, it appeared to imply a 'top down' view of the company. The following comment by one industrial training manager is telling:

> To achieve that (i.e. a high level of under-
> standing) you'd have to be sitting with the
> managing director.

This respondent went on to make the point, however, that the level of understanding achieved by the teacher was 'good enough for teachers'.

UNDERSTANDING THE COMPANY, UNDERSTANDING INDUSTRY

If one accepts that the level of understanding of the company implied in both teacher and industrial personnel responses is an appropriate one for the scheme, the question still remains, of course, as to the degree to which such understanding is applicable to industry generally. The scheme's 'formal curriculum' stressed objectives relating to industry in general, rather than to specific individual companies. 'Company understanding' is thus a means to an end - that of more general industrial understanding.

When the teachers were asked what they had learned about the company and more generally about industry, the responses almost invariably focussed upon two areas. The first one was that their role had enabled them to develop insights into what was variously termed 'the culture of working life', 'the human side of industry', 'the feel of in-dustry'. This was achieved through introspection on their own reactions to their roles and the observation of industrial colleagues. It was quite noticeable from their replies that it was an 'industrial' rather than a 'company' perspective which was stressed, although, in fact, their ex-perience was of one company. No teacher talked of the possibility that their experience might have been idiosyncratic or that their reaction to their roles was not typical of other 'employees'. The other area most frequently stressed concerned the technicalities of business organisation and prod-uction, in particular departmental organisation, management practice and company training policy and procedures. Here, however, the teachers generally recognised the limitations of their experience and the expressed perspective was a 'company' as op-posed to an 'industry' one.

The scheme itself made attempts to broaden the
teachers' experience by bringing together the
teachers as a group on a number of occasions during
the year and subsequently. At these times,
teachers were able to discuss and make comparisons
across participating companies. Additionally,
some teachers made contacts with other companies
through the jobs they performed.

The industrial personnel from several
companies also argued that certain features common
to a broad range of companies, especially those
relating to organisational structure and commercial
outlook, could be identified. One company training manager expressed the following typical view-
point:

> I think that any medium sized company would
> have a similar range of functions and depart-
> ments as us. There will probably be a
> different emphasis, but I'm sure you'll find
> most companies have similar values and
> structures.

Hence, it was felt that experience of one company
did constitute a rudimentary basis for an understanding of the broader perspective.

However, while there were felt to be broad
similarities, it was the fairly general feeling
of both teachers and company personnel that
companies differed quite considerably in detail.
Although personnel from some companies expressed
the view that their company could be said to be
representative of a particular type of company,
it was generally felt that a company typical of
industry as such was a chimera.

Even if it were possible to gain a high level
of technical understanding of one company, it is
clear that this could not necessarily be translated
into a high level of understanding of industry
generally.

THE PROCESS OF UNDERSTANDING AND EXPERIENTIAL
LEARNING

The teachers were asked to comment on their
industrial year from the point of view of the
manner in which they learnt about their company and
about industry. It was not surprising that
practically all were strongly in favour of learning
through experience. Understanding was perceived to
have 'emerged' over a period of time partly as a

result of immersion in particular tasks, and partly
through discussion with company personnel. Almost
all the teachers attended a company induction
course which, in many cases, treated such topics as
company history, organisation, working conditions
etc. Nevertheless, it was the perception of
practically all the teachers that any understanding
so acquired only became meaningful through subsequent experience. One teacher put this position
quite neatly:

> I got a feel of the company through the
> course, but it was only at the end of the year
> that I'd managed to put flesh on the bones.

Almost all the teachers believed that they would
not have been helped by any formal learning prior
to the secondment on theoretical aspects of industrial organisation and production or on critical
tools of analysis. In fact, most teachers made
sharp distinctions between the 'theoretical' and
the 'practical' and only a small minority believed
that a theoretical component on the nature of
industry and its role in society would have been
useful in furthering the formal objectives of the
scheme. There was an unexpectedly strong anti-
academic feeling and great stress was put upon the
value of experiential learning. The following
observations made by one teacher fairly accurately
reflect this generally held position:

> I didn't think it a bad thing to be thrown in
> at the deep end and to float around for a
> while. If I'd had a formal introduction to
> industry, I'd probably have found myself
> doing a lot of reading of stuff that would not
> have made much sense in any case.

The practical, anti-academic bias of many responses
emerges again quite explicitly in the following
comments:

> Once you've been in industry, that's when the
> issues emerge. One of the values of the year
> is to be out of an educational framework, to
> be able to immerse yourself in industry. It
> shouldn't be too much of an academic exercise.

Even where there was support for a formal intro-
ductory course, it was generally felt that it
should be of short duration and taught by

industrial personnel.

However, the responses of one of the teachers highlighted the limitations of experiential learning and uncovered a deeper level of industrial understanding which the secondments barely appeared to have developed. This particular teacher approached his secondment already academically equipped with the tools of critical analysis. He had previously worked in industry and had an academic background of political science. His major contention was that interaction with industrial personnel and the direct experience of doing a job would not raise what he considered to be pertinent and important issues relating to the wider role of industry in society. He felt that much of value had been gained by him through contact with industrial personnel, but that their perspective was largely determined by the functional requirements of running a successful business enterprise. Clearly, exposure to such perspectives was an integral part of coming to an understanding of industry, but it was his contention that company personnel were predominantly concerned with the role of industry as a wealth creator, and that issues such as the ownership of industry, its differential reward structure, and the moral dimension to certain types of industrial production were not raised or discussed.

Reviewing the evidence of the teachers' responses, it does appear quite striking that such issues as these did not appear to inform their appreciation and understanding of industry. This is perhaps all the more surprising when it is remembered that the secondments took place at a time of rapid change in industry in the West Midlands, and when youth unemployment was rapidly rising.

This teacher was, in fact, one of the few who argued for the inclusion of a formal academic component to the secondment on the grounds that through such a component, issues of political economy could be systematically analysed and discussed.

THE INFORMAL CURRICULUM

Almost all the teachers asserted that their overall view of industry became more favourable as a result of their experiences. Practically without exception, the teachers were particularly impressed by the management and organisation of their

companies. Furthermore, many of the teachers
stated that the secondment had dispelled certain
stereotypical views they had held about industry
prior to their year. For example, several teachers
maintained that their general conception of industry had been to a degree unwittingly influenced
by the media presentation of it as a site of
conflict between management and work-force. However, by the end of their year, practically all of
the teachers felt that the 'two sides' view of
industry was an antiquated one and that industrial
relations were characterised as much, if not more,
by cooperation than hostility. A consensus, as
opposed to a conflict model of industry, was
proposed.

Additionally, several teachers also focussed
on the question of profit. They asserted their
attitude had changed. This position was put
unequivocably by one of the teachers:

> I know there's profit and profit, but before
> my year, I'd thought of profit as a bit of a
> dirty word. What struck me forcibly was the
> small percentage of turnover profit was.

Even where teachers went into a nationalised
industry, making a profit was considered to be the
overriding objective.

A number of teachers also commented that,
although many industrial jobs appeared dull and
repetitive, employees nonetheless seemed to derive
social and personal satisfaction from them.

It is interesting that when defining their
attitude towards industry, many of the teachers
appeared, implicitly, to rebut certain of the
classic criticisms of capitalism - the moral un-
acceptability of profit, the notion of worker
alienation, the basis of conflict of the social
relation of the work place. These teachers were,
in effect, taking up a political position in
relation to industry, but few of the teachers would
have conceded that their attitudes were in any way
political.

Favourable teacher attitudes towards industry
were, paradoxically, implicit in many of the
negative statements which the teachers made about
school. It is interesting that the experience of
the company as an organisation highlighted for
the teachers certain alleged organisational
deficiencies of schools. The teachers were, in
fact, encouraged by both UBI and industrial

personnel to make analogies between schools and
companies, and practically always, it was felt that
it was schools which could learn from industry
rather than vice versa.

The following propositions were made about
industry and schools by various of the teachers:

- industry is generally well managed; schools
  are not.
- industry generally trains its managers
  effectively; schools do not.
- industrial activity is structured by agreed
  objectives; educational activity is
  generally 'ad hoc'.
- industry develops its human capital; schools
  do not.
- industry processes and acts upon research
  information; schools generally do not.
- the profit motive stimulates effectiveness;
  schools lack this discipline.
- industry resources change effectively;
  schools do not.
- industry plans long term; schools do not.

Hence, effective industrial organisation was
counterposed against ineffective school organisation.

Such glowing perceptions about industry can be
of course related to the way in which the secondments were set up and structured. Manifestly, the
initial selection procedures had a bearing. No
company representative expressed the view that any
of the teachers embarked upon the year with strongly unsympathetic views towards capitalist organisation and production. It is quite likely that
teachers holding such views would not have applied
for the secondment in the first place, and that,
had they done so, the various selection procedures
would have eliminated them. One teacher, in fact,
asserted:

> I don't think anyone with left wing views
> ought to get on the scheme. I don't suppose
> they would . . . and they'd never cope in the
> company.

There was thus a strong element of self-
selection to the scheme. The manner in which the
teachers were allocated to the host companies may
also have been significant. The companies had the
right of veto over candidates selected by UBI and

LEAs. Some companies did, in fact, exercise their veto. Personality traits and attitudes deemed necessary and useful in the company were important aspects of selection criteria used by companies. Particularly stressed was the teachers' ability to fit into the company. The importance attached by the company to 'matching' procedures may be gauged by the fact that most frequently senior managers and directors were involved. Generally, intellectual capacity, subject background, level of formal qualification were considered unimportant, and it was the teachers' ability to fit in with the company which constituted the keystone of selection procedures. From the point of view of the smooth running of the company, this is no doubt understandable. It is, however, questionable as to whether it forms the most effective basis for the achievement of the fundamental objective of the formal curriculum of industrial learning. Learning about industry, as indeed learning about anything, is surely maximised by the spirit of enquiry and critical independence.

As has already been seen, the teachers occupied in many senses a privileged position within their companies. They were 'normal' employees only in a limited number of aspects. They differed in many ways. For example, they had been specially selected, and they were in industry for a specified and limited period of time. They were not threatened by the pressures of redundancy, and how they coped in their industrial roles could not radically affect their long term careers in teaching. In short, they were secure in a very insecure world. Their most frequent contacts with the company were at the levels of managers or industrial trainers, and many of the teachers perceived themselves as operating at a managerial level in the company. Their views on industrial and educational matters were sought both formally and informally, and they had freedom of access to a range of personnel, of departments, and in many cases, to relatively confidential information. A number of the teachers also received a considerable amount of media publicity, appearing on television and making educational radio programmes. As one teacher asserted, 'the whole thing was a tremendous ego boost'.

The context of the secondments in the teachers' professional lives must also be borne in mind. Many of the teachers had been in their posts a quite considerable number of years. The secondments took place at a time of severely curtailed opportunities within the education service for its employees. Although the teachers were unsure as to the worth of their year in strictly career terms, there is no doubt that their experience considerably enlarged the range of their social and professional contacts. The scheme involved the partnership of the school, the LEA, the company and UBI. Hence, during the year the teachers came into fairly extensive contact with personnel from each of these spheres. Frequently they formed close ties with industrial personnel, LEA inspectors and administrators and in some cases with their own headteachers. Not only was the teacher's reference group extended, but it was perceived by them as containing a greater number of higher status members than formerly.

Given these very unusual circumstances within which the teachers worked in the companies it is not surprising that teachers identified closely with 'their' company and developed a powerful sense of loyalty to it. The selection and matching procedures had ensured that no teachers with any major questioning attitudes would be seconded, but initially those selected did still express some doubts about the benevolence with which industry and commerce acted. Such doubts were largely assuaged by the end of the secondment year. The informal curriculum of the encouragement of more positive attitudes towards industry on the part of these teachers was thus extremely successful.

DISCUSSION

It has been shown that rather than being complementary there was often a conflict between the formal and the informal curricula for these teachers on secondment. In terms of the formal aim of increasing understanding, the scheme was successful in transmitting information about a wide range of aspects of the organisation and operation of the particular companies to which the teachers were seconded. Teachers became aware of career opportunities, industrial training procedures, labour policy, uses of new technology etc. within that company, but information on wider issues was less easily available.

General industry issues, as opposed to specific <u>company</u> issues are, of course, more economically, systematically and impartially addressed by more formal, organised and academic procedures rather than through experiential learning.

General issues such as:

- an appreciation of the role of industry in society,
- a knowledge of different forms of industrial organisation and production,
- a knowledge of economic and political issues relating to industry,
- a knowledge of different types of industry (manufacturing, extractive, service),
- a knowledge of alternative forms of industrial organisation employed in other societies,

can not be adequately dealt with through an experiential learning year in a single company. Yet information on such issues is surely vital for teachers who are to return to their schools as 'experts' on industry or who are to become education/industry liaison officers. It is thus clear that the formal curriculum objectives of enabling the teachers on the scheme to acquire a better understanding of industry and commerce were only partially met by the scheme.

However, the scheme was almost totally successful in meeting the objectives of the informal curriculum. Even though these teachers already had positive attitudes towards industry, the particular experiential learning programmes used by the scheme increased their positive attitudes and decreased any doubts that they may have held prior to the secondment.

It is our contention that this is not accidental. Although the scheme advertises itself largely in terms of the formal curriculum objectives and the informal aims of changing teacher attitudes is rarely voiced, the scheme is constructed in such a way that it is the informal curriculum objectives that are largely successful.

It is instructive to draw comparisons between the ideology behind this particular UBI teacher secondment scheme and that of the compensatory education programmes of the 1960s and early 1970s. Compensatory education programmes, such as Hardstart in the United States and the Educational Priority Areas in Britain, were specific intervention programmes introduced in an attempt to ameleorate inequalities in educational attainment which were perceived to be due to cultural 'deficits' in various 'disadvantaged' groups. They were directed towards pre-school and primary aged

school children who were seen as being able to
benefit from positive discrimination in attempts to
counter social, cultural and economic disadvantage.
In the late 1970s and early 1980s such compensatory
education schemes had shifted their target to
school leavers. Atkinson et al (1982), for example,
argue that many of the Manpower Services Commission's programmes for unemployed teenagers, especially those concerned with social and life skills,
are often informed by a similar underlying ideology
of cultural deprivation. There, unemployment is
seen in terms of individual deficiencies in the
'social skills' required in the workplace such as
communication, behaviour, appearance, attitude and
ability to take orders, and also in terms of 'life
skills' such as getting information or advice,
handling money and coping skills. It is worthy of
note here that the curriculum emphasis of these
courses has gradually changed from what would be
traditionally regarded as formal curriculum areas
such as writing, arithmetic and mechanical skills,
to the informal curriculum areas of behaviour,
attitudes and even appearance. A key element of
the cultural deprivation ideology is, of course,
that those cultural competences that these
teenagers do possess, which may be to some extent
oppositional, are negated.

Clearly, as many researchers like Keddie
(1973) have argued, the concept of 'cultural deprivation' is a nonsense, in that the groups involved are not deprived of their own culture, it is
simply that their culture is disvalued by groups
within the ruling class culture who have power to
ensure that their interpretation of the situation
is maintained. The work of Labov (1972) on
American black non-standard English, though with
its limitations, is still a prime example showing
the lack of any inherent communicational disadvantage in terms of linguistic deficit.

What is of interest is that there are marked
similarities between these compensatory education
programmes and the UBI teacher secondment scheme.
In this case, however, it is the teachers who are
seen as being deficient - lacking an understanding
of industry and commerce. These compensatory
education programmes can also be seen as having
both formal and informal curricula objectives with,
in practice, more emphasis being given to the
informal goals. Here, just as with Hardstart, EPAs
and the various MSC programmes, the objectives of
the formal curriculum in terms of specific skills

and knowledge serve to partially mask those of the
informal curriculum which demand changes in
attitudes and behaviour. The dominated culture is
devalued by the dominant to serve its own interests.

In the case of the UBI scheme, understanding
of industry is redefined as that which comes
through experience rather than through systematic
study or open debate. Teachers are seen to lack
experience of the 'real world' of commerce and
industry, and their own cultural competences in
terms of their academic knowledge and rigorous
study are systematically disvalued in contrast to
the 'reality' of experience. At root, it would
seem that it is not the lack of 'knowledge' about
industry that is the key target of the scheme, but
the whole academic culture of the school. It is
not simply that teachers are seen as deficient,
but that their whole culture is deficient.

Leaflets and documents published by UBI and
aimed primarily at teachers and educationalists
are careful to conceal this attack by phrasing the
aims and objectives of UBI in terms of increasing
understanding.

Leaflets aimed more at industrialists and
published by the CBI Educational Foundation (the
parent body of UBI) are less coy, as the following
extract shows. It comes from a four page glossy
pamphlet, undated, but actually published in 1982.
The text is in the form of a question/answer
session with Stephen Mullaly, Vice-Chairman of the
CBI Educational Foundation. The first question is,
'How and why was the Educational Foundation
started?' Mr Mullaly replies:

> During the '70s awareness grew that a major
> cause of poor industrial performance and
> declining national morale was the prevailing
> lack of understanding of the role of industry
> and commerce in the generation of wealth and
> resources. On this depends the country's
> social as well as economic well-being.
>
> Behind this lay, it was thought, a culture
> peculiar to Britain which gave status to
> intellectual performance and developed an
> educational system placing heavy emphasis
> on academic achievement. This had been
> compounded since the War by the apparent
> feeling that personal endeavour and self
> reliance was no longer sensible when 'they',
> the state, was the universal provider.

> Education was clearly the key to assess and
> if necessary change this attitude.
> (Educational Foundation, no date)

The message is stark. Teachers are not only
deficient in their knowledge and understanding of
industry and commerce, their culture is to be disvalued. Academic culture is a deprived culture.

The UBI scheme may thus be seen as a further
indication that the power relations between education and industry have been challenged and are
changing. The dominant interpretations of any
situation, in this case the nature of educational
understanding, learning and knowledge itself, are
a reflection of the interpretations held by those
with the most power to define. We believe it is
not accidental that a scheme such as the UBI
teacher secondment scheme reflects an ideology
which discourages systematic information gathering,
the drawing of comparisons, the analysis of dif-
fering viewpoints and the questioning of the basic
structure of social relations and perpetuation of
inequalities. At a time of increased attacks on
the social welfare provision (in particular education), growing authoritarianism and repression by
the State and structured unemployment, we find it
of no small concern that so many teachers appear to
be ready to flee from providing pupils with the
very tools that might encourage them to bring about
change, towards an unquestioning industrial
'relevance'.

It is not that we would wish in any way to
exclude learning about industry and commerce from
the school curriculum. On the contrary, we feel
that it is vital that schools encourage pupils
to gather information on our industrial, or perhaps
post-industrial, society and to engage in discussion about the role of industry and commerce based
upon that evidence. We would certainly wish pupils
to be informed on questions of, for example,
deskilling and automation and the effects that
these may have on their lives both in and out of
the workforce. What is clear, though, is that
teachers have to be systematically prepared to
enable them to handle these issues in a fair and
competent manner; they need to know what sources
of information are available and to be given the
academic tools necessary to be able to analyse and
evaluate that information and present it to pupils.

If this were done we have little doubt that
individualistic answers to our economic problems

which rest upon questions of 'attitudes towards
industry', on which we have shown the informal
curriculum of the UBI scheme to be based, would be
seen to have little relevance.

NOTES

1.   An early, less developed, version of this
paper was published by Thompson (1984).
2.   Since October 1983 the University of
Warwick, in conjunction with UBI, has offered a one
year Advanced Diploma course in Industrial Studies
in which seven months are spent in industry and
three at the University. This development does
not, however, fundamentally change our argument
for, as far as we can see, the university input is
mainly concentrated on practical aspects of
curriculum development and the sharing of experiences. It would seem, in fact, that the attack
on academic culture has been extended to the
universities. Perhaps it is not accidental that
the university most strongly involved is Warwick
(Thompson, 1970).

ACKNOWLEDGEMENTS

We wish to thank British Petroleum Ltd., for
financial support through its Schoolteacher Fellowship Scheme, the members of the evaluation Advisory
Group for their encouragement and many helpful
comments during the time of the research, and the
many people involved in the secondment scheme who
gave their time to be interviewed. The views
expressed in this article are our own, and not
necessarily those of UBI, BP or the Advisory Group.

REFERENCES

Atkinson, P., Rees, T.L., Shone, D. and
     Williamson, H. (1982) 'Social and life
     skills: the latest case of compensatory
     education' in T.L. Rees and P. Atkinson (eds.),
     Youth Unemployment and State Intervention,
     Routledge and Kegan Paul, London.
Bell, G.H. (1981) 'Industrial culture and the
     school: Some conceptual and practical issues
     in the schools/industry debate', Journal of
     Philosophy of Education, 15, (2), 175-189.
Callaghan, J. (1976) 'What the PM said', Report of
     Ruskin College speech, Times Educational

Supplement, 3203, 22nd October, 1
Cathcart, H. and Esland, G. (1983) 'Schooling and industry: Some recent contributions', British Journal of Sociology of Education, 4, (3), 275-83.
Cooper, N. (1981) School-Industry Link Schemes. A Study and Recommendations. Unpublished report commissioned by the Secretary of State for Education and Science.
Department of Education and Science (1977) Curriculum 11-16. HMI Series: Matters for Discussion, HMSO, London.
Educational Foundation (no date) Understanding British Industry. A Potent Force for Changing Attitudes, Educational Foundation, London. (Actually published 1982).
Ginsburg, M.B., Meyenn, R.J. and Miller, H.D.R. (1979) 'Teachers, the 'Great Debate' and education cuts', Westminster Studies in Education, 2, 5-33.
Jamieson, I. and Lightfoot, M. (1982) Schools and Industry, Derivations from the Schools Council Industry Project, Schools Council Working Paper 73, Methuen, London.
Keddie, N. (1973) Tinker, Taylor . . . The Myth of Cultural Deprivation, Harmondsworth, Penguin.
Labov, W. (1972) Language in the Inner City: Studies in Black English Vernacular, Pennsylvania University Press, Philadelphia.
Methven, Sir J. (1976) 'What industry wants', Times Educational Supplement, 3204, 29th October, 2.
National Economic Development Council (1982) Education and Industry: Memorandum by the Director General, NEDC, London.
Nisbet, J.W. (1979) 'Schools and industry - specialized in-service training for teachers', Trends in Education, 2, 4-7.
Parlett, M. and Hamilton, D. (1972) Evaluation As Illumination: A New Approach to the Study of Innovatory Programmes, Centre for Research in Educational Sciences, Occasional Paper No. 9, University of Edinburgh, Edinburgh.
Reeder, D. (1979) 'A recurring debate: Education and industry' in G. Bernbaum (ed.), Schooling in Decline, Macmillan, London.
Salter, B. and Tapper, T. (1981) Education, Politics and the State. The Theory and Practice of Educational Change, Grant McIntyre, London.

Thompson, E.P. (ed.) (1970) _Warwick University Ltd_, Harmondsworth, Penguin.

Thompson, R. (1984) 'Teachers into industry: Reflections on a one year secondment scheme' in I. Jamieson (ed.) _Industry and the Curriculum: Case Studies and Practice_, Longmans, London.

Thompson, R. and Walford, G. (1983) _Teachers into Industry. An Evaluation of an Understanding British Industry Teacher Secondment Scheme_, Aston Educational Enquiry Monograph No. 11, University of Aston, Birmingham. Also published in _Collected Original Resources in Education_ (1984), _8_, (1), 1-178.

Understanding British Industry (1978) _Annual Review 1977-78_, UBI, London.

Understanding British Industry (1980) _Industrial Secondment of Teachers. A Progress Report of the UBI One Year Scheme_, UBI, Oxford.

Understanding British Industry (1982) 'LEA responses to a survey on teachers and industry schemes'. Unpublished mimeo by Ian Jamieson, resulting from a meeting between UBI, SCIP and the National Centre for Schools Technology.

Watts, A.G. (ed.) (1983) _Work Experience and Schools_, Heinemann, London.

Wood, B. (1983) _School Industry Liaison: The Development of Policy and the Role of the Schools/Industry Liaison Officer_. Unpublished MEd thesis, Worcester College of Higher Education, Worcester.

Chapter Four

SCHOOLING IN RURAL ENGLAND - JOBS FOR THE GIRLS?

Kristine Mason

This article begins by discussing three issues in relation to schooling in the rural areas of England. The first of these focusses on the trend of school closure and amalgamation which has been occurring on a massive scale in the rural areas over recent years. The second is to indicate that sociologists of education in this country, unlike their counterparts in many other European countries and North America, have tended to ignore schooling in the rural areas. It would appear that some form of urban hegemony has blinkered sociologists from addressing this issue: this has been neglectful to say the least in view of the large proportion of this country which continues to be described as rural. The third issue is that, whereas the question of gender as an organising principle has come to the forefront of research in the sociology of education, such research has focussed almost exclusively, and often implicitly, upon the urban areas.

The article then presents findings from a recent empirical study of schooling in a rural location which has specifically addressed the problematic of gender. It concludes by suggesting that further theoretical development is required to explain the particular relation between gender and schooling in the rural areas, and that such development is necessary in order to examine the implications for girls and boys of the relentless trend of school closure and amalgamation which has been occurring in rural England.

SCHOOL CLOSURE AND AMALGAMATION: THE CONTINUING TURMOIL
The publication of the Gittins Report(1967),and of the

Plowden Report of the same year which both
recommended a minimum sized primary school of three
teachers and sixty pupils, meant that thousands of
small rural primary schools in Wales and England
were under threat. It is probably not surprising
therefore that the focus of the somewhat limited
amount of literature on rural schooling has been
subsequently directed towards the primary sector.
From the University of Aston Final Report on the
Social Effects of Rural Primary School Reorganization (Comber et al., 1981), quite astounding
figures related to school closures are revealed.
The authors say that there are not any official
figures which show the extent of rural primary
school closures in the ten years following the 1944
Education Act, and that there is only incomplete
data from 1955 to 1977. However the Report estimates that:

> As many as 800 small schools may have dis-
> appeared since 1967, and the number could turn
> out to be over a thousand (p. 8).

In projecting the results of its survey data
collected as part of its research programme, the
Report states that,

> Around 1,000 'rural' or village based schools
> were closed between 1955 and the publication
> of the Plowden Report in 1967; approximately
> 660 between Plowden and the reorganization of
> Local Government in 1974, and approximately
> 275 in the period since 1974 (p. 10).

Such estimates suggest then that in the last thirty
years some two thousand primary schools have been
closed in the rural areas of England alone. This
figure clearly represents a very considerable degree
of educational disruption in the rural areas.
Information regarding rural secondary schools
is extremely scant. In a brief chapter on this
sector, Nash (1980) makes the point that, 'Villagers
have become accustomed to sending their children to
town secondary schools'. He goes on to say,

> The official statistics do not allow urban-
> rural differences to be discerned easily, but
> figures on the size of school are available.
> In 1975 there were 8 schools with up to 100
> pupils on roll, 51 between 101-200, 130 between
> 201-300 and 227 between 301-400. It is also

possible to calculate that the average size of school - implying that there are many smaller - in a sample of predominantly rural counties, was 590 in Northumberland, 639 in Norfolk and 641 in Cumbria (p. 71).

Since that time one may discern a considerable reduction in the number of small secondary schools, as the following table reveals:

Table 1: Number of secondary schools with the following numbers of full-time pupils

	Up to 100	101-200	201-300	301-400
1975:	8	51	130	227
1981:	7	35	67	144

(The 1981 figures are taken from the DES figures in Statistics of Schools).

In calculating for 1984 the average size of secondary schools in the three predominantly rural counties selected by Nash for 1975 an increase in average school size is clearly discernable.

Table 2: Average size of school in three predominantly rural counties:

	Northumberland	Norfolk	Cumbria
1975:	590	639	641
1984:	957	825	783

(The 1984 figures are calculated from The Education Authorities Directory and Annual, 1984).

Although falling roles will undoubtedly have accounted for some of the closures of the smaller rural schools, a further factor is amalgamation. The decrease in the number of small schools resembles the similar tendency in North America where the trend has also been to amalgamate small schools. The view expressed by Rosenfeld and Sher (1977: 42) concerning this trend in North America could apply very pertinently to the situation

Schooling in Rural England - Jobs for the Girls?

in this country in that it represents,

> . . . an ideology of growth, efficiency and
> conformity designed to support the nation's
> rising commitment to industrialism, corporate
> capitalism and urban life.

URBAN HEGEMONY IN THE SOCIOLOGY OF EDUCATION

In spite of this upheaval in the countryside,
sociologists of education have tended to ignore the
question of schooling in the rural areas of England.
There are some notable exceptions to this assertion,
for example the work of Hart (1973), Nash (1980),
Clarricoates (1980), and Comber et al (1981),
however such work represents an extremely small
proportion of the overall amount of sociological
activity devoted to schooling.

One reason for this apparent lack of interest
could be that if sociologists of education were to
focus on the rural areas then their work might be
tinged by some form of geographical determinism.
Such forebodings have not of course deterred rural
sociologists and, as Newby (1978: 5) has pointed
out, rural sociology might learn from 'urban
sociology' by,

> . . . adopting a more holistic approach which
> addresses itself explicitly to the question of
> rural change under the conditions of a pre-
> dominantly capitalist society.

Clearly this approach of political economy is one
which has for some years fruitfully dominated the
study of schooling in urban areas; it would seem
unreasonable, therefore, that schooling in the rural
areas should be so completely marginalised.

A second possible explanation as to why
sociologists of education in this country have
eschewed the rural areas might be due to problems
encountered in defining what is meant by the term
'rural'. Writing of OECD member countries, Sher
(1981: 22) asserts,

> Actually, most countries have either not been
> able, or have simply not bothered to define
> rural areas at all. Rather the common practice
> is to carefully define the urban (and semi-
> urban) population and consider any place left
> over to be rural.

This non-specificity, however, may be avoided by selecting a particular index, or set of indices, and then proceeding to conduct the research in the rural area so defined.   An example of this approach is provided by Comber et al. (1981: 4) in whose study,

> rural or village-based primary schools were defined as comprising all primary schools located in areas of scattered developments as well as free-standing hamlets, villages and small towns with a population of 10,000 or less.

I have suggested two possible reasons then why schooling in rural areas might have been overlooked by sociologists.   However, there must undoubtedly be other reasons why sociologists have so evidently placed rural schooling on the periphery, such as perceived problems of access to such schools, and the problems of funding empirical research.   Perhaps sociologists of education fear tainting their discipline by trespassing into the perceived atheoretical empiricism of rural sociology.   Yet whatever the reasons and rationalisations, unstated though they are, they cannot be sufficient to so thoroughly marginalise the country's rural school children.

GENDER: THE FORGOTTEN FACTOR

In the same way that sociologists have largely concentrated on the urban rather than the rural, they have also concentrated on men rather than women.   The work by Newby (1979), for example, on agricultural workers hardly mentions women at all. There are exceptions to this trend such as the work of Chamberlain (1975), Whitehead (1976) and Gasson (1980) who have each focussed upon the differential position of women in rural areas.   However, the small amount of research focussed on women is illustrated in Neate's (1981) annotated bibliography of deprivation in rural areas.   He states that:

> It is crucial to recognize that the population of rural areas is seldom socially homogeneous ... the environment impinges on different groups in different ways ... In addition to the less well off, women and the elderly have consistently been identified as especially vulnerable (p. 10).

However, despite this apparent 'consistent identification', the bibliography itself, containing over three hundred entries, reveals only <u>one</u> reference to a study of the particular situation of women in the rural areas - that of Chamberlain (1975).

Studies of schooling in rural areas frequently omit gender as an organising principle, there is a preference to refer to 'children' and 'pupils' rather than boys and girls. Elsewhere in studies of rural education it is evident that women have been patronised; Trollope (1973) for example, reports on a view concerning,

> The undesirability of a woman teacher (and a women teacher is essential in a school which contains infants) being required to live alone, often in an isolated and remote situation (p. 78).

In Morris's (1973) work on the 'Role of the County College of Agriculture in the Rural Community', there is one heading entitled 'The Countrywoman' who is straight away assumed to be a 'housewife'. The very next heading used by Morris is 'The Adult Farm Worker' who is immediately assumed to be male. Fortunately not all of the work on rural schooling has entirely disregarded gender (see for example Hart (1973)) however a perusal of the published literature reveals an urgent need for this question to be systematically addressed.

THE SCHOOLING OF RURAL GIRLS

The first part of this section is based upon an ethnographic study conducted in a village in Herefordshire during 1980. The objective of the research was to inquire into the schooling of girls in a rural area. Some of the ethnographic data has appeared elsewhere (Mason, Meyenn and Small, 1981).

The research was conducted in the village of Headleigh (1) which is situated in the southern district of Herefordshire, referred to by Hale (1971: 2) as 'one of the most rural of all counties'. It was not a village in which tourists to the area would linger, flanked as it was with a development of small modern new houses, which were referred to by local farmers as 'pidgeon houses'. However, the valley in which Headleigh is

situated is itself extremely beautiful, and when
passing through, it is hard to avoid subscribing to
the ideological view of pastoral England so well
criticised by Newby (1979).   A letter from the
District Planning Office received by a resident in
March 1980, highlights what the ideology of the
rural idyll serves to mask,

> The problem of rural depopulation and
> deprivation, as you are no doubt aware, has
> been a cause of concern for a number of years
> and it is thought that this area ... suffers
> more than any other within ... district ...
> the present economic depression has further
> exaggerated rural hardship, i.e. the fuel
> crisis, rising transport costs and cuts in
> public transport, migration to the town for
> housing and employment and the resultant
> closure of schools, shops and post offices in
> the villages has further deprived country
> folk (sic.)

The social mix of the population of 375 males
and 379 females was considerable, with the 'locals'
occupying a range of positions from farmers to
council house tenants, and the 'incomers' who were
made up of elderly people, referred to by locals as
'retired townies', and young couples living in the
'pigeon houses', as well as couples mainly in their
thirties who had come from towns and cities during
the mid-seventies aiming for varying degrees of
self-sufficiency by, for example, establishing themselves in a craft; this latter group was referred
to by 'locals' as 'those hippies'.   According to
official returns, it would appear that the proportion of men and women in officially recognised
employment was 59% and 30% respectively.   Such
official figures do not, however, present the true
picture of employment, particularly in relation to
women.   They do not take account of the work of
women such as 'farmer's wives' nor of the part-time
seasonal work which they perform, for example,
fruit picking.   Another point about the inaccuracy
of these figures may be discerned from a village
primary school teacher who said, 'nearly everybody
moonlights, practically everybody has two jobs.'
    For men the main forms of local employment
were farming on their family farm, and work related
to transport, such as motor vehicle mechanics.   Some
worked in the market town some twelve miles distant.
For women the main forms of regular paid employment

were in the local plastics factory, and doing
domestic work for old people and in the primary and
secondary village schools.

Among the villagers there was evidence of a
clear emphasis on the work ethic. As the vicar,
who had lived in the village for twenty years, put
it, 'we have very hard working people here; and
also over here people who are a bit workshy are
looked down upon. If you're workshy you won't have
the respect of the community'. Certainly within
the village, people seemed to have a very good idea
of each other's activities; as one incomer ruefully
said, 'Here, if you sneeze, everybody knows about
it, and what kind of handkerchief you use.'

There were two schools in the village, a primary school for 5-11 year old boys and girls, and a
coeducational county comprehensive school for 12-16
year olds. The comprehensive school drew upon a
catchment area of some 160 square miles, so this
necessitated many pupils being bussed in to school.

In the course of the fieldwork it was evident
how the functioning of the school was impaired by
factors which might not impinge so drastically on an
urban school. Heavy snows meant that children in
the outlying areas could not get to school, and when
the river overflowed its banks, a recurring event
(and referred to as far back as the primary school
log book of 1894), the school had to be closed.

A historical perspective reveals that schooling
had traditionally been viewed with some indifference
by the people in this rural area. In an interview
with the retired first head teacher of the secondary
school he related how he had to,

> keep a reasonably low profile and wait until
> people came to see me, to complain or whatever,
> and I'd show them round and watch their eyes
> pop out of their heads as they'd see the labs
> etcetera. There was no antagonism, no
> enthusiasm; really they were just neutral.

He went on to describe how three market days
affected the process of schooling, those of
Abergavenny, Hereford and Hay:

> You get kids staying away to escort cattle to
> market. After all it was fair enough because
> all the farms were small. There wasn't a farm
> labouring class of any sort. They were all
> independent people.

91

Schooling in Rural England - Jobs for the Girls?

Not only was schooling disrupted, but the kinds of
events which schools tend to mount to encourage
parental and community involvement had also been
given very low priority by the rural population.
The first head teacher told of how in the 1950s he
arranged a school Christmas entertainment, and he,

> invited all the parents, all the school
> governors and all the people in local govern-
> ment who had dealings within the county. One
> governor turned up because he was the verger and
> landlord of the pub next to the school. Nobody
> came from the County, two parents came because
> they were driving the school buses, and three
> others of their own free will. When I com-
> plained, people said it was feathering time -
> you can't expect them to come.

This head teacher had seen his role as being one of
trying to get the school 'to fit in with the
community'. He had felt that formal examinations
would be 'alien', though not only, it would seem,
because of the culture of the community, but also
because of his perceived capabilities of the
children.
   From the views expressed by the first head, it
appeared that in the early years the school was
viewed as something of an irrelevant institution,
to be viewed with some tolerance. Further
investigation revealed however that this was not so
much the case with the female pupils. The words of
one retired teacher who had spent all her working
life in the area were indicative. She related how
the first head had not wished the children to take
public exams, but how in fact she had been pressurised from girls who complained to her about the
school not preparing and entering them for the
examinations. This desire to take external
examinations was borne out in talking to women who
had been former pupils of the school, one of whom
said,

> I loved school. I'd have stayed there if it was
> humanly possible. I went to Agricultural
> College to do a three month course. Lots of
> farmer's daughters were doing the course. It
> was a filling-in thing. I remember wishing
> we could take exams at school.

It might be suggested then that over the years
the school was perceived to be of greater

importance by the females than by the males in the
rural area under study. The extent, if any, to
which this apparent gender differentiation has
continued up to the present time was examined among
pupils at the Headleigh schools.
An interview with the head of the primary
school revealed that he considered the primary girls
to be 'more intelligent than boys' and he pointed
out that there were no girls in the school receiving
remedial attention. In the view of the reception
class teacher.

> The little girls work more conscientiously and
> more neatly and in general they tend to read
> more quickly. Little girls tend to be with
> mothers who talk. Boys tend to go outside and
> deal with things.

The teacher of the eight to nine year olds said,

> The higher standards are achieved by the girls
> in test type things. I have a lot of backward
> boys, boys with problems. The girls are
> achieving ones and the quantity of work they do
> is far greater. I've got one boy who asks to
> take work home and about six girls. It's hard
> to generalise, but on the whole the girls seem
> to fit in much quicker and knuckle down.

These and similar comments made by the teachers in
the primary school showed that the girls seemed to
be achieving more highly than were the boys. The
differential achievement fits in with the similar
pattern documented in Britain as a whole (Reid and
Wormald, 1982). With regard to secondary age pupils
in the area under study,certain features of gender
differentiation become apparent during the course of
the research.
The first of these was in relation to the
girls' higher degree of motivation towards secondary
schooling. This was evident to teachers as well as
to the pupils themselves. One of the teachers
pointed to the fact that 'There are more boys than
girls in the lower (streamed) classes', and another
teacher said of his subject, mathematics, that,

> The girls are more motivated. It's usually
> the boys I've found more motivated in the city
> schools. Yes I think there is a reversal here.
> I think that the good boys are good, but it
> seems to bring the girls out.

Schooling in Rural England - Jobs for the Girls?

This difference in motivation towards school was shown in interviews conducted with the whole fifth year of girls and boys. Many of the girls considered, further, that boys could be very disruptive of their work efforts, for example.

Ann:
> I think most farmer's boys are interested only in the farm and they don't want anything else.

Interviewer:
> Mmmm. Does this seem obvious at school at all?

All the girls:
> Yes.

Jane:
> Yes, they've got jobs already, they join really with their fathers and then they make trouble for the rest of us. You know, they're silly and that.

Carol:
> They disrupt everything.

Interviewer:
> They disrupt everything?

Carol:
> Yes.

Interviewer:
> How do they disrupt?

Ann:
> Well, if you're doing private lessons up there (i.e. the private study room) they'll just come in and start strangling you and throwing the books round the place and stupid things like that.

Interviewer:
> Really?

Ann:
> Yes, there's no point in it. Just because they've got nothing to do they disturb.

Jane:
> Yes, the lessons ... now there are higher and lower classes so most of these are in the lower ones now, so we've got out of that anyway.

Carol:
> There's first, second and third years here you know, and we're all together, and you know it was almost impossible to do anything.

Interviewer:
> How did you cope with that? What did you do if you wanted to get on with your work?

Ann:
> Well you had to just sort of go in a corner by yourself or do it at home when you can. You

just sort of get the teacher's attention ...
the teacher has to teach you in a private
group.

Interviewer:
Did you do that, did you get hold of a teacher
sometimes and say ...

Ann:
Yes, sometimes.

Interviewer:
How did you arrange that?

Ann:
Well just ask him for problems and just say
'Sir I don't understand what you was on about'
... just he'll explain it to you on your own,
just to a couple of you. Like most of the
time the teachers are telling the other boys
off for messing around so you lost out all the
time.

The following interview with fifth year boys
indicated a common indifference towards school:

Interviewer:
What do you think about school?

Tom:
I don't like it. I just aren't interested in
school. I'd rather be at home working on the
farm.

Interviewer:
And is that what you're looking forward to
doing?

Tom:
Yes.

Interviewer:
And Steven?

Steven:
I don't like school at all.

Interviewer:
Why not?

Steven:
I'd rather be at home.

Interviewer:
Have you always felt that or was it ...

Steven:
Yes. I even used to think it at primary
school.

Interviewer:
Is there anything you particularly like at all.
Any subject?

Steven:
No, not really.

Schooling in Rural England - Jobs for the Girls?

Interviewer:
    Barry?
Barry:
    I don't mind school, it's not too bad.
Interviewer:
    What sort of things do you like doing?
Barry:
    Practical. Metalwork and woodwork.
Bob:
    I don't mind school, but I won't be sorry when
    I leave.
Interviewer:
    You won't.
Anthony:
    It ain't so bad once you get used to it. You
    can do without school really. I reckon you
    learn more outside than you do inside.
Interviewer:
    Some of you are nodding, do you agree that you
    do more outside than inside?
Barry:
    Yes, practical things. But you got to have
    schools to do reading and that.

During the interviews it became clear that both boys
as well as girls viewed schooling as being of
greater importance to the girls as the following
transcript illustrates,

Joss:
    I think a girl should have a good education
    really.
Interviewer:
    Why?
Joss:
    Well it's more important I reckon for a girl to
    have a good education than it is for a bloke.
Interviewer:
    Why is that?
Joss:
    Well a girl, there isn't so many jobs for a
    girl which she's going to need, like. Any boy
    can, specially round this part of the country,
    can go and be a farmer without ... well even
    if he's as thick as two short planks
Interviewer:
    Mmmm.
Joss:
    And a girl like, well she hasn't got much of a
    job round this part of the country ... If she
    wants a decent job, like, she wants some decent

96

education.

Quite clearly the local employment situation in and
around Headleigh favoured the boys rather than the
girls. For many of the boys there appeared to be a
complex informal labour market in operation whereby
employment could be found through family and
neighbourhood connections with regard to farming
and transport. For the girls, local employment
opportunities were absolutely minimal. Although
many of the girls expressed the desire to undertake
traditionally female forms of employment, for
example, nursing, child care and secretarial work,
there was a clear recognition among the girls
themselves of the lack of local opportunity for
them to fulfill their work aspirations; as one fifth
former put it,

> Around Hereford there's no catering jobs at all.
> You have to go further afield.

This lack of local employment opportunities for
women in rural areas has been emphasised by Bracey
(1971: 36) who said,

> Opportunities for employment of women,
> especially young women, in remote rural areas
> are few and many have no choice but to take up
> permanent residence in a town if urban employ-
> ment cannot be secured by commuting. The pull
> is clearly greater the smaller the hamlet or
> village and the greater the distance from urban
> employment. It appears greatest in young fem-
> ale adults up to the middle twenties.

It would seem then from the above that the
boys' and girls' differential perceptions of their
schooling were influenced by the structural
features of employment within the local economy.
It became evident during the research that there
were also important cultural features which
affected the boys' and girls' views on whether
they hoped to remain in the area or whether they
wanted to leave it. Moving away from the area was
seen by the girls not only as a likely necessity,
but it was also regarded as a preference. The boys
however expressed strong preferences to remain in
the area, and those boys who recognised that they
might have to move away to find employment were
very regretful of the prospect. The following are
typical of comments made by fifth year girls and

boys.

GIRLS:
Mary:
>I'd rather travel around than stay here.

Interviewer:
>And Jane, would you prefer to stay here or ...

Jane:
>I'd like to go to a town that was fairly small.
>I wouldn't like to stay round here really. I
>wouldn't want to stay round here, it's too
>quiet.

Interviewer:
>Is it?

Jane:
>There's not much to do really.

BOYS:
Brian:
>I wouldn't like to move. I wouldn't mind, you
>know, going somewhere fairly close but I
>wouldn't want to go far.

Interviewer:
>So you're happy to stay here.

John:
>I'm happy to stay here too. It's alright
>here.

This gender difference in willingness to move away
was very pronounced among the Headleigh pupils.
This differs from the earlier work by Hale (1971)
who in her research in the late sixties on school
leavers' work aspirations found a preference
expressed by both males and females to remain in
Herefordshire. This change in the girl's willingness to remain at home as wives and mothers who
would content themselves with whatever work was
available (usually part-time, low-paid and
seasonal) was one in which the girls appeared to
receive their mothers' support. The following
comments from girls and mothers illustrate the
point,

>My mum regrets all her life that she didn't
>get qualifications, that's why she gets on at
>me. She didn't do anything. She worked on the
>land. She really, really regrets (Fifth year
>girl).

>She (mother) won't want me doing too much hard
>work. She said if she lived her life again

she'd never be a farmer's wife (Fifth year
girl).

I often think that I missed it by ten years.
I often think that I was born ten years too
soon educationally. If there was a chance
again I'd be more educated, that's why I've
got hopes for her. (Indicating her 14 year old
daughter). (Woman married to a farmer of 600
acres. She had left home when she was 15 and
had worked on the home farm before marriage).

I'd like to see them (her two daughters are
12 and 14) learn a trade so they have something
to fall back on when they get married ... I
want Amy to go into the forces so that she can
get a training and see something of the world.
If they have to go away I won't try to make
them stay. (Woman married to a tenant farmer
of twenty acres. She was the youngest of 12
children. Her father had been a gardener and
she had done domestic work before marriage.)

Linked to the girls' desire to move away, there was
obviously the question of how girls and boys
perceived rural life. It became clear that boys
considered the experience of living in a rural area
to be much more satisfactory than did girls as
statements like these suggest,

Boys:
I play sports; cricket, snooker, darts and
table tennis.

I go to Young Farmers in my spare time, and I
like woodwork and shooting.

Girls:
It's terrible if you haven't got transport,
it's awful. It's alright if all you want to
do is stay at home and sew and knit and take
the dog for a walk.

It's the boringness of the village, that's why
I like to go to school. In the summer holidays
I walk round the village bored.

In summary, the qualitative research described above
has shown that gender differences occurred in three
major areas in relation to the girls and boys in
this Herefordshire secondary school. Firstly, girls

viewed schooling more positively than did boys since they regarded it as being of considerable importance to them in gaining future employment. Secondly, girls and boys differed in their motivation to move away from the area. Thirdly, girls and boys differed in their perceived satisfaction with life in the rural area under study.

In order to test the extent of gender differences related to these three issues, and to ascertain whether they had endured over time, it was decided to employ a triangulation approach and gather some quantitative data from a wider population. Thus in 1984 during school time, I administered a questionnaire at the comprehensive school in Headleigh to its entire fifth form of boys and girls. This questionnaire, consisting of 46 questions, was completed by 21 girls and 17 boys. The pupils were asked to provide information concerning such details as their length of residence in the area under study and parental occupation and land holding. In this article, however, information relating to gender alone will be discussed.

The pupils' orientation towards schooling was ascertained from nine questions related to such areas as their opinions of school, how much home-work they did, and how hard they considered they worked at school. Their responses were scored on a 1-4 point scale with 4 indicating the most positive orientation towards school. The mean ratings derived from these questions were analysed using a Mann-Whitney test which analyses the difference between two sets of ratings. As expected, a significantly higher rating for girls was found $(u = 88.5 \ (17,21) \quad z = 2.65, \ p < 0.05)$. The mean ratings for this and the other analyses to be described are shown in Table 3.

With regard to the second issue, pupils were asked in the questionnaire whether they would in future prefer to work in the area where they were living, or in an area 'quite far from where I live now'. Analysis of the girls' and boys' preferences in relation to this question indicated a significant gender difference in the pupils' desire to remain in the rural area under study $(u = 48 \ (15,18), z = 3.46, \quad p < .001)$; the boys prefer to remain where they are while the girls want to move to a different area.

The third issue which was addressed by the questionnaire was that of the degree of satisfaction which was experienced by girls and boys with their lives outside school time. The qualitative research

had suggested that the boys derived more enjoyment
from life outside school than did the girls. The
pupils' responses to this question were assessed by
a 4 point scale with 4 indicating a positive view
of their life in the rural area. Analysis of the
pupils' responses to this question again showed a
significant difference in girls' and boys'
satisfaction with life outside school (u = 122
(17,21) z = 1.83, p < .05). This also supports
the ethnographic data which had indicated that boys
found more activities outside school from which they
derived enjoyment.
      The research in this Herefordshire rural area
thus showed a considerable variation between girls
and boys in relation to the three main issues
already discussed. In order to ascertain whether
this gender differentiation occurred in other rural
areas, the questionnaire was also administered
during the same period in 1984 to all fifth formers
in two other secondary schools in rural settings.
The two schools selected from the non-metropolitan
counties were chosen as the most comparable to the
Herefordshire secondary school. These schools
were situated in rural locations in Lincolnshire
and Cumbria. Analysis of the responses to the
questions relating to orientation towards school
supported the finding from the Herefordshire school
(Lincolnshire, u = 144 (19,22), z = 1.73, p < .05;
Cumbria, u = 81 (17,18), z = 2.39, p < .01). The
preference of boys to remain in the rural area
where they now live was also evident, although the
difference was only marginally significant in
Lincolnshire (Lincolnshire, u = 88.5 (15,17),
z = 1.57, p = .06; Cumbria, u = 78.5 (17,16),
z = 2.21, p < .02).
      In relation to the question about how
satisfactory life outside school was perceived, no
significant difference between boys' and girls'
responses was obtained in either Lincolnshire or
Cumbria. In other questions such as availability of
part-time work, the results did not follow the
pattern of the Herefordshire pupils' responses
either. This of course may be explained by the
variability of the rural areas under study; with
regard to part-time work, for example, the presence
of a large public school next to the Cumbria
school provided a substantial amount of part-time
domestic work which was undertaken by the girls.
This highlights the necessity of studying rural
schooling in particular settings: as Whitfield and
Nisbet (1982:2) remarked, 'rural regions differ

and problems and solutions are sometimes specific to local conditions'.

Table 3: Mean Ratings of Boys' and Girls' Responses to Questionnaire for Pupils in a Rural School

		Hereford-shire	Lincoln-shire	Cumbria
Orientation to school: (4 = positive orientation)	Boys	2.55	2.88	2.73
	Girls	3.12	3.13	3.09
Satisfaction with life outside school: (4 = very satisfied)	Boys	3.65	3.00	3.24
	Girls	3.19	2.82	2.78
Preference for remaining in the area: (4 = strong preference)	Boys	3.60	3.13	3.41
	Girls	2.83	2.71	2.81

Note: for numbers of responses contributing to each cell see text.

Having said this, however, there remains a remarkable degree of consistency in the analysis of the three populations of pupils in terms of gender differentiation: in all three schools the girls were more positively oriented towards school and more highly motivated to move away.

CONCLUSION

The empirical research described above has shown quite conclusively that gender is an extremely important factor with regard to school in the rural regions in England. The school, for the rural girls in particular, is perceived as a domain wherein qualifications are to be acquired to better enhance opportunities for future employment. It is

arguable then that schooling itself is an important
component of the 'pull' factor of female migration
from the countryside, referred to earlier in
Bracey's (1971) work. The research has shown too
that the rural girls studied would prefer to move
away from their area of residence. This suggests
that there are cultural as well as economic factors
which are influencing the girls' desires to move;
the stereotyped ascribed role of 'The Countrywoman'
is evidently not one to which young rural women are
aspiring. In this respect the Herefordshire
ethnography revealed that they are being supported
in their resistance to this role by their mothers.

In the light of continuing school closure and
amalgamation, sociologists of education need to
consider the possible differential consequences for
boys and girls, particularly with regard to
secondary schooling. Two of the three schools in
which the questionnaire was administered in the
research described in this paper, have been, or are
currently, under threat of closure. The implications for the boys and girls may be considerable.
It is possible that larger secondary schools with
greater curriculum choice may be viewed as
advantageous by the girls in order to better
facilitate their gaining the qualifications they
need in their quest for work elsewhere. It is
possible too, that as employment opportunities in
the rural areas continue to decline for males too,
that the larger school may be increasingly perceived by boys as offering the means towards finding
alternative employment.

It would be a truism to state that rural areas
in this country vary considerably in their social,
cultural, political and economic formations. Such
variability will undoubtedly have implications for
schooling in the rural regions. It is extremely
likely, and indeed suggested in the recent work by
the rural sociologist, Terry Marsden (1984), that in
the rural areas where capitalist farming pre-
dominates, education is both valued and paid for
by capitalist farmers in order to maintain, to
use Marsden's term, 'social selectivity'. In this
instance it would appear that schooling is, indeed,
reproducing existing class relationships. Along
the small family farms around Headleigh, however,
the relation between schooling and the existing
social structure was more problematic, especially
with regard to gender relations.
Clearly it is necessary for sociologists

of education to shed their urbancentric outlook and address the fertile fields of education in the rural areas.

NOTE

1.   'Headleigh' is a pseudonym.

ACKNOWLEDGEMENTS

Geoffrey Walford and David Miall have provided invaluable assistance in the production of this paper.

REFERENCES

Bracey, E.E. (1971) People and the Countryside, Routledge and Kegan Paul, London
Chamberlain, M. (1975) Fenwomen: A Portrait of Women in an English Village, Virago, London
Clarricoates, K. (1980) 'The importance of being Ernest ... Emma ... Tom ... Jane. The perception and categorization of gender, conformity and gender deviation in primary schools' in R. Deem (ed.) Schooling for Womens Work, Routledge and Kegan Paul, London
Comber, L.C., Joyce, F.E., Meyenn, R., Sinclair, C.W., Small, M.A., Tricker, M.J. and Whitfield, R.C. (Study Team) (1981) The Social Effects of Primary School Reorganisation. A study on behalf of the Department of the Environment and the Department of Education and Science, Final Report, University of Aston.
Department of Education and Science (1967) Primary Education in Wales (The Gittins Report), HMSO, Cardiff
Department of Education and Science (1967) Children and their Primary Schools (The Plowden Report), HMSO, London
Department of Education and Science (1977) Falling Numbers and School Closures, Circular No 5/77, HMSO, London
Department of Education and Science (1982) Statistics of Schools, January 1981, Department of Education and Science
Education Authorities Directory and Annual (1984) The School Government Publishing Company, Redhill

Gasson, R. (1980) 'Career opportunities for women in British agriculture', Agricultural Administration, 8, 241-253

Hale, S. (1971) The Idle Hill. The National Council of Civil Service, Bedford Square Press, London

Hart, P.L. (1973) 'The background interests and attitudes to the curriculum of a group of rural children attending a Cambridgeshire village school' in P.W. Warner (ed.) Rural Education, University of Hull Institute of Education

Marsden, T. (1984) 'Capitalist farming and the farm family: A case study', Sociology, 18, (2), 205-224

Mason, K.M., Meyenn, R. and Small, M.A. (1981), 'The schooling of girls in rural England. Paper presented to the 41st Annual Meeting of the Society for Applied Anthropology Rethinking Applied Anthropology, April, University of Edinburgh

Morris, P.W. (1973) 'The role of the County College of Agriculture in the rural community' in P.W. Warner (ed.) Rural Education, University of Hull Institute of Education

Nash, R., Williams, H. and Evans, M. (1976) 'The one teacher school', British Journal of Educational Studies, 24, 12-32

Nash, R. (1980) Schooling in Rural Societies, Methuen, London

Neate, S. (1981) Rural Deprivation: An annotated Bibliography of economic and social problems in rural Britain, Geo Abstracts, University of East Anglia

Newby, H. (1978) 'The rural sociology of advanced capitalist societies' in H. Newby (ed.) International Perspectives in Rural Sociology, Wiley, Chichester

Newby, H. (1979) The Deferential Worker, Penguin, Harmondsworth

Newby, H. (1979) Green and Pleasant Land? Social Change in Rural England, Hutchinson, London

Reid, I.R. and Wormald, E. (1982) Sex Differences in Britain, Grant McIntyre, London

Rosenfeld, S.A. and Sher, J.P. (1977) 'The urbanization of rural schools 1840-1970' in J.P. Sher (ed.) Education in Rural America - A reassessment of conventional wisdom, Westview Press, California

Sher, J.P. (1981) 'Education in the countryside. Overview of conditions and some conclusions' in J.P. Sher (ed.) Rural Education in

Urbanized Nations: Issues and Innovations,
OECD/CERI Report, Westview Special Studies in
Education, Westview Press, California
Trollope, M.H. (1973) 'Problems of reorganization
in a rural countryside since 1944' in P.W.
Warner (ed.) Rural Education, University of
Hull Institute of Education
Whitehead, A. (1976) 'Sexual antagonism in
Herefordshire' in D. Barker and S. Allen (eds.)
Dependence and Exploitation in Work and
Marriage, Longmans, London
Whitfield, R.C. and Nisbet, J. (1982) 'Changing
provision of rural primary education in England
and Scotland'. Paper presented at conference
on Education and Local Development, April,
and also published in J. Sher (ed.) Education
and Rural Development in the United Kingdom,
OECD, Paris

Chapter Five

COMMUNITY ACTION AND COMMUNITY SCHOOLING: THE
CAMPAIGN TO SAVE CROXTETH COMPREHENSIVE
Phil Carspecken

Demographic decline and economic pressures have
stimulated a contraction in educational provision
throughout Britain. In Liverpool these forces
precipitated stormy debates over secondary reorganisation between two competing policies:
'parental choice' and 'community comprehensives'.
Croxteth Comprehensive was officially closed in
1981 by advocates of the 'parental choice' policy.
In response, residents of this working class estate
mounted a three-year campaign to win their school
back. On 13 July, 1982 their protest culminated
in the illegal take-over of the school buildings.
For the next twelve months, the Croxteth Community
Action Committee ran its own school with help from
volunteer teachers. In this chapter, I analyse
the development of their campaign and the educational
issues it raised.

EDUCATION IN LIVERPOOL

1) The Effect of Falling Rolls on Secondary
      Provision: 'Parental Choice'
The national fall in birth rates, which began in
1964, was accelerated in Liverpool by a trend of
outward migrations dating back to the 1930's
(Brown and Ferguson, 1982) and a slum clearance
programme implemented during the late 1960's which
decanted large numbers of people into outlying
districts like Runcorn and Kirkby. The result
has been an unprecedented decline in births, dropping
from 16,479 in 1962 to 6,166 in 1977.
    The effect of the falling birth rate on school
rolls can be seen in figure 1. The primary sector
was first affected in 1969, to be followed by the
secondary sector in 1973. In the primary sector,
over-all rolls dropped from 76,000 in January 1969

to 39,800 in January 1984 - a drop of 48 per cent.
In the secondary sector, rolls dropped 23 per cent
from their peak in January 1974 to 40,200 in
January 1984.   Secondary rolls will continue their
decline through the 1980's (Liverpool Education
Department, 1965-1977, 1978-1984).

When the decline in Liverpool school rolls was
first noticed in 1970 it was welcomed as a beneficial trend.   Schools built to minimum standards in
the 1950's and 1960's had been very full and declining rolls meant more space and lower pupil-teacher
ratios.   More importantly, lower numbers increased
the opportunities for parents to choose schools
of their liking.   Admission areas surrounded each
school to ensure places for children living nearby,
but parents were allowed to apply for empty places
in other schools.   As rolls declined, increasing
numbers of pupils began to attend schools outside
their neighbourhoods.   A pattern of attendance
resulted in favouring comprehensives located in
buildings of old grammar schools which lay, for
the most part, in middle-class suburban sections
of the city.

Of course, this pattern of choice meant that
schools lacking the prestige of former grammar
schools were left to bear the brunt of population
decline.   Several of these unfortunate schools
were in the inner city, others, like Croxteth
Comprehensive, in outer city working class estates.
By 1975, Liverpool had a suburban belt, the 'Queens'
Drive District', of well-attended, high status
comprehensives sandwiched between seriously depopulated schools in the inner and outer city.
Figure 2 compares roll declines in schools
representing each area.   Paddington Comprehensive
lay in the inner city, Yew Tree, Speke and Croxteth
in the outer city.   Ellergreen Comprehensive, the
site upon which Croxteth was to be amalgamated in
1982, lay just two miles towards the city centre
from Croxteth.   Between 1975 and 1982, city-wide
secondary rolls dropped by 18 per cent.   Quarry
Bank lost only 7 per cent of its numbers during
this period, Childwall Valley lost 8 per cent, and
Queen Mary (a voluntary school) actually gained
1 per cent.   Croxteth and Ellergreen, meanwhile,
both lost 41 per cent.   Speke lost 48 per cent and
Paddington lost 36 per cent.   Most of the
differences can be attributed to the effects of
parental choice.

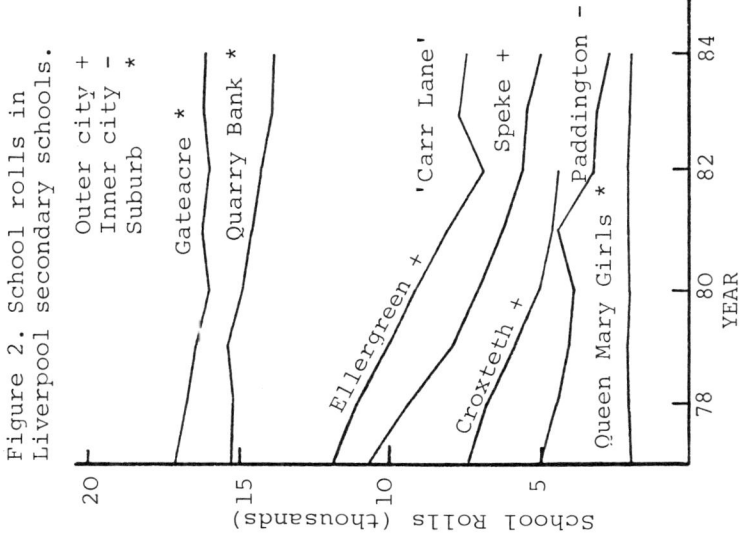

Figure 2. School rolls in Liverpool secondary schools.

Outer city +
Inner city −
Suburb *

Gateacre *
Quarry Bank *
Ellergreen +
'Carr Lane'
Speke +
Croxteth +
Paddington −
Queen Mary Girls *

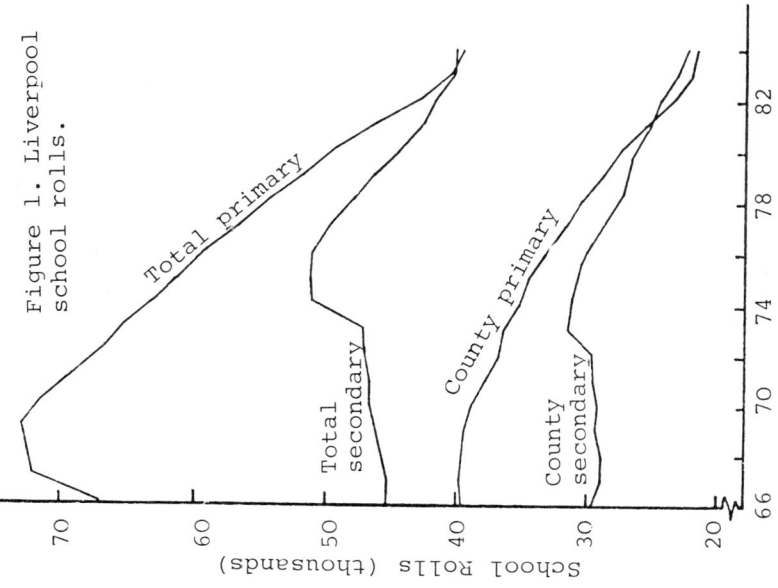

Figure 1. Liverpool school rolls.

Total primary
Total secondary
County primary
County secondary

2) Political Struggles over Reorganisation: 'Choice' vs 'Community'

By 1975 it was clear that reorganisation was necessary. A system of staffing according to pupil numbers meant that a contraction in subject options would follow the rapid pupil depopulations in the inner and outer city schools. There was also concern over the amount of money being lost through the inefficient use of school buildings (Liverpool Education Committee, 1978/79). By 1978 there were 7,500 surplus places in LEA secondary schools and the local papers claimed that between £1 million and £1½ million could be saved through reorganisation (Liverpool Daily Echo, 21/7/78).

The demographic trend and the pattern of parental choice suggested two basic approaches to city-wide reorganisation. One was first formally proposed by the Director of Education, Kenneth Antcliffe in 1976 for the consideration of a newly formed 'Reorganisation and Development Subcommittee'. It suggested that parental choice be curtailed in order to protect the rolls of the inner and outer city schools. The result would have been a number of rationalisations, amalgamations and closures designed to retain a roughly equal geographical distribution of schools throughout the city. This approach, with a number of elaborations not necessarily consistent with Antcliffe's personal views, was also to become the basis of Labour Party proposals for 'district comprehensives' (1978) and later for 'community comprehensives' (1983). The Labour Party was aware that this policy meant a restriction of choice, but argued that this would be offset by making 'education more closely linked to the local community' (Daily Echo 1/7/78).

The second basic approach sought to use parental preferences to guide reorganisation. Under the slogan of 'parental choice' it became the policy of the Liberals: 'The key to our proposals was that parents should vote with their feet, that reorganisation should actually be carried out by the parents themselves' (David Alton, Liberal councillor on the Education Committee during the 1970's) (1). This principle, with the addition of selective schools, was basic to the Conservative Party's position as well. The Liberals were the second largest party in Liverpool during the 1970's, the Conservatives were the third.

In practical terms, 'parental choice' meant that the school depopulation trends summarised in figure 2 ought to be the basis for deciding

closures. It argued that the depopulated schools
were effectively being 'voted against' by parents
and ought to be closed down.

3) Controversy and Stalemate: 1975 - 1980
Antcliffe's 1976 proposal was leaked to the press
before the Reorganisation Subcommittee even met to
discuss it and a great public outcry resulted.   A
city-wide organisation of parents immediately formed
to ensure a parental voice in policy decisions.
As the subcommittee meetings proceeded during 1977
and 1978 at least seven parent action committees
were formed around schools whose names had been
proposed for possible closure.   Parents even
lobbied the DES in London before Liverpool Council
had agreed on any plan.

Agreement on a city-wide plan was nearly
impossible because of the incompatible policy
positions of the three political parties and
because Liverpool's Council had been 'hung' since
1973 - no party having the overall majority necessary to pass controversial proposals through.
General agreement on the primacy of parental choice
enabled the Conservatives and Liberals to collabor-
ate on a number of piecemeal proposals and in 1978
these two parties voted together on a 'partial
solution' based on the closure of Paddington
Comprehensive and the creation of a sixth form
college in its buildings.   A number of other
closures in the inner city area were part of this
plan.   In March 1979, the Secretary of State for
Education, Shirley Williams, rejected the bulk of
the resolutions, allowing only one small inner city
school to close.   Liverpool thus entered the 1980's
with virtually no progress made on its badly needed
reorganisation.

THE CLOSURE OF CROXTETH COMPREHENSIVE

In 1980 the Liberal Party produced a new list of
recommended closures and amalgamations.   The chief
architect of the plans was Michael Storey, Liberal
chairman of the Education Committee and councillor
for the Norris Green ward.   Included in the plans
was the amalgamation of Croxteth Comprehensive with
Ellergreen Comprehensive on the latter's site.
Ellergreen Comprehensive lay within Michael Storey's
Norris Green ward.   General details of the resulting protest and eventual occupation of Croxteth
Comprehensive can be found in Carspecken and Miller
(1983, 1984a, 1984b).   Below I analyse the devel-

opment of the protest along four parameters,
isolating the factors which allowed it to succeed
and noting changes in the 'educational philosophy'
of the participants. I also consider implications
of the events in Croxteth for the 'community
schooling' concept.

1) The Croxteth Estate

The Croxteth housing estate is one of the most
deprived sections of Liverpool. It lies within
the Gillmoss electoral ward, five miles outside
Liverpool City Centre, which had an unemployment
rate of 29.4 per cent (calculated against the
number of 'economically active people') in 1981
compared with 19.8 per cent in the city over all
(Liverpool Planning Department figures). Decline
in local industry, particularly along the East
Lancashire Road which flanks one side of Croxteth,
has accounted for a 153 per cent increase in
unemployment for Gillmoss from 1971 to 1981. The
corresponding figure for Liverpool as a whole was
104 per cent.

Croxteth itself is the most deprived portion
of Gillmoss. Figures from the Croxteth-Gillmoss
Federation estimate adult unemployment to have been
58 per cent in 1983 and unemployment among 16 to 19
year olds to be as high as 95 per cent. Housing
conditions in Croxteth are extremely bad, though
improvements began in 1982 and continue to this day.
In 1983, requests for housing repairs averaged 274
a week for 7,108 houses, 30 per cent of which were
vacant (Croxteth Area Working Party, 1983).
Houses designed for coal fire heating have suffered
high levels of damp since the introduction of gas
fires in the 1960's. Black and green mould abound,
as do diseases related to damp.

In 1973 a Liverpool Policy and Finance Committee
report stated:

> For various reasons, when the Croxteth Estate
> was constructed emphasis was given to the
> provision of housing accommodation and the
> provision of many of the associated environ-
> mental and social facilities necessary to
> provide the basis for a balanced and integrated
> community had lagged behind.

To this day Croxteth has no swimming baths, no
cinema, job centre, or adequate shopping centre.
It lacked any recreational facility at all until
the completion of a YMCA in 1983. The Croxteth
Area Working Party Report (1983) describes prevalent

depression and high rates of marital break-ups
which can be partially attributed to the combination
of unemployment, poor housing, and few facilities.

2) The School

Croxteth Comprehensive was formed in 1966 by amal-
gamating two secondary modern schools: Croxteth
Secondary Girls and Croxteth Secondary Boys. The
two buildings are separated by a 22 acre playing
field. It was the only LEA secondary school on
the 24,000 person estate (until 1983 there were
four Catholic secondary schools and two of these
remain after the 1983 Catholic reorganisation).
    As we have seen (figure 2), Croxteth Comprehen-
sive experienced much decline in its rolls during
the latter half of the 1970's. Designed for 750
pupils, it had only 513 or 68 per cent of its places
filled in 1982. Designed for five forms of entry,
Croxteth had just under three forms of entry every
year from 1977 to its time of closure in 1982. The
number of pupils entering the school was stable
during this period, however, remaining in the high
seventies and low eighties, which indicates that
the school's population would most likely not have
continued to drop much further had it remained open.
    One of the reasons for the small number of
pupils entering Croxteth each year was the effect
of 'creaming'. Because Croxteth Comprehensive
was based on the sites of two former secondary
modern schools it could not compete with the
prestige of former grammar schools. Director of
Education, Kenneth Antcliffe said that in Liverpool
'no comprehensive based in the buildings of former
secondary modern schools really got off the ground'.
The Croxteth Estate itself has suffered from a
stigma in Liverpool. Local resident Pat Brennan
explained that most people in Liverpool 'think that
only people who'd been evicted or come out of jail
or something live in Croxteth'. It is therefore
not surprising that some parents would want to
send their children to schools outside Croxteth.
Approximately one third of parents with children
in Croxteth Comprehensive's main feeder primary
were doing so in 1980.
    Croxteth Comprehensive, however, was well
regarded by those parents who sent their children
to it, by its staff and by the Director of Education
who called it 'Excellent given its area and
circumstances'. The school was used as a youth
club and operated services for the elderly at times
during the year. It arranged transportation for

children during bad weather and the head teacher,
George Smith, often counselled adults in the
neighbourhood.   It was regarded as a 'highly
disciplined' school by parents, staff and pupils
alike, with much emphasis on school uniforms.   The
cane was used 'when necessary'.   George Smith
summarised the atmosphere of the school as being
traditional and respected:

> It wasn't progressive in any way ... the
> staff were beautifully dressed and the
> children were beautifully dressed ... the
> local cowboys will perhaps break every
> window in the district, but not at the
> school.

3) Closure

The Liberals justified their decision to close
Croxteth Comprehensive with two main arguments:
the school was under-populated and parents were
choosing to send their children to other schools.
Sir Keith Joseph summarised the arguments in a
letter to Labour Councillor Bob Wareing in May
1982.   The low numbers meant:

> the inefficient use of buildings with con-
> sequent wastage of funds,
> the reduction of staff which would either
> contract the curriculum (which in fact
> didn't happen) or put extra strains on the
> smaller staff with educationally deleterious
> effects,
> disadvantages to the less-able according to
> the HMI which insists on a minimum of four
> forms of entry to maintain standards.

He also pointed out that 'no less than a third of
the 11+ children in the area stated and took up
a preference for schools other than Croxteth'.
    Key dates and events in the closure of Croxteth
Comprehensive are listed below:

28 January 1981	Liverpool Council votes in favour of the amalgamation with majority of three.
3Q November 1981	Keith Joseph announces his approval of plan.
November 1981 – March 1982	Action Committee carries out a number of direct actions to publicise cause (see below).

The Campaign to Save Croxteth Comprehensive

1 March 1982	Conservatice Party visits estate. Struck by the deprivation, change position to favour the school.
3 March 1982	Conservatives and Labour vote together to pass a resolution to 'reopen' a school in Croxteth. Majority of 31.
May 1982	Keith Joseph announces his rejection of the new resolution. Croxteth Comprehensive to close in July.
13 July 1982	The Action Committee occupies the school buildings.
July - September 1982	The Action Committee runs a 'pilot' summer school programme.
20 September 1982 - 19 July 1983	The Action Committee runs classes for 150 secondary pupils of the Croxteth estate with the help of volunteer teachers.
5 May 1983	The Liverpool Labour Party wins an over-all majority in the council with a campaign pledge to re-open Croxteth Comprehensive.

The Labour Party was not able to re-absorb Croxteth Comprehensive immediately, however, because of legal problems. Instead, it funded the school for half of its budget in the 1983/84 school year as an independent. It is being run under slightly more supportive conditions in 1984-85 and will become a full county secondary comprehensive in September 1985.

4) Resistance
Resistance to closure went through three rough stages distinguished by four variables: 1) The people/groups involved in protest, 2) the goals and aspirations of the protest, 3) the tactics used in pursuit of those goals, and 4) the justifications/ explanations used with respect to tactics and goals.

PHASE I: November 1980 to November 1981: Two main groups organised after the 10 November 1980 announcement to oppose the closure: teaching staff and parents. The school governors were also active in protest, but affiliated themselves primarily with the staff. Teachers formed a committee under the leadership of George Smith and immediately protested about the total lack of consultation preceding the formulation of the plan. They drafted several alternative plans to the closure for the consideration of the Education Committee.

By and large, the staff accepted the Liberal arguments on the detrimental effects of low numbers at Croxteth Comprehensive. Although they pointed out that subject options in the school had not contracted, and that disadvantaged pupils were receiving sufficient attention, they were in agreement that low numbers meant unacceptable wastage of educational monies, and they based their proposals on <u>alternative solutions to the depopulation problem</u>. They pointed out that a new housing estate was being built next to Croxteth which would total 4,000 new homes by 1996, claiming that the new housing estate would produce sufficient numbers of secondary pupils to fill both buildings by the early 1990's. Meanwhile, several means of keeping the buildings cost-effective were available. The school could move entirely into one of its buildings, for example. It could be amalgamated with Croxteth Junior School, or it could be run alongside an expanded Return and Learn scheme.

The staff argued, furthermore, that if an amalgamation of Croxteth and Ellergreen was absolutely necessary, <u>it should be Ellergreen, not Croxteth, which closes</u>. Several reasons were given for this. Croxteth had larger playing fields (Ellergreen actually had no playing fields at all), Croxteth had modern dining facilities in both its buildings, Ellergreen in only one. Ellergreen's split site was divided by a dangerously busy dual carriageway, and so on. A major argument of the teaching staff for retaining a school in Croxteth was <u>the special need of the area for a school</u> because of its general deprivation. The school was one of the only assets in the community.

Parents organised a parallel campaign using the same arguments as the teachers. Pat Rigby, secretary of the Croxteth-Gillmoss Federation which has its office in the heart of the estate, claimed that after the closure announcement 'for the first time the whole community reacted to something, and they all reacted in the same way, with total disbelief and shock'. According to Pat, this included many parents who were not sending their children to the school. John Dunne, a Croxteth parent with two children in the school, expressed his own reactions:

> It was just sheer indignation that they could close your neighbourhood school down like that

overnight! To say that that school just
doesn't exist any more and you've got to send
your kids two or three miles away. It was
just amazement, indignation and anger on
everybody's part.

Six hundred and fifty people attended a protest
meeting at the school four days after the announcement. An action committee was formed and a
campaign of lobbying with letters and personal visits
to councillors begun. The goal of both teachers
and parents during this first phase was simply to
prevent the closure of their school, even if that
meant Ellergreen would close instead. Tactics
were entirely institutional: submitting alternative
proposals and lobbying politicians. The justification of the campaign has already been outlined above:
the basic arguments of the Liberals and Conservatives
for closures were not contested, only the specific
decision to close Croxteth was.

PHASE II: December 1981 to July 1982. The teaching
staff withdrew from the campaign after Keith Joseph's
announcement in November that he approved the closure.
Interviews with former staff members, who wish to
remain annonymous, indicate at least three reasons
for this. First, all legal means of protest
appeared to have been exhausted and many teachers
were reluctant to participate in civil disobedience.
Second, the staff had been assured that they would
have jobs with the LEA after the amalgamation and
the time to apply for posts was approaching. Many,
in fact, had to apply to Ellergreen, and it was
feared that further protesting would endanger their
chances. Third, George Smith, the head teacher,
who had been very much a leading figure in the
protests of the staff, had taken an early retirement
due to poor health.
    The parents, however, re-organised themselves
and adopted new tactics. Phillip Knibb, currently
the chairman of the Action Committee, joined the
struggle at this time, bringing many years of trade
union experience with him. Cyril D'Arcy, secretary
of the Action Committee since its formation, also
had a trade union background and helped Phillip Knibb
lead the way for a heightened campaign. The
Committee was renamed 'Croxteth Community Action
Committee' and meetings were now held outside the
school buildings in local pubs and churches in order
to try to broaden membership beyond parents of
children in the school. The new tactics included:

The Campaign to Save Croxteth Comprehensive

December 1981	Occupation of the Liverpool Daily Echo, Daily Post and local radio offices in a demand for more publicity,
2,3,4 February 1982	Blockage of traffic on the East Lancashire Road,
3 March 1982	Blockage of traffic in the city centre,
22 May 1982	Blockage of city bus routes at Pier Head, Liverpool's largest bus terminal,
6 July 1982	Occupation of offices in the Department of Education buildings,
13 July 1982	Occupation of the school buildings.

These tactics were successful in drawing public attention to Croxteth. Several newspaper features on the estate appeared during the early months of 1982 along with pictures of some of the worst housing. The longest feature, published by the Echo 2 March, described the role of the school to be 'one of the threads holding the community together'. It was this argument, that Croxteth Comprehensive was a sort of oasis in a desert of deprivation, which won over the Conservative Party in March. One member, who had been on the Education Committee at the time, explained the change of heart: 'We became convinced that it was more than just a school'.

Hence the argument of the campaign shifted during Phase II. The parents were no longer echoing the teachers in their efforts to show how the problem of low numbers could be solved in other ways than by closing the school down. They were bringing forth what had formerly been one of several arguments into an almost exclusive position – the exceptional social need for a school in Croxteth. The other arguments developed during the first year were retained, but remained in the background – to be drawn upon when needed.

Also during this phase the argument that Ellergreen Comprehensive should be closed instead of Croxteth was dropped altogether. A leaflet dated February 1982 states: 'We don't oppose the amalgamation, only the choice of site'. But a few months later the Action Committee supported a school in every community:

We consider that Norris Green, where Ellergreen is, and Croxteth or Gillmoss, where Croxteth Comprehensive is, are two separate communities,

and they are both entitled to have their own
local comprehensive school.
Cyril D'Arcy, Secretary of Action Committee

The emphasis on 'community' was evident in
another way during this second phase. After the
3 March council vote in favour of the school, the
Action Committee was convinced the battle had been
won. But rather than disbanding, it formed a
number of subcommittees concerned with other
problems on the estate, like housing and recreation.
It actually managed to get one resident rehoused
by putting pressure on the housing department. But
in May, when Keith Joseph rejected the proposal to
're-establish' a comprehensive in Croxteth, the
Action Committee dropped its new activities and
refocussed its energies on the school.
Tactically, as we have seen, this phase
employed a number of techniques of civil disobedience.
By this time, Action Committee membership had
stabilised at about thirty, though many more
attended demonstrations. Most of these were women
who had never before demonstrated or picketted.
Many brought along their infants when the East
Lancashire Road was blocked and the papers headlined
the event as 'Petticoat Blockade' (Daily Post,
3/2/82). The leaders of the Action Committee,
however, were men with much previous experience in
picketting and demonstrating. Nothing in the
tactics of Phase II was outside their experience.

PHASE III: August 1982 to July 1983. When the
school buildings were occupied in July a number of
sympathetic outsiders offered their help. Several
of these were teachers, and it is from their ranks
that the first suggestion to actually run the school
was made. While the occupation of buildings is
a well-known trade union tactic with plenty of
precedents, running a school for children was
totally beyond the experience of the Action Committee.
They realised that it would be impossible without
the help and advice of teachers and put out a call
for more volunteers. In August, a pilot summer
school programme was run and by September enough
volunteers had arrived to open the school for the
1982/83 year. Two hundred and seven pupils turned
up for the first day of classes, indicating extensive
support from parents in Croxteth.
The strategy of the Action Committee took on
new features during the occupation. Phase II
strategy had concentrated on community mobilisation

119

to mount highly visible public demonstrations.
Public attention made it easier to pressurise all
three political parties to vote in favour of the
school.   Initially the occupation represented a
continuation of the public visibility approach,
dramatising the committee's determination not to
yield its school.   But after a November council
vote which narrowly defeated a proposal to reopen
Croxteth Comprehensive, the Action Committee began
to concentrate primarily on the electoral victory
of the Labour Party in the forthcoming May elections.
     In late November a rally was held inside the
school which featured several Labour Party and trade
union leaders.   It was meant to promote a new
organisation, formed in August in order to aid
Croxteth Comprehensive, called the 'Merseyside Trade
Union-Community Liaison Committee'.   In contrast
to phase II, when public meetings over the school
were announced through loud hailers on top of cars,
no effort had been made to invite members of the
community.   They were not excluded from the meeting,
but its purpose was more to plan opposition to Tory
cuts by united trade union and Labour Party efforts,
than to address residents of Croxteth.   Despite the
name of the committee, little was said about
mobilising communities.   Instead, the anti-cuts
policies of the Labour Party were stressed.
     The 'Merseyside Trade Union-Community Liaison
Committee' became the lifeline of the occupation.
Through its efforts enough money was collected from
various (primarily manual) union branches to keep
Croxteth School running for the entire year.
Expenses during the winter, when heating and lighting
costs were highest, went as high as £400 per week.
Without trade union support the occupation would not
have been possible.   It is remarkable that such
support was mustered.   Most writers on urban and
community politics stress the typical absence of
union-community links (Cockburn 1977:168;   Saunders
1981:27).   I asked Eddie Roberts, Merseyside
District Secretary of the TGWU, who was the TGWU's
representative on the Merseyside Liaison Committee
and one of its most active members, why Croxteth was
supported when such support is said to be rare.   He
answered that the TGWU has often supported community
struggles (such as the Tower Hill rent strikes) and
added:

> It depends on the style of campaign that you've
> chosen to run.   Trade union activists, people
> like Phil Knibb, they're working class lads,

trade union members. It's natural to them to
say who could be counted on as their natural
allies - our unions.

This raises an important point. Studies of city
politics indicate the existence of informal 'rules
of access' to power which are usually learned and
played most successfully by middle class communities
(see Saunders 1983:62-65). The case of Croxteth
demonstrates the existence of such 'rules of access'
to alternative sources of power, such as the trade
unions. The existence of community leadership
capable of establishing contacts and of understanding
what 'style' of campaign is most likely to attract
union sympathies is important. Cockburn (1977)
makes a similar observation when she describes how
the style of campaign adopted by squatters in
Lambeth obstructed the sympathies of the Labour
movement.

After Christmas 1982, the Action Committee set
up a 'campaign office' inside the school to coordinate fund raising and to organise a 'national'
march against the Tories to take place in April,
which would end with speeches outside the school
buildings. When this demonstration actually took
place, most of the speakers were from the Labour
Party and the dominant message was to 'vote Labour'
in the May election. As May 1983 approached, many
Action Committee members and some of the teaching
staff canvassed for the Labour Party. Throughout
this period of close coordination between the
Action Committee and the Labour Party good informal
relationships were established between the Action
Committee leadership and key members of the Party.
These informal links later proved very useful by
giving the Action Committee a negotiating voice in
the private discussions held on reorganisation after
the May election victory. They also kept the Action
Committee informed of various constraints and
problems facing the Labour Party and contributed to
the development of a city-wide perspective in the
Action Committee's leadership. Once again, access
was established through the informal contacts of
the community leaders. It is important to note,
however, that this success on the part of the Action
Committee corresponded to a shift of attention away
from community mobilisation, the leaders' energies
becoming more bound up with city politics. Recently
Phillip Knibb has shifted his energies back to
mobilising community participation in Croxteth
Community School.

Both the goal of the Action Committee and the justification used for its campaign changed as well during phase III. The 'exceptional need' argument was not used after the Labour Party's city-wide community comprehensive plan was accepted by the Action Committee. In April 1983, Phillip Knibb stated in a staff meeting that he was not interested in any measure to re-establish a school in Croxteth if it endangered the school of another community. The justification of the fight to save Croxteth now lay within an over-all plan guaranteeing 'a school in every neighbourhood' (Liverpool Education Committee, 1983). In the case of Phillip Knibb and several other members of the Action Committee, the goal itself had shifted to the city-wide plan.

However, the close links with the Labour Party and full acceptance of their policy meant that the Action Committee had to accept the same financial constraints to planning that the Labour Party did. 'Staffing by curriculum', rather than by numbers of pupils, was sometimes argued for during phase II, but by phase III this was considered impractical, though still desirable. The Labour Party's plan called for the closure of nine schools, chosen to leave schools evenly distributed across the city and to shift resources in favour of the city's deprived areas rather than away from them (Liverpool Education Committee, 1983). The Action Committee effectively approved the closure of 9 schools by giving its support to this policy in phase III.

Figure 3 summarises the phases of the struggle of Croxteth Comprehensive. In the main, the goals and educational arguments characterising each period were those of the 'official face' of the campaign as presented by its leaders to the press and in interviews. I was only able to compare the personal goals and attitudes of different members of the Action Committee during the last phase, when I was present as a participant-observer. I found that some differences existed between the attitudes of the membership and leadership: the members tending to think more in terms of the single issue of saving their school than in terms of reorganising education across the city. However, all the members opposed education cuts in general and none, by the time of the occupation, argued that Ellergreen should close.

FIGURE 3

PHASES OF THE CAMPAIGN FOR CROXTETH COMPREHENSIVE

Time Period	People/Groups Involved	Goals/Aspirations	Tactics	Justification
Nov. 1980 – Nov. 1981	Parents Action Committee. Old teaching staff.	Prevent school closure.	Use of established channels, submission of alternative plans and lobbying. Low public visibility.	Objection to lack of consultation. Deprivation in Croxteth warrants an exception to closure policy. The existence of alternatives to closure which will solve low numbers problem.
Dec. 1981 – Jul. 1982	Croxteth Community Action Committee.	Reverse closure. (briefly) Better Croxteth estate in all ways.	Civil disobedience. Lobby of all parties. High public visibility. High community mobilisation.	Exceptional deprivation of Croxteth. Opposition to closures generally.
Jul. 1983 – Jul. 1984	Croxteth Community Action Committee. Volunteer teachers. (indirectly) Local trade unions. (indirectly) Local Labour Party.	(initially) hold school until campaign succeeds. (later) support reorganisation of education in city. (later) question traditional school experience.	Occupy and run school. Aid party-political electoral campaign. Link to trade unions. High public visibility. Low community mobilisation.	Community school ideology of Labour Party. (developing) community school ideas of Action Committee.

COMMUNITY SCHOOLING AND THE OCCUPATION OF
CROXTETH COMPREHENSIVE

1) Community Schooling: Principles and Problems
When the Croxteth Community Action Committee adopted
the 'community comprehensive' policy of the local
Labour Party they were essentially supporting a plan
for the even geographical distribution of facilities
throughout Liverpool.   What was actually to take
place inside those facilities was not an issue.
      In contrast, most of the literature on community
schooling is specifically concerned with improving
the quality of educational experience, especially
for pupils from deprived urban areas (Halsey 1972;
Midwinter 1972, 1973, 1975).   Hatch and Moyland
(1972) identify what they call a 'radical interpretation' of the community school concept which seeks
to offset class-biased socialising functions of the
school by:

1)   using an alternative 'community curriculum'
       which makes use of the immediate social
       environment and employs actual 'community
       action' where possible;

2)   establishing a high degree of community control
       over the school with local adults taking part
       in key decisions.

This 'radical interpretation' has also been identified in more recent studies of community education
(e.g. Williams and Robins 1980).   In addition to
the above two points, most advocates of community
schooling stress the importance of:

3)   changing the relationships between teachers,
       pupils and parents in the direction of more
       informality.
       (See Moon 1983:148;   Fletcher and Thompson
       1980.)

The aim of informal relationships is to give pupils
more self-direction and to generate maximum input
from parents.
      Educators attempting to practice these ideas
have encountered many problems, two of which are
highly typical and appear as actual dilemmas from
the stand-point of educational planning:
      First, there is frequently a conflict between
the 'progressive' ideas of educators and what
are usually described as the 'conservative'

attitudes of parents (see Hargreaves 1982:124).
This constitutes a dilemma if community education is to mean, simultaneously, community
control and an alternative curriculum.

Second, there is a problem with respect to
power.   As Boyd (1977:16-17) expresses it:

Involvement of those living in the neighbourhood so that they cease to perceive themselves
as recipients, and see themselves as agents
bringing out change would seem to be a necessary
condition ... yet, paradoxically, it would seem
that people in the inner city are powerless
to bring about change of and by themselves.

Boyd cites Halsey (1972) and Midwinter (1972) for
evidence of the powerlessness typifying deprived
urban areas.   Some theorists claim that the problem
of power will never be resolved on the side of the
community unless the actual class structure of society
as a whole is changed (e.g. Merson and Campbell
1974:44).

2) Power, Curriculum and Community-School
Relationships in Croxteth

The occupation of Croxteth Comprehensive takes on
special interest in the light of the above discussion
for it reversed the usual order of problems encountered in community education programmes.   The
Action Committee had an unusual degree of power,
but began the occupation without any plan or desire
for an alternative curriculum.   The power of the
Action Committee rested upon four factors:

1)   The Action Committee had an alternative base of
     resources (the trade unions) out of the reach
     of the local government.

2)   The Action Committee had political representa-
     tion on the council through the support of a
     political party (Labour) and excellent links
     between community leaders and party
     representatives.

3)   The Action Committee had high public visibility
     which served as a deterrent to the threatened
     use of bailiffs.   (An example of this occurred
     in December 1982 when a politician informed
     the Action Committee of a plan to send in
     bailiffs during the Christmas holidays.   The

threat was immediately publicised in the papers
and on the radio along with objections from the
community and Labour Party representatives.
No attempt to use bailiffs was actually made
in the end.)

4)   The Action Committee had <u>formal control over
      the school</u>. The teaching staff was subordin-
      ate to the committee and committee members were
      present 24 hours a day, both observing the
      activities of teachers and taking part in many
      educational activities themselves.

The first three points enabled the Action Committee
to succeed in winning back their school.   The
fourth unintentionally opened up a new dimension to
their campaign.   Now that they had complete formal
control over their school the question of curriculum
and school relationships suddenly arose.   I examine
developments in curriculum and relationships during
the occupation below.

A) A 'Proper School'

A number of factors ruled out the possibility of a
'community curriculum' in Croxteth Community School
during its occupation.   The most obvious one was
the lack of any desire on the part of the Action
Committee to run an alternative school.   The
question of educational experience was one they
simply had not considered before.   In addition,
the political enemies of the Action Committee began
to accuse them of gross irresponsibility – using
children as political pawns and endangering their
education.   The Action Committee was therefore
quick to inform the media that traditional subjects
were being offered and that CSE and O level examinations would be taken by pupils in the summer.
      Yet it would be incorrect to describe the
attitudes of Action Committee members as 'traditional'.
None of them really had any clearly articulated
views on education at all.   Rather, a sort of
'folk model' (Holy and Stuchlik 1981, 1983) of what
constitutes 'proper' education was at work.   The
elements of this folk model can be deduced from the
many recorded comments and conversations in my
field notebooks.   Most basic was a concern with
<u>discipline</u>.   If children were seen to be working
quietly in classrooms it was assumed that they were
being properly educated.   Next was a concern that
<u>visible products</u> result from school work (worksheets,
essays, etc.).   Third was a strong belief in the

powers of a proper head and of proper teachers.
Fourth was the belief that pupils 'bright enough'
be taught towards external examinations.   Associated
with these four elements was the widespread belief
that the main purpose of an education was to help
pupils get jobs.

Aside from these few basic requirements, however,
the Action Committee was very open to the 'progressive'
suggestions of staff and probably would have approved
a 'community curriculum' if the teachers had formula-
ted one and if it did not appear to threaten the
basic principles of their folk model.   The committee
readily agreed, during the first few weeks of school,
to have the cane abolished and to have parents work
alongside teachers inside the classrooms when requested.   They also accepted proposals for project work
which would have integrated subject areas, like the
running of a community auto-repair business by
pupils.

But for a number of reasons the teachers were
never able to carry out such ideas and had no hope
of formulating a community educational philosophy.
They were a very diverse group, only 30 per cent
of whom had had previous training and experience in
teaching.   Forty per cent were recent university
graduates with no previous teaching experience and
another 30 per cent came from Croxteth itself with
no qualifications apart from a few O levels.   This
last group taught 'non-academic' subjects like P.E.,
woodwork and needlework, and substituted for absent
teachers.   None of these volunteers had had
previous experience with alternative schooling and
only one had ever administered a school before
(a retired deputy head).   Furthermore, there were
extra demands on time in the occupied school,
especially for the core ten teachers who had to
locate materials, constantly revise the time-table,
advise the lesser experienced teachers, advertise
for more volunteers and often prepare lessons in
subjects they had not taught before.   In such a
situation, traditional subjects, syllabi and text
books were inevitably relied upon.

Another constraint operated upon the teachers
which went beyond the particular situation in
Croxteth.   Most of the teachers agreed with the
Action Committee that examinations were important -
many, in fact, placed much more emphasis on them
than the Committee members.   This meant that streaming had to be introduced in order to provide enough
attention and teaching time to the examination pupils.
The most consistent and experienced teachers were

then allocated to the examination streams, leaving
the non-examination pupils with less consistent
teachers and poorer quality lessons.   Acceptance
of the external examinations thus virtually determined the organisation of classes, the content of
lessons, and the allocation of teachers.

B) Pupil-Teacher Relationships

In terms of teaching practice, the large majority
of volunteers established very informal relationships with pupils at the start of the first term.
Pupils were allowed to call teachers by their first
names, uniforms were not insisted upon, the teachers
themselves dressed informally, and pupils were
often allowed to cluster desks together in classrooms
so that they could talk to each other while working.
This informal approach was so different from the way
the school had previously been run that it was seen
as very radical by pupils and parents alike.   A
large minority of the pupils responded with disruptive behaviour which soon forced teachers to return
to more traditional methods.   Complaints from the
Action Committee also pressurised teachers to
adopt more formality.   Sanctions were soon put into
use which included detentions, suspensions, even
expulsions, and the establishment of a 'discipline
room' (run by parents) to which pupils could be sent
during school hours.   Disruptions came under control
with these methods.

     Many parents were dismayed when teachers con-
tinued to allow pupils to use their first names,
but interviews taken during the last two months of
the occupation indicate that this attitude changed.
Pupils, parents and teachers almost unanimously
approved of first name usage by that time.   On a
questionnaire administered during the final week,
over 90 per cent of the pupils rated their teachers
highly in terms of their helpfulness and approach-
ability.   'The teachers are kind and helpful',
'You can talk to them', and 'Some of them understand
your feelings, a lot of them do' were typical
comments.   Nearly all the community volunteers
also expressed preference for the warm relationships
established by most of the volunteer teachers over
the stiffer relationships which had previously
characterised the school.   On the same questionnaire,
however, most of the pupils simultaneously expressed
the wish that teachers had been 'stricter'.

     Volunteers from the local community were
particularly adept at achieving this desired
combination of warmth and firmness.   Mick Checkland

and Joey Jacobs took the P.E. and games classes
for the entire year. Both had grown up in Croxteth
and both were extremely effective teacher's. Mick
described his technique:

> Put fun into it, you know, you let them do it,
> you make the kids think that it's their idea
> all the time and they'll work like mad, they
> really will.

Mick thus shared the progressives' goal of self-
motivation, but he didn't achieve it with what is
usually understood by 'informality'. It rather
seemed to be his ability to 'speak the language' of
the children, a language that combined plenty of
gruff handling with 'a laugh and a joke'.

It is worth noting that the original response
of Croxteth pupils to informality with disruptive
behaviour is not unique. Many innovative schools
have had to endure a period of frequent disruptions
before pupils began to become more self-directing
(see Moon 1983:148 for summary of six such schools).
It is during such 'transition periods', moreover,
that the 'conservative' views of parents are reported
with much dismay. The experience of Croxteth
Community School suggests three things with respect
to teacher-pupil relationships:

- First, if parents are present and in communication with teachers their attitudes towards
  formality and informality may change.

- Second, it is by no means certain that 'informal'
  relationships are entirely desirable. Warm
  and supportive relationships mixed with a high
  degree cf firmness seemed to be called for in
  Croxteth.

- Third, the form of effective relationships
  will probably be different in different communities. In this respect, teachers stand to
  learn much from residents of the school's
  neighbourhood.

C) 'Conscious Dissatisfaction': Community-School
Relationships and Educational Change
The most 'community' feature of Croxteth Community
School was not its curriculum nor its pupil-teacher
relationships but the 24 hour presence of local
residents. They ran the kitchen, cleaned the classrooms, worked in the office and substituted in the

classrooms when teachers were absent.   Some of the
helpers from the community discovered that they could
keep discipline better than many of the trained
teachers and university graduates, and confidence
in their own perceptions and opinions on education
grew as a result.   As the year progressed, several
parents became critical of traditional education.
Margaret Gaskell was a local parent with two children in the school.   When interviewed in 1984 she
said:

> When I first came in, I just was interested in
> a school, and being involved during those
> 12 months, that's when I started to . . .
> I mean, you were trying to decide if you should
> have exams, you should have that many O levels,
> CSEs, and the kids would turn around and say,
> well Why?, and I started to think about it,
> you know, and then I said to myself, Well, Why?
> You know, they're leaving school, the kids
> with O levels, A levels, what have you, and
> they're still on the dole.

Margaret was responding to the frequent complaint of pupils over the uselessness of what they
were being taught.   This complaint contrasted with
the almost unanimous feelings of loyalty to the
school and enthusiasm for the campaign against its
closure which pupils expressed in interviews
throughout the year.   The only purpose they could
see to learning subjects like mathematics, English
and history was to better their chances of getting
a job later in life.   In a community with over
95 per cent of school leavers unemployed and one
out of every two adults (economically active adults)
drawing dole, such an exercise seemed pointless to
many.
Teachers and parents alike found it difficult
to answer the 'there's no jobs anyway' argument.
'I know what they mean' was a frequent remark in
the staffroom (all the volunteers, from inside and
outside Croxteth, were unemployed).   Alternative
explanations for the worth of an education were
offered to the pupils but with little effect.
Statements like 'education will help you change
society so that there will be jobs' or 'education
is a way of getting stronger - a tool for surviving'
must have sounded hollow when the curriculum was
not backing them up - was not giving the children
a sense of growth or strength.
Educational policy thinking on the national

level has long taken employability as a basic
purpose. especially since the late 1970s (CCCS 1981
: 239).   This has absurdly continued into the 1980s,
a period of unprecedented unemployment in Britain.
In Croxteth this notion seemed prevalent in the
common conceptions or folk models of the Action
Committee and pupils.   It was an effective constraint
on educational innovation.

Parents in Croxteth were also becoming critical
of the examination system and especially of the
related division of pupils into streams.   Ann Pine,
a local parent, established a very close relationship with the non-exam 4B class.   She was very
bitter over the 'second rate' treatment they were
getting as resources and time were concentrated on
the 4A1 and 4A2 groups progressing on examination
syllabi.   Ann expressed her bitterness at several
staff meetings and to several teachers personally and
was joined by Phillip Knibb, his brother George,
Margaret Gaskell and parent Pat Brennan.   Margaret
saw it as a general problem, produced by the examination system: 'That's very unfair, and I found
out it wasn't just going on in this school, it is
happening in other schools'.

It is interesting that the staff, in total
agreement with the point, responded by attempting
to do project work with the 4Bs, taking them out on
field trips and running a photography project with
them which contrasted a wealthy nearby estate with
the poverty of Croxteth.   The 4Bs were also given
their own form room with table tennis and a tea
kettle.   The staff were essentially recapitulating
the history of 'community curricula' which began in
the 1960s as an attempt to motivate and provide
relevant experiences for 'slower' streams (Boyd
1977, ch. 2).   In Croxteth, as in England generally,
it was discovered that the lower status of such
projects and privileges in comparison with examination work greatly limited their benefits: the
4Bs eventually destroyed their own form room and
continued to feel bitter about the attentions given
the 4A groups.

Thus the examination system was a powerful
constraint on the power held by the Action Committee
over their school.   Keddie (1971) argues that
unless the organisation of knowledge in a school
is changed the experience of the pupils will not
be fundamentally altered despite other innovations.
Salter and Tapper (1981:71) write 'whoever controls
the organisation of knowledge also controls the
experience of schooling'.   Given the role of

public examinations in the organisation of knowledge
it is not surprising that some advocates of community
education call for their abolition (Hargreaves 1982:
12).   No-one in Croxteth actually came to the point
of thinking that the O level and CSE examinations
ought to be ignored, however.   As long as British
society as a whole places so much emphasis on them,
it is extremely unlikely that any single community
would decide to reject them.

Examinations, the popular conception of education as a way of becoming employable, and the
absence of 'alternative folk models' of education
made alternatives difficult to conceive:

> I think we should be offering something.
> Maybe there are no jobs, but there must be
> something else they could be doing worthwhile,
> that'd make them feel as though they're not
> a burden on society, which is what a lot of
> the kids feel they are.   What I don't know.
> I know there should be something.
>
> Margaret Gaskell

Pat Brennan continued Margaret's thoughts: 'I
think what we'd have to find out really is what a
community school is.'

Toward the end of the third term a joint meeting
of teachers and committee members was held to discuss
forms the school might take in the future.   All the
community representatives present expressed the
desire to continue working in the school and some
ideas about possible courses and ways of organising
them were discussed.   A constructive dialogue had
begun between teachers and community which may have
generated answers to the question of 'what a
community school is', at least an answer for
Croxteth.

Boyd (1977:21) drawing on Halsey (1972),
describes how community education would ideally
develop:

> The notion of change which has been discussed
> here has everything to do with a conscious
> dissatisfaction with the status quo developing
> in the neighbourhood.

But Boyd points out that this constitutes a dilemma
for the educational planner: 'conscious dissatisfaction' cannot be imposed from above.

In Croxteth the dilemmas of community education
seemed on the verge of being resolved because

community power and participation had first been
established. With this condition met, dissatisfaction definitely had begun to grow and the
community and teachers had begun to look at
educational problems together (see also Poster
1982 on the usual difficulties of parent-teacher
problem solving). The situation seemed to be an
excellent way to 'set the agenda of inquiry'
(Johnson 1983:25) into appropriate forms of education. But, from a planner's point of view, the
problem of how to 'establish' community power
remains. In Croxteth it occurred by the spontaneous protest of community residents leading to an
illegal occupation of school buildings - not the
sort of foundation a planner is likely to draw
blueprints on.

CONCLUSION AND POSTSCRIPT

The campaign to save Croxteth Comprehensive developed
through a number of phases, partly characterised
by the broadening goals and educational arguments
of its participants. The experience of actually
running a school occupation suggests:

1)   Community power over its school may be
      constrained by popular notions of the main
      purposes of education.

2)   Community power over its school may also
      be highly constrained by the 16+ examinations.

3)   An otherwise powerful position of a community
      over its school, in combination with a high
      degree of community participation, can lead
      local residents to become critical of
      traditional education and establish a construc-
      tive dialogue between themselves and teachers.

Postscript:
In September 1983 Croxteth Community School began
a new year with 50 per cent funding from the local
council as an independent school. The funding
allowed the school to hire new teachers and a Head,
the hiring being carried out by a committee of three
former volunteer teachers, the new Head, and
Phillip Knibb, still chairman of the Action Committee.
Only four of the former teacher volunteers remained
with the school. Oddly, despite their nearly
unanimous desire to stay involved, former community
helpers were not invited back into the school.

The reason was the belief that it would be better educationally if the parents left. As a resident explained: 'Because the school was getting a proper Headmaster, proper staff, we thought it was going to be run like a normal school. I mean we thought ... it would be better to let the teachers on their own.' The notion of a 'proper school' ruled in the end.

The Action Committee met very few times during the following year and then only to discuss financial matters, leaving education to the 'proper' staff. But for those few who retained close contact, like Margaret Gaskell, Pat Brennan and Phillip Knibb, the year was a disappointment. Margaret is more than ever critical of the examination system, streaming, and a content of education which has little relevance to the children of Croxteth. Phillip Knibb has expressed the desire to bring back the involvement of community residents, and has begun taking steps in this direction in the 1984/85 school year.

NOTE

All non-textual quotations in this chapter are from taped interviews conducted by the author in 1982-84.

ACKNOWLEDGEMENTS

I wish to thank the many people of Croxteth who gave me many hours of time in interviews. I also wish to thank Kenneth Antcliffe, Director of Education in Liverpool, Eddie Roberts, District Secretary of General Worker Trade Group, TGWU, Phillip Knibb, Chairman of Croxteth Community Action Committee, Cyril D'Arcy, Secretary of Croxteth Community Action Committee, Margaret Gaskell, Pat Brennan, Mick Checkland, Joey Jacobs, Pat Rigby and John Dunnee for their special contributions. Special thanks also to Tony Williams, Librarian of Liverpool Education Department for his help in compiling educational statistics.

REFERENCES

Boyd, John (1977) Community Education and Urban Schools, Longman, London
Brown, P.J.B. and Ferguson, S.S. (1982) 'Schools and Population Change in Liverpool' in W.T.S. Gould and A.G. Hodgkins (eds.) The Resources of Merseyside, Liverpool University

Press, Liverpool
Carspecken, P. and Miller, H. (1983) 'Parental
    Choice and Community Control: the Case of
    Croxteth Comprehensive', in Ann-Marie Wolpe
    and James Donald (eds.) Is There Anyone Here
    from Education? Pluto Press, London
Carspecken, P. and Miller, H. (1984a) 'Community
    Education in Croxteth', Forum, Autumn
Carspecken, P. and Miller, H. (1984b) 'Croxteth
    Comprehensive - Curriculum and Social
    Relationships in an Occupied School,
    Socialism and Education, 11, (1)
CCCS (1981) Unpopular Education, Hutchinson,
    London
Cockburn, Cynthia (1977) The Local State,
    Management of Cities and People, Pluto Press,
    London
Croxteth Area Working Party (1983) Croxteth Area
    Working Party Report, City of Liverpool
Evans, Bob (1983) 'The Countesthorpe Team System:
    Towards the "Mini School"' in Bob Moon (ed.)
    Comprehensive Schools: Challenge and Change,
    NFER-Nelson Publishing, Slough
Fletcher, Colin and Thompson, Neil (eds.) (1980)
    Issues in Community Education, Falmer Press,
    Lewes
Halsey, A.H. (ed.) (1972), Educational Priority,
    Vol. 1, HMSO, London
Hargreaves, D.H. (1982) The Challenge of the
    Comprehensive School: Culture, Curriculum
    and Community, Routledge and Kegan Paul,
    London
Hatch, S. and Moyland, S. (1972) 'The Role of the
    Community School' in J. Raynor and J. Harden
    (eds.), Equality and City Schools: Readings
    in Urban Education, Vol. 2, Routledge and
    Kegan Paul, London
Holy, L. and Stuchlik, M. (eds.) (1981) The
    Structure of Folk Models, Academic Press,
    London
Holy, L. and Stuchlik, M. (1983) Actions, Norms
    and Representations, Foundations of Anthro-
    pological Inquiry, Cambridge University Press
Johnson, Richard (1983), 'Educational Politics:
    the Old and the New', in Ann-Marie Wolpe
    and James Donald (eds.), Is There Anyone Here
    From Education? Pluto, London
Keddie, N. (1971) 'Classroom Knowledge', in
    M.F.D. Young (ed.), Knowledge and Control:
    New Directions for the Sociology of Education,
    Collier Macmillan, London

Liverpool Education Committee (1965-1977)
Statistics of Education, City of Liverpool
Liverpool Education Committee (1978/79) Reorgan-
isation of Non-Roman Catholic Secondary
Schools, Education Book number 8A.
City of Liverpool
Liverpool Education Committee (1983) Proposals for
County Secondary Reorganisation, a Consul-
tative Document, City of Liverpool
Liverpool Education Committee (1978-1984) Form 7
Statistics, City of Liverpool
Liverpool Policy and Finance Committee (1973)
Provision of Amenities on the Croxteth Estate
Report of the Chief Executive and Town Clerk,
TC/181, 73, City of Liverpool
Merson, M. and Campbell, R. (1974) 'Community
Education: Instruction for Inequality',
Education for Teaching, 93, Spring
Midwinter, Eric (1972) Priority Education,
Penguin, Harmondsworth
Midwinter, Eric (1973) Patterns of Community
Education, Ward Lock, London
Midwinter, Eric (1975) Education and the Community,
Allen & Unwin, London
Moon, Bob (ed.) (1983) Comprehensive Schools:
Challenge and Change, NFER-Nelson, Slough
Poster, Cyril (1982) Community Education, Its
Development and Management, Heinemann
Educational Books, London
Saunders, Peter (1981) Social Theory and the Urban
Question, Hutchinson, London
Saunders, Peter (1983) Urban Politics, a Sociolog-
ical Interpretation, Hutchinson, London
Williams, Wyn, and Robins, Wayne R. (1980)
Observations on the Californian Case, in
C. Fletcher and N. Thompson (eds.), Issues
in Community Education, Falmer Press, Lewes

Chapter Six

THE ENGLISH MIDDLE SCHOOL - THE BIRTH AND DEATH
OF A DREAM
Colin A.A. Marsh

Middle schools first appeared in England in 1968.
Until the Education Act of 1964 was passed such
schools were not permitted as they contravened the
1944 Education Act which required a break between
Primary and Secondary education to occur at the
age of eleven. Once middle schools became a legal
possibility their growth was rapid. By 1973 six
hundred and eighty seven had been established and
according to Hargreaves and Tickle (1980) there
were over one thousand two hundred by April 1974.

THE BIRTH OF MIDDLE SCHOOLS

Burrows, formerly Chief Inspector of Primary and
Middle Schools, stated that this new type of
school came into being because of the 'combination
of the observations of perceptive primary school
teachers and of child psychologists and paedia-
tricians.' (1978)
     Such a view is not supported by the evidence
contained in the literature. The main reason for
the creation of middle schools was the response of
Local Authority administrators who were grappling
with the problems that they were encountering in
the reorganisation of their education system on
comprehensive lines.
     The most acute problem confronting the intro-
duction of the comprehensive system was that of
accommodation. In the selective system, schools
had been comparatively small with a population of
three hundred being quite normal for a secondary
modern school. In the immediate post war years
the projected size for a comprehensive school was
very much larger with some suggestions reaching a
figure of two thousand pupils. The difficulties
and dangers inherent in such large units were

recognised at an early stage in the discussions.
Ellen Wilkinson, Minister of Education,
warned local authorities to think carefully of the
practical problems involved in the proposed size of
unilateral schools and this warning was repeated
by Florence Horsbrugh, Minister of Education (1952),
who saw enormous disadvantages in large schools.
Even if the Local Authority Administrators had
accepted the difficulties foreseen in large units
they were still confronted by the even greater
problem of procuring the funds to build large and
sophisticated schools.   The major pre-occupation
of the Ministry of Education in the immediate post-
war years had been in providing 'roofs over heads'
for a rapidly expanding school population.   In
order to cope with the acute problem at a time of
economic stringency it was essential that every
school was used to its full capacity.   Local
Authorities wishing to introduce a comprehensive
system were forced to think in terms that fully
utilised their existing plant.
     Commenting on the problem confronting Local
Education Authorities and the debate concerning
secondary education, Pedley (1959) stated:

> The tripartite and comprehensive giants were
> opposed in head-on conflict ... Each was too
> big, too committed, to give way.   Ever since
> 1944 however a small minority of people had
> held the view that the drawbacks of selection
> at 11+ on the one hand and of large comprehen-
> sives on the other, could be resolved - and
> moreover quickly and economically resolved by
> using existing small and medium sized schools
> to provide secondary education in two stages.

     The Leicestershire Authority evolved such a
plan.   Mason (1957) stated that the generally
accepted size of a viable comprehensive school was
very large and would create problems that would
outweigh the advantages.   He also recognised the
fact that a special building programme would be
prohibitively expensive.   His solution lay in
dividing children of secondary school age not
vertically as in the selective system but horizon-
tally.   Writing at a later date Mason (1967)
pointed out that his original plan, which retained
a break at 11, had been dictated by the legal
requirements existing at the time.   The introduction
of the Leicestershire Plan was an important step in
the evolution of the Middle School as it

demonstrated a system that provided comprehensive education by utilising the existing stock of buildings and it also introduced the vital concept of a two-tier organisation for secondary education. Pedley (1958) claimed that:

> the introduction of the Leicestershire scheme had torn a rent in the mesh of ministerial powers that is unlikely to be repaired for some time.

He added that if one authority could do it why not others? Once Local Authorities began to think in terms of an end-on organisation for secondary education it was only a small step for them to begin to question the break at 11+. Marsh (1980) has documented how one Local Authority did just this in the late fifties and prepared a Plan (which was rejected by the Ministry) that would have introduced a 3-tier system of comprehensive education.

The West Riding of Yorkshire Education Authority published in October 1963 a pamphlet entitled 'The Organization of Education in Certain Areas of the West Riding' and sub-titled '5 - 9, 9-13, 13 - 18'. The report had been written in response to some of the Divisions in the Riding requesting comprehensive education but who could not

> have it in large schools for children aged 11 - 18 because there already exists in those areas a number of smaller schools which cannot easily be extended, which are unsuitable as primary schools and which are so sound that they will have to continue in use for the foreseeable future.

The strong influence that buildings were having on the plans for comprehensive reorganisation was recognised in Curzon Street. Wilma Harte (1969), Assistant Under Secretary of State, said that:

> lacking a Special Building Programme (for comprehensive reorganization) the most intractable element is the stock of buildings designed for other purposes. The Local Authorities draw up their own solutions to fit local needs and we give respectability to their needs.

Bullivant (undated) was convinced that tiered systems were the inevitable result of compromising with the accommodation available and that a system utilising middle schools was the most flexible form of organisation to meet local needs.

The West Riding proposals, published in 1963, were against the existing law but owing to the strong feelings within the Authority it was decided to continue with the planning and to offer the scheme as a challenge to the Ministry. This challenge did not occur in isolation as other Local Authorities were also making strong representations to the Ministry for a greater degree of flexibility within the legal framework of education. This increasing pressure had its effect on the Ministry as Sir Edward Boyle stated:

> It became perfectly clear (in the Ministry in 1963) that we would have to have some changes in the law to allow middle schools. (Boyle and Crossland 1971)

The change came with the passing of the 1964 Education Act on the 31st July 1964. However, during the debate on the act it was made clear in Parliament that the proposal was seen as being limited in scope to facilitate an experiment. This view was reiterated in Circular 12/64 which stated that:

> The intention is to permit a relatively small number of experiments in educational organiz- ation (DES 1964).

Shortly after the passing of the 1964 Education Act by the Conservative Government, a Labour Govern- ment came to power in October 1964 having made a pledge to introduce comprehensive education through- out the country. In July 1965 Circular 10/65 appeared requiring all local authorities to prepare and submit plans for reorganising secondary education in their areas on comprehensive lines. It suggested six possible schemes, the most favoured of which was the all-through 11 - 18 comprehensive school. The sixth suggestion which included middle schools was again seen as a very limited option. Circular 10/65 pointed out that each local authority would have to adopt a form of organisation that best suited its own area and that the available options would be limited by the existing stock of buildings.

> The disposition, character and size of existing schools ... must influence and go far to determine the shape of secondary education. (DES 1965)

Both the Government and the Department of Education and Science failed to appreciate the attractiveness that a 3-tier system of education held for local authority administrators. It is rather extraordinary that having acknowledged the strong influence that the existing stock of buildings would have on plans for reorganisation they failed to foresee the popularity that would be achieved by schemes involving middle schools amongst local authority administrators who in the words of Bryan and Hardcastle (1977) had been:

> put in a straight-jacket by Circular 10/65 because they were not given any additional funds or an extended building programme.

Circular 10/66 (DES 1966a) issued on March 10th 1966 made it clear that because of a balance of payments crisis, money would be extremely limited and that reorganisation would have to be carried through without the allocation of additional financial resources. More and more local authorities came to see that their only possible course of action lay in following the sixth option of Circular 10/65 and introducing a form of 3-tier organisation. This realisation and the increasing number of proposals for 3-tier systems placed the Government under increasing pressure. By the 20th April 1966 when Circular 13/66 was issued it became apparent that the reluctance concerning the introduction of middle schools had dissipated in the face of local authority pressure. Paragraph 4 of Circular 13/66 states:

> It has become increasingly apparent since the issue of Circular 10/65 that for some authorities the early change over to a comprehensive system in all, or part, of their areas, would be facilitated by the adoption of an age of transfer other than eleven. It is also likely to be the case that in some areas the operation of raising the school leaving age can be carried through more easily if it is accompanied by a change in the age of transfer and a consequent reduction in the age range of the secondary schools which will have to

accommodate the extra pupils. The Secretary
of State has therefore decided that ... there
are urgent practical reasons why a greater
degree of flexibility should be allowed now
to authorities. He will therefore regard a
change in the age of transfer for the time
being as a matter for local option and is
prepared to consider proposals from authorities
on this basis. (DES 1966b)

This statement marked the capitulation of the
Government to the pressure exerted by local authority administrators. It was they, and almost
entirely they, who had been responsible for the
creation of a situation in which the middle school
could emerge. However, the change in the law
permitting the introduction of middle schools did
more than solve an administrative problem. The
possibility of creating a new type of school catering for a new age group focussed attention on the
characteristics and needs of children in their
middle years of schooling. It provided an
opportunity for ideas to be put forward as to the
form and content of a curriculum for the middle
years. As the National Union of Teachers (1979)
stated it provided a 'unique opportunity' for
development and was 'one of the most exciting
products of reorganization'.

THE BIRTH OF THE DREAM

The opportunity was not ignored. Many educationists put forward their ideas and it was remarkable
how alike their ideas were. As will be shown
the 'dream' was based very largely on the so-called
'progressive' approach to education for which the
English primary school had become internationally
famous. However, there has never been a clear
and precise definition of the term 'progressive'
and the situation has been exacerbated by the
introduction and general use of other terms equally
vague and often overlapping or encompassing the
same broad ideas. Tunnell(1975) and Crowl (1975)
expressed the opinion that terms such as 'progressive' were so vague as to be virtually 'valueless
in terms of educational practice' and that they
were used as slogans to convey general ideas.
Komisar and McClellan (1961) expressed the view that
educational slogans summarise a set of assertions
which are associated with the general impact of the
slogan, whilst Scheffler (1960) stated that such

slogans

> neither claim to define terms in educational
> discourse or to facilitate such discourse but
> act rather as "rallying symbols" of the key
> ideas and attitudes of educational movements.

For the purpose of this article a 'progressive'
approach to education will be taken to indicate one
in which the aim is to give the child a greater
degree of freedom and autonomy in his, or her, own
learning and one which advocates a significant shift
in the balance of control over the learning situation from the teacher to the child.
    The origins of this approach to education can
be traced back to Socrates, Plato and Aristotle.
In his book Selleck (1972) traced the evolution of
this idea up until 1939 when he concluded that:

> though they (the progressives) had not won all
> to their cause they had captured the
> allegiance of the opinion-makers ... by that
> time a person who was being initiated into the
> educational culture of the English primary
> school, who read his textbooks and journals,
> took part in discussion or listened to the
> lectures at his teachers college, such a
> person found that he was being constantly
> confronted with the ideas and practices which
> have been called progressive.

In an examination of some official publications,
March (1984) illustrated how the progressive approach
had been consistently supported from the introduction
Morant wrote for the 1902 Elementary Code, through
the various Handbooks of Suggestions, the 1931 Hadow
Report and the Plowden Report which appeared just
as the first middle schools were being opened. The
latter was seen by Watson (1981) as giving the single
greatest impetus to the extension of progressive
education. But it was not only the official
publications that were advocating a progressive
approach in English primary schools. Many other
publications pursued a similar and equally strong
advocacy which helped to develop a very clear
impression that in very large measure English primary
education was progressive. This is an important
point as many saw the emerging middle schools as
being an upward extension of the progressive primary
school. For example the Plowden Report states:

If the middle school is to be a new and progressive force it must develop further the curriculum, methods and attitudes which exist at present in junior schools.

The N U T (1964) saw 'advantage in extending a primary-type regime for pupils to a later age' whilst Hargreaves (1980) identified in the debate on middle schools that a

major justifying theme was that a delay in the age of transfer could lead to an extension of primary school methods beyond the age of eleven.

It is possible to gain a picture of the middle school as it was envisaged before a significant number were opened, from three sources. These are the official publications; the recorded suggestions of educationists and the first reports from groups of teachers who worked together prior to the opening of middle schools in their areas.

The most important official publication was that provided by the Central Advisory Council for Education, the Plowden Report (1967). It summarised its philosophy in these words:

A school is not merely a teaching shop, it must transmit values and attitudes. It is a community in which children learn to live first and foremost as children and not as future adults. In family life children learn to live with people of all ages. The school sets out deliberately to devise the right environment for children, to allow them to be themselves and to develop in the way and at the pace appropriate to them. It tries to equalise opportunities and to compensate for handicaps. It lays special stress on individual discovery, on first hand experience and on opportunities for creative work. It insists that knowledge does not fall into neatly separate compartments and that work and play are not opposite but complementary.

In discussing the practical implications of the approach they were advocating, the Committee stated that if there had to be a time-table in the middle school it would be composed of lengthy periods of time which would be easily adjusted to suit the needs of the children. They advocated

a flexible curriculum which would make good use
of the interests and activity of the children, one
that would minimise the idea that subject matter
can be rigidly compartmentalised and one that
required the teacher to act in a consultative,
guiding and stimulating role rather than a didactic
one.

Building Bulletin 35 (DES 1966c) contained a
plan of a purpose built middle school designed to
accommodate a progressive approach. The designers
from the Architects and Buildings Branch of the
Department of Education and Science, envisaged a
wide variety cf group sizes being used in a wide
variety of teaching and study activities. In the
design they provided for both the individual child
and for groups larger than the conventional class.
They believed that the year group with its own
small group of teachers would be the basis on which
the school would operate in order to create a
highly flexible and individualised approach to
education. In two other DES publications
(Launching Middle Schools (1970a) and Towards the
Middle School (1970b)) similar ideas were advanced.
The authors believed that in the middle schools
class teachers would take their own class for a
large proportion of the time and that the children
would never have to experience the secondary school
system of having different teachers for each subject
as it would fragment the day and sever the natural
connections between aspects of the curriculum.

Many individual educationists also put forward
their ideas and suggestions for the new middle
schools and their views are recorded in a variety of
publications. Many stressed the individuality of
the child and it was stated repeatedly that all
planning for middle schools had to acknowledge this
fact. Burrows (1967) expressed the opinion that
the whole strength of the school would depend on
the teachers having a detailed knowledge of the
individual child and in recognising that different
children have different needs and would respond in
different ways and at different times to the stimuli
and experiences they received.

Such a view conditioned the suggestions made
for the approaches to education in the middle school.
It was strongly argued that the starting points for
the education of children in the middle school would
have to be the child's individual interests (Adams
1968) and it would be the child's individual method
of learning, his or her individual level of understanding as stimulated, provoked and extended by

teaching of the best quality that would determine
the approach adopted (Ross 1968).
      Very strong support was given to the view that
the methods of teaching established in good primary
schools and identified and supported by the Plowden
Committee had to be adopted in the middle school,
with a dedication to the ideal of an individually
tailored curriculum providing for each pupil a sequence of learning experiences that would enable him
or her to develop to the full his or her powers of
learning.   It was felt that every good middle
school would accept the task of catering for the
individual child's needs and potential and that
this could only be achieved through broad enquiry
based learning (Clegg 1967), with discovery methods
and project work playing a large part in the programme of the school (Sproule 1971).   The view
was expressed that such an approach would require
the child to be given freedom to choose his or her
work from the many activities made available and
to have open access to all the facilities in the
school.   It was thought that as the range of interests would be wide the curriculum would not fit
neatly into either subject or time-table compartments.
Duncan (1967) stated that learning had to be rooted
in enquiry and interest and proceed by discovery in
order to assist the child to discover and recognise
his own interests, aptitudes and talents.   Many
speakers such as Clegg (1967) and Johnson (1968)
argued that there had to be an integrated approach
to the curriculum as a subject based approach would
inhibit and restrict the child in the pursuit of
its own interests.
      Flexibility in grouping children in the middle
school was stressed by many speakers.   Adams (1968)
stated that in his view working groups would seldom
consist of the conventional class unit and this
view was supported by Burrows (1967) who expressed
the opinion that the full class had ceased to be
the teaching unit for many purposes in primary
schools where work was organised on an individual
rather than a class or group basis.
      Although some speakers conceded the need for
a time-table to control the use of major facilities,
there was very strong and uniform opposition to the
'tyranny of the bell'.   'The bell-controlled period
was seen as restrictive, artificial and inappropriate and that every effort had to be made to avoid
the excessive fragmentation of the day as this would
kill the capacity of the child to become interested.
      Marshall (1968) was emphatic that middle

schools would be:

> staffed by primary school trained teachers who
> are <u>au fait</u> with all that is best of the
> changes brought by the creative revolution.
> In this way the benefits of the new progressive
> thinking would be applied up to the age of 12
> or 13.

Teachers were not seen as purveyors of information but as organisers of structured learning
experiences and providers of recognition of achievement, security, stimulation and guidance.
Many speakers commented on the design of
schools for the middle years. The general view was
that whilst offering the individual child security
it had to be able to offer great flexibility of use.
Ross (1968) did not think individual classrooms were
appropriate and he believed that the designs should
be based on modern primary schools that offered
facilities for a wide variety of groupings and
would not impose patterns of organisation but would
cater for the experimental, investigative and
individualised work that would develop. Many
speakers favoured the open plan design as offering
the ideal facilities and the greatest flexibility
in use.
In putting forward their ideas for the middle
school these early speakers made frequent references
to good, i.e. progressive, junior school practice
and the need to make the new middle schools
developments and extensions of the best Plowden-type
schools. Taylor (1969) summarised the characteristics of good junior schools as follows:-

1. They afford many avenues for learning.
2. Learning begins from the mode of experiencing
   which comes naturally to the child and is not
   held within rigid boundaries of time or subject
   matter.
3. The motives which provide the drive for such
   learning are either intrinsic in the child
   or intrinsic in the experience which is open
   to him.
4. Active involvement of the learner in learning
   by doing.

Once a Local Authority had made the decision
to introduce middle schools the usual practice was
to set up working parties of teachers and advisers
in the areas to be reorganised to discuss the

implications of the change and to make suggestions
for the curriculum and organisation of the new
schools.   For the first of these working parties
there were considerable difficulties to be faced as
the middle school was an entirely new element in
the education system and there was little experience
for them to draw on.   Little or no use was made of
the experience gained in other countries such as
America or in the private sector (Marsh 1972) and
this left the groups largely dependent on the
advisory officers or guest speakers from University
Departments of Education and Colleges or members of
the Inspectorate to suggest ideas and innovations.
The earliest documents, i.e. those that appeared
before any signficant number of middle schools had
been opened, supported a progressive approach.
For example, following discussions with teachers,
officers of the Dorset Authority prepared a brief
for the architect responsible for designing the
first middle school in the county.   In the brief
it is stated that:

> The newer open-ended approach to educational
> activity characteristic of the best junior
> schools will prevail over formalism.   Individ-
> ual enquiry, varied forms of self and corporate
> expression, learning born of interest - the
> full use of the whole environment - these will
> be the keynotes throughout the school.   The
> fragmentation of both matter and time (fixed
> subject divisions in a rigid time-table)
> common in many secondary schools will not
> obtain here, even at the top of the age range
> (Dorset County Council 1967).

The Droitwich Working Party Report (Worcestershire County Council 1968) similarly advocated an
approach to education in the middle years which was
based on the belief that:

> Children generally learn best by working at
> that which interests them and by working at
> their own pace and in a fashion which provides
> the maximum possible opportunity for practical
> experience using materials readily to hand.
> This unrestricted learning situation can only
> arise where a teacher or teachers have contin-
> uous responsibility for a group of children and
> where subject barriers are diminished.   It
> flourishes through enquiry and discussion.
> Class groups under the direction of class

teachers in continuous contact with their pupils are organizationally the simplest method of providing such learning opportunities.

This type of approach based largely on primary style class teaching with a small group of teachers having total responsibility for a year group, was supported in almost all the early documents. Such an approach was seen as giving the greatest degree of flexibility in organisation and curriculum in order to cater for the varying needs of the children consequent upon their varying rates of development.

The picture that emerges of middle schools from a review of the earliest material available on them is in the words of Nias (1980) a 'powerfully consistent one' and that a striking feature is the 'degree of agreement about the nature of the middle school'. The picture is one of schools highly committed to the individual child, with an organisation and curriculum based on the concept of individualised learning and with the children being given the freedom to actively pursue their individual interests in an educationally rich, varied and informal situation; guided, supported and encouraged by a small team of teachers that knew them well and who provided a secure base for individual exploration and discovery.

It would therefore seem that many educationists saw that the administrative pressures that made possible the middle school provided an ideal opportunity to introduce the progressive approaches to education that had been established, it was said, in primary schools into the early years of traditional secondary education.

THE DEATH OF THE DREAM

The available evidence suggests strongly that despite all the urgings, promptings and encouragement poured out by educationists to help and guide middle school teachers the latter have not taken the 'highroad of educational progressivism' (Lynch 1980). In a survey he made of six 9 - 13 middle schools (three purpose built and three converted secondary modern schools) in 1970, Marsh (1972) found that a progressive approach, as defined in this chapter, had not been adopted. Similarly, as a result of the national survey of middle schools, Taylor and Garson (1982) spoke of 'the gap between the rhetoric of the early pioneers and the reality of actual

middle school development.   They stated that middle
schools had not been particularly innovative and
had not adopted radical new methods.   They claimed
to have noted at the Warwick Conference (Schools
Council 1967) a marked difference between 'the
optimism and visionary zeal of the speakers' and
the 'more jaundiced views from the floor of the
conference', and they stated that practising
teachers perceived an entirely different world to
that portrayed by the platform rhetoric.
    The H.M.I. Survey published in 1983 (DES 1983)
also confirmed that few middle schools had adopted
a progressive approach.   For example they stated
that:

> much of the children's time in school is
> spent in listening and writing.   Not many
> opportunities are provided for extended
> discussion, for collaborative work in groups,
> or for the exercise of choice, responsibility
> and initiative within the curriculum.

They also stated that 'the content and pace
of work and the teaching approaches used were most
often directed towards the children of average
ability in a class' and that 'in many schools able
pupils are often not challenged sufficiently'.
    Reporting on a survey of five 9 - 13 middle
schools accommodated in almost identical purpose
built open plan buildings, Marsh (1984) concluded
that there was:

> a high degree of similarity ... in their way
> of working, but that this common style was
> very different to the preferred progressive
> style of teaching which formed the basis for
> the design of the schools.

Explanations have been provided by various
writers as to why middle schools have not developed
and adopted the progressive style of education which
had been so vigorously advocated in their early days.
For example Lynch (1980), Taylor and Garson (1982)
and Wallace and Tickle (1983) all advance a range
of reasons.   However, a more fundamental question
is why was it that so many educationists felt
convinced that the progressive approach was right
for the newly emerging middle schools?   What made
them so certain, in marked contrast to practising
teachers, that this particular style was the correct
basis for classroom practice?   For many, the answer

could well be given in the words of the Plowden Committee:

> If the middle school is to be a new and progressive force it must develop further the curriculum, methods and attitudes which exist at present in junior schools.

The Plowden Committee, and many other education-ists, were certain that the English primary school had advanced a long way along the progressive road. However, the evidence now available indicates that the much acclaimed primary school revolution never took place. It was in fact a much publicised myth. Bennett (1976),Galton (1979),Simon (1979) and Boydell (1981), for example, all question the real-ity of the progessive revolution, whilst both Harris (1974) and Wicking (1974) state that it was a non-event. Richards (1980) in an article demythol-ogising primary education stated:

> the primary school revolution has not been tried and found wanting but never tried at all except in a small number of schools.

The dream of a progressive middle school was therefore based on a myth. What was advocated was an approach to education that had never been tried on any significant scale and an approach which had never been evaluated and one that had failed to gain the support of the vast majority of teachers in England.
Herein lies danger and a recipe for turmoil. On the one hand we have the 'opinion-makers' (Selleck 1972) advocating one approach, whilst on the other we have the teachers in the classroom operating another and very different approach. Such a situation is harmful in a number of ways and certainly does nothing to help the middle schools withstand the present pressures to eliminate them. It is bad for relationships within the service. For example, as early as 1967 Pulman was stating disdainfully that the middle school idea was the creating of the 'non-combatants and refugees from the classroom', whilst more recently Roy (1983) talks of the real expert in education being seen 'as the person who works away from the classroom and the school'. Such views generate suspicion and distrust. There are also practical outcomes from this separation that created difficul-ties. For example, members of the Architects and

Buildings Branch of the Department of Education and Science were convinced that the progressive approach was the correct one for the middle school and in Building Bulletin 35, and other documents, they advocated the open-plan design as being most appropriate. Their advocacy influenced Local Authorities (see March 1984) and the result has been that some middle schools are operating an approach which runs contrary to the theory on which the design of the school was based.

The situation would seem to indicate that a great deal of thought and attention needs to be given to the whole question of innovation in education. New ideas are required to ensure a healthy developing service but it would seem that unless more effective ways are developed for evaluating and implementing worthwhile new ideas the chasm between rhetoric and practice will continue to exist, and will leave the education service open to attack from people such as Midwinter (1966) who states:

> the so called alternatives in education have been, when not mythical, superficial. They have flattered to deceive. They may change the facade but not the substance of education.

THE DEMISE OF THE MIDDLE SCHOOL

We are now witnessing the un-scrambling of three tier systems and the disappearance of middle schools. However, middle schools are not disappearing because they have been subjected to an educational evaluation and found wanting. Indeed in the 9 - 13 Middle School Survey (DES 1983) it is stated that the schools:

> revealed many of the same strengths and weaknesses found in inspections of primary and secondary schools.

Neither is it true that middle schools are disappearing because they failed to implement a progressive approach. Bearing in mind the ardent advocacy of the progressive approach that dominated the early rhetoric, one would expect to find in the current literature a flood of criticism aimed at this failure. No such flood exists. The advocates of the progressive approach have been remarkably reticent with their criticism. The demise of the middle school is being brought about by the very same factor that brought it into being - pupil numbers in the secondary schools. Created initially to relieve the pressure of numbers in the upper schools, middle schools have disappeared, and will continue to disappear where falling rolls bring into question the viability of the upper school with viability being largely determined by the number of vacant pupil spaces within the upper school building.

Thus in a very short period of time we have seen the emergence and demise of a new type of school. In its brief life the rhetoric of the 'experts' and the practice of the teaching staff failed to coincide. For many teachers and for many parents the episode has created feelings of confusion and resignation.

REFERENCES

Adams, F.J. (1963) 'Delf Hill Middle School', Comprehensive Education Bulletin, 9, 12-14

Bennett, N. (1975) Teaching Styles and Pupil Progress Open Books, London

Boydell, D. (1981) 'Classroom organization 1970-77' in B. Simon and J. Willcocks (eds.) Research and Practice in the Primary Classroom, Routledge and Kegan Paul, London

Boyle, E. and Crossland, A. (1971) The Politics of Education, Penguin, Harmondsworth

Bryan, K.A. and Hardcastle, K.W. (1977) 'The growth of middle schools : Educational rhetoric and economic reality', Journal of Educational Administration and History, 9, (1), 49-55

Bullivant, A. (undated) The How and Why of Comprehensive Reorganization, CASE and Ashton-under-Lyne AASE

Burrows, L.J. (1967) 'What's in store for the children?' in The Middle School - A Symposium, Schoolmaster Publishing, London

Burrows, J. (1978) The Middle School - High Road or Dead End? The Woburn Press, London

Clegg, A. (1967) 'The middle school cometh' in The Middle School - A Symposium, Schoolmaster Publishing, London

Crowl, T.K. (1975) 'Examination and evaluation of the conceptual basis for open classrooms', Education (USA), 96, 54-56

Department of Education and Science (1964) Circular 12/64 The Education Act, HMSO, London

Department of Education and Science (1965) Circular 10/65 The Organization of Secondary Education, HMSO, London

Department of Education and Science (1966a)
    Circular 10/66 School Building Programmes,
    HMSO, London
Department of Education and Science (1966b)
    Circular 13/66 The Age of Transfer to
    Secondary Schools
Department of Education and Science (1966c)
    Building Bulletin 35 New Problems in School
    Design - Middle Schools, HMSO, London
Department of Education and Science (1970a)
    Launching Middle Schools, Education Survey
    No. 8, HMSO, London
Department of Education and Science (1970b)
    Towards the Middle School, Education Pamphlet
    No. 57, HMSO, London
Department of Education and Science (1983)
    9-13 Middle Schools. An Illustrative Survey,
    HMSO, London
Dorset County Council (1967) 'Ferndown Middle School',
    Architects' brief and schedule of accommodation,
    unpublished
Galton, M. (1979) 'Strategies and tactics in junior
    school classrooms', British Educational Research
    Journal, 5, (2), 197-210
Hargreaves, A. (1980) 'The ideology of the middle
    school' in A. Hargreaves and L. Tickle (eds.)
    Middle Schools : Origins, ideology and practice,
    Harper and Row, London
Harris, D.E. (1974) Open Plan Primary Schools,
    unpublished M.Sc. thesis, University of Aston
    in Birmingham
Harte, W. (1969) 'Behind the Curzon Street curtain'
    Times Educational Supplement, 2 May
Horsbrugh, F. (1952) 'Report of Conservative
    Conference' Education, 17 October, 513
Johnson, J. (1968) 'Block study could solve middle
    school problem', Times Educational Supplement
    18 October
Komisar, B.P. and McClellen, J.E. (1961) 'The logic
    of slogans' in B.O. Smith and R.H. Ennis (eds.)
    Language and Concepts in Education, Rand,
    McNally, New York
Lynch, J. (1980) 'Legitimation crisis for the
    English middle school' in A. Hargreaves and
    L. Tickle (eds.) Middle Schools : Origins,
    ideology and practice, Harper and Row, London
Marsh, C.A.A. (1972) The Reorganization of Education
    in the County of Worcestershire with special
    relation to 9-13 middle schools, unpublished
    M.Ed. thesis, University of Birmingham

Marsh, C.A.A. (1980) 'The emergence of nine-thirteen middle schools in Worcestershire' in A. Hargreaves and L. Tickle (eds.) Middle Schools : Origins, ideology and practice, Harper and Row, London

Marsh, C.A.A. (1984) Middle School Design and Educational Practice, unpublished M. Phil. thesis, University of Aston in Birmingham

Marshall, S. (1968) 'Middle schools : they must be staffed by progressive primary school teachers', Times Educational Supplement, 14 June

Mason, S.C. (1957) The Leicestershire Experiment : A New Venture in the Organization of Secondary Education, Councils and Education Press, Leicester

Mason, S.C. (1967) Leicestershire Plan - the next step. Four year high schools, unpublished

Midwinter, E. (1966) 'Non-events in the history of education', Education for Teaching, 71

National Union of Teachers (1964) First things first: a memorandum of evidence submitted to the Plowden committee, NUT, London

National Union of Teachers (1974) Middle Schools - deemed or doomed? Schoolmaster Publishing, London

Nias, J. (1980) 'The ideal middle school : its public image' in A. Hargreaves and L. Tickle (eds.) Middle Schools : Origins, ideology and practice, Harper and Row, London

Pedley, R. (1958) 'Lord Hailsham's legacy', Journal of Education, 90, 4

Pedley, R. (1959) 'Two-tier secondary education' in E. Blishen (ed.) Changing Schools, Council for Children's Welfare, London

Plowden Report (1967) Children and their Primary School, Central Advisory Council for Education, HMSO, London

Pullman, W.A. (1967) 'Some arguments challenged' in The Middle School : A Symposium, Schoolmaster Publishing, London

Razzell, A.G. (1969) 'The curriculum of the middle school' in The Middle Years of Schooling, Schools Council Working Paper No. 22, HMSO, London

Richards, C. (1930) 'Demythologizing primary education', Journal of Curriculum Studies, 12, (1), 77-8

Ross, A. (1968) 'The middle school', Comprehensive Education Bulletin, 9, 7-10

Ross, A. (1969) 'Round up on the whole curriculum'
    in The Middle Years of Schooling, Schools
    Council Working Paper No. 22, HMSO, London
Roy, W. (1983) Teaching Under Attack, Croom Helm,
    Beckenham
Scheffler, I. (1960) The Language of Education,
    Charles Thomas, London
Schools Council (1967) The Middle Years of Schooling,
    Schools Council Working Paper No. 22,
    HMSO, London
Selleck, R.J.W. (1972) English Primary Education and
    the Progressives 1914-1934, Routledge and
    Kegan Paul, London
Simon, B. (1974) 'The primary school revolution :
    Myth or reality' in Education in the Sixties,
    History of Education Society, London
Sproule, A. (1971) 'Taking the middle school plunge'
    Resources for Education, November
Taylor, M. and Garson, Y. (1982) Schooling in the
    Middle Years, Trentham Books, Keele
Tunnell, D. (1975) 'Open education : an expression
    in search of a definition' in D. Nyberg (ed.)
    The Philosophy of Open Education, Routledge
    and Kegan Paul, London
Wallace, G. and Tickle, L. (1983) 'Middle Schools :
    the heart of schools in crisis', British
    Journal of Sociology of Education, 4, (3), 223-
    240
Watson, K. (1981) 'The growth of progressive
    education in the twentieth century', Spectrum,
    14, (1), 81
Wicking, B. (1974) 'An open and shut case', Times
    Educational Supplement, 14 June
Worcestershire County Council (1968) Report of the
    Droitwich Working Party on Middle Schools,
    Worcestershire

Chapter Seven

MIDDLE SCHOOLS THROUGH THE LOOKING GLASS

Gwen Wallace

> 'I know what you're thinking about,' said
> Tweedledum; 'but it isn't so, nohow.'
>
> 'Contrariwise,' continued Tweedledee, 'if it
> was so it might be; and if it were so, it
> would be; but as it isn't, it ain't. That's
> logic.'
> (Lewis Carroll, 1872)

INTRODUCTION; 'IF IT WAS SO IT MIGHT BE ...'

It is now part of the historic record, that when
James Callaghan launched the Great Debate into
education, with a speech at Ruskin College, Oxford,
in October 1976, he signalled a formal change in
the orientation of government policy on state
schooling. The rhetoric of the speech signalled
the closure of an era of general consensus on
schooling policy, in which it had been argued by
both political parties that investment in education
was investment in human capital, which would draw
into the ladder of opportunity those who had been
neglected by social and geographical inequalities
(OECD, 1965). As the Conservative Minister of
Education 1962-1964 expressed it:

> The Ministry of Education wants to be the
> sponsoring Department for as many young people
> as possible going up the ladder as far as
> their potential abilities can carry them..
> (Kogan, 1971, p. 65)

Following the 1973 world oil crisis, the intervention into the British economy by the International Monetary Fund, and cuts in public

expenditure, there were growing fears for a system
which could not deliver what had been promised.
As the Organisation for Economic Cooperation and
Development (OECD)put it in 1976, 'the guarantee
provided by credentials in a time of scarcity of
education is no longer valid.' Endorsing this view,
Taylor (1980) talked of, 'the problem of 'un-
governability' that arises from what are seen as the
denial of entitlements'.

Seen in this context, the Callaghan speech can
be seen as an attempt to establish a new set of
criteria of 'entitlement'. These criteria would
throw doubt on the value of the existing credentials
and reorientate 'entitlement' to the economic
'realities'. It would also legitimate the redis-
tribution of resources away from the public sector
of the economy and into the private sector, as
monetarist economic doctrine dictated.

Hence the shift from a rhetoric of equality of
opportunity, to a rhetoric of efficiency, is merely
a shift in the rhetoric which legitimates the
unequal distribution of socially produced wealth,
as being in the 'general interest'.

Much of the political and ideological activity
which heralded, surrounded and followed the
educational Great Debate, has been variously
defined, recorded, analysed and interpreted already
(Kogan, 1978; Lawton, 1980; Salter and Tapper,
1981; Holt, 1981; Baron et al, 1981; Ahier and
Flude, 1983). There has also been some published
work which has identified ways in which this
activity has reverberated into schools (Ginsburg
et al, 1979; Wallace et al, 1983; Wallace and
Tickle, 1983; Campbell, 1984). Furthermore, the
concern of the present Secretary of State for
Education, Sir Keith Joseph, for a 'more secure'
system of stratifying pupils, has also attracted
scrutiny (Ransom and Walsh, 1982; Hunter, 1983).

The general view in the political analyses of
the shift from the rhetoric of equality of
opportunity to that of efficiency, has conceded that
the shift is related to more efficient forms of
technical-managerial control. This form of control
involves every level of the organisation in a
participative endeavour to achieve the goals of the
organisation. Hence, each level of the organisation is expected to perform its task efficiently,
in accordance with the overall goals of the enterprise. In the case of schooling, efficiency is a
matter of deploying resources and credentials in a
legitimate fashion, so that the inequalities of the

wider society are justifiably reproduced because
they are grounded in the concept of 'ability'. The
socio-cultural rationale unites economy with
politics.

The problem with such a rationale in the
context of rapid economic changes is that the
political ordering of society is under constant
attack from the economic environment within which
it must operate. In a more stable age, the concept
of innate intelligence sufficed to legitimate the
differential spread of wealth and income. Under-
mined by the post-war growth of opportunity and the
evidence of mismatch between intelligence and
opportunity (Jackson and Marsden, 1963; Halsey
et al, 1961), the ideology switched to one of human
potential which took into account both natural and
environmental factors (Plowden, 1967). The problem
remained of how to measure such potential, in a way
which legitimated differences of ability, without
associating such differences with failure. The
ladder of opportunity must offer the hope that
motivates as well as the order that stabilises
expectations within the economic 'realities'.

In this paper, I shall examine the way in
which the managerial approach to this problem since
the mid 1970s has involved attempts to introduce
into schools a curricular order of sequenced
learning which was intended to provide the rational,
technical criteria whereby pupil ability could be
directly related to progression through curricular
programmes, thereby increasing the efficiency of
resource distribution. Yet in the context of the
corporate management systems which had opened up
schools to unpredictable market forces, the
resources for such a curriculum were under attack,
leaving management reacting to events rather than
planning for change. The curriculum in different
schools was being differentially affected by these
events in a spiralling context of decline.
Furthermore, the criteria necessary for linking the
level of difficulty of subject items, to levels of
pupil ability do not exist, in spite of twenty
years of research. Yet field research in six
middle schools shows evidence of growing pressure
on teachers to teach pupils to answer test questions
accurately, in ways which make little sense in the
substantive conditions in the schools.

In other words, I shall argue that the notion
of 'efficiency' operates at one level to justify
financial cuts in the 'general interest', at
another level to imply that there are clear,

attainable objectives with regard to standards of
ability, which could be attained if only those
given the task of attaining them acted efficiently,
and thirdly to turn the problem of legitimating
policy changes onto teachers, rather than to locate
it at the level of government.

It is in examining the way in which this
ideological apparatus has been erected and sustained that we can begin to unravel the interplay
of class interests and socio-cultural negotiations
which appear 'contrariwise' through the looking
glass.

FINDING THE TECHNICAL CRITERIA: ... IF IT WERE SO
IT WOULD BE ...

Hunter (1981) marks 1974 as the significant year
when the Labour Party shifted its policies towards
positive support for industry and containing public
expenditure. Holt (1981, pp. 38-39) notes
significant comparisons between the changing role of
NAEP (National Assessment of Educational Progress) in
the United States and that of the APU (Assessment
of Performance Unit) in Britain, in the same year.
Both organisations switched from a concern with
sub-cultural or ethnic groups, to the problem of
monitoring the achievement of mainstream pupils.
Lawton (1980) takes a similar line of argument and
draws attention to an article by Kay (1975) in
which the emphasis is on an 'interest and concern'
... 'related in the minds of many people to some
anxiety about standards'. Kay then defines the
six 'kinds of development' in skills and knowledge
which are familiar from the work of Hirst (1965)
and Phenix (1964), and which have subsequently
framed much of the thinking of Her Majesty's
Inspectorate on the curriculum.

Holt (1981) has provided a penetrating account
of the origins and development of the APU, but
there are two points which he misses. The first is
that there is an even earlier article by Kay (1974)
in which he begins by establishing subjects as the
starting point of curriculum development and
rehabilitates the notion of pupil learning as a
linear process, tied to a structured programme of
objectives, which can, through training and
practice, bring pupils to 'as high a level of
proficiency as possible'.

There is no reason why adequate practice in all

> the skills necessary to the pupil should not
> be built into an interdisciplinary course, but
> if this is to be achieved there is need for a
> more sophisticated analysis of objectives, a
> more structured planning of the individual
> pupil's programme and a closer monitoring of
> his development than is usually found.
> (Kay, 1974, pp. 8-9)

Now this passage is clearly framed within the
ideology of the Plowden (1967) Report, insofar as
it concerns the individual's progress to the limit
of his or her potential. The major additional
assumption is the association of pupil proficiency
with his or her progress through a programme of
learning.

It is also worth noting that Kay was concerned
to avoid confusion between methods and objectives
and to present skills as 'tools supplied by subjects' which children could be trained to use. He
argued that using the tools for multi-disciplinary
work in problem solving in adult life might require
multi-disciplinary techniques, but it was not
'secure' to deduce from this that it was appropriate
for pupils.

If Lawton (1980) is correct, Kay was already
heading up the APU, which, in turn, was establishing links with the NFER (National Foundation for
Educational Research), in order to link the national
monitoring of standards with the item banks of tests
which were being constructed for local authority
use (Holt, 1981, p. 69).

The second point missed by Holt, however, is
that the NFER had been involved with the production
of test items since 1966, when it had been asked
by the Schools Council

> to carry out a pilot study into the feasibility
> of establishing banks or libraries of exam-
> ination questions or items suitable for
> measuring the achievement of 16-year-olds
> taking examinations in various subjects.
> (Wood and Skurnik, 1969, p.1)

The idea behind the project was to produce
items, with the cooperation of teachers, which
would provide a national bank for teachers of mode
3 CSE (Certificate of Secondary Education) with
'comparability built in from the outset'. The
pilot study concentrated on mathematics and provided teachers recruited to it, with a classification

of behavioural objectives covering:

    A. <u>Knowledge</u>: recall of definitions,
       notations, concepts.
    B. <u>Technique and Skill</u>: computation,
       manipulation of symbols.
    C. <u>Comprehension</u>: capacity to understand
       problems, to translate symbolic forms, to
       follow and extend reasoning.
    D. <u>Application</u>: of appropriate concepts to
       unfamiliar mathematical situations.
    E. <u>Inventiveness</u>: working creatively in
       mathematics.
            (Wood and Skurnik, 1969, pp. 17-18).

These classifications drew on the work of Bloom <u>et
al</u> (1956) on tne cognitive domain, and Husen (1967)
<u>International Study of Achievement in Mathematics</u>.
verbs were 'suitable' in choosing objectives
(Choose, Name, Describe, Select, Write, Solve,
Underline, Order, Construct) and others were not
(Infer, Analyse, Associate, Contrast, Demonstrate,
Relate, Compare).
    The authors warn that 'one cannot be sure that
(the behaviours) correspond with real mental
functions' (p. 23) and quote criticisms of
behavioural objectives by, among others, Asubel
(1967). They declare (p. 25):

> critics of behavioural objectives should not
> be allowed to derail the movement. There is
> no evidence that it is harmful and some that
> it is beneficial. It is only when one forgets
> that these behaviours are only useful con-
> structs which help us to conceptualise
> intellectual achievement and starts thinking
> of them as real and independent functions, as
> the so-called 'faculties' of the mind were
> once regarded, that the mischief begins.

However, by 1974 there is evidence of a link
between the NFER, the APU and the item banks of
tests which were being constructed for local
authority use, in order that the national norms,
which the APU would discover, could be linked to
local authority testing processes (Holt, 1981,
p. 69).
    Furthermore, the APU adopted the Rasch model;
a mathematical model which assumes that the
'likelihood of a person getting a test item right
depends on only one factor (or trait ...)' (Holt,

1981, p. 68). In other words, there is a presumed link between the level of ability of the pupil and the level of ability of the item; what Goldstein and Blinkhorn (1982) call, the assumption of 'unidimensionality'. Goldstein and Blinkhorn argue (p. 168):

> the Rasch model ... requires that all items appear in the same order of difficulty to all children whatever their exposure to different curricula ...

> ... an alternative unidimensional model can 'fit' a set of data just as well as Rasch but give very different ability estimates ...

We have then, yet another link in the apparatus of testing. The logic of a nationally available bank of test items, standardised to national norms through the work of the APU, required some standardisation of curricula. Yet, doubtless the similarity of this process to that of the 1862 Revised Code, could alert teachers to the dangers posed by politicians keen to tie payment to 'results'. Following Kay's (1975) paper, the debate about the curriculum was conducted in a different arena.

Her Majesty's Inspectorate (HMI) incorporated the (slightly modified) areas of development in Kay's (1975) paper in their (DES, 1977a) document, Curriculum 11-16. The Inspectorate were critical of the options systems which had developed in secondary schools, on the grounds that they gave pupils the freedom to opt out of important experiences. In the same year (DES, 1977b) they concluded a language survey of eighty three schools and reported 'the haphazard and infinitely varied provision' they encountered. They called for less diversity on the grounds that the population was a mobile one (p. 45). They also called for teachers to specify precise objectives for pupils of different ages and abilities. A further document on 'gifted' children (DES, 1977c) used a wide ranging and somewhat vague set of definitions on 'giftedness' to attack middle schools and their egalitarian ethos. They noted (p. 34):

> ... an understandable reluctance ... (for) ... the school to categorise pupils too early. Mixed ability groups are frequently found in the early years of a receiving school ... because such an organisation avoids early

>   categorisation <u>based on inadequate information</u>
>   ...
>   (All emphasis mine)

In defining the problem thus, the solution had to
be found in better and more efficient documentation
of pupil progress. Pupils could then be categorised earlier. The curricular-test-selection
link was forged.
        The teachers, however, continued to reject the
APU/NFER link up (Holt, 1981, pp. 97-98). They
also suspected that it would affect the curriculum.
This was explicitly denied by the then Secretary
of State, Shirley Williams, when she addressed the
Consultative Committee of the Assessment of Performance Unit, a body with considerable representation from the teacher unions. The NUT (National
Union of Teachers) reported her as saying:

> The significance of the APU's work was that
> it was not based on the exhaustive testing of
> everything or of crude-blanket testing. The
> APU would help by making a distinction bet-
> ween valid and invalid criticisms ...
>
> ... there were fears that blanket testing
> would lead to a narrowing of the curriculum
> and teaching to the test ... (but) ... the
> outcome of the APU's light sampling would
> largely avoid these pitfalls while giving
> useful information about the weighting of
> the curriculum. The procedures to be used
> whereby only a small number of pupils in any
> one school would complete different tests
> would provide safeguards ...
>   (NUT, 1979a, p. 92).

Surprisingly, the NUT then gave over a whole
edition of its Secondary Education Journal to
articles concerned with assessment techniques,
apparently convinced of their usefulness (NUT,
1979b). Quoting the Schools Council Examinations
Bulletin No. 31, Evenden (1979) argued the
benefits of criterion referenced testing for
building up a 'continuous judgement' of pupils
and for understanding the process whereby any
pupils achieved particular learning objectives.
He quoted Bloom, Krathwol and Gagné, as academic
authorities (p. 19). In the same journal, Evans
argued that testing not only provided valuable
information for parents, employers and higher

education authorities and so on, but also demonstrated to pupils that teachers valued their work.
Not to test, 'by extension ... could be seen as a
lack of regard for it' (p. 21).

All of the Journal articles were written by
authors with connections with the Welsh Examinations Boards, and we can only speculate that the
NUT had decided to concede the struggle whilst
attempting to rescue its professional image. The
editorial declared:

> Several ... authors ... suggest the time is
> ripe for Headteachers and their staffs in
> secondary schools to develop their own
> individual policy on assessment. Such pol-
> icies recognise the supremacy of the curric-
> ulum and its aims and objectives, but they
> stress the vital role of assessment as a truly
> professional tool of fundamental importance to
> effective teaching and learning.
> (NUT, 1979b, pp. 1-2)

The NUT accepted the technical process, but
rejected its use as a means of assessing national
norms or of measuring teacher efficiency. It was
all right to use it for a 'continuous judgement'
of pupils, but not to measure teachers. The NUT
appeared to be in danger of losing its head to the
Knave of Hearts, to 'help' pupils.

The issue turns, however, on the problem of
what can be assumed from the results of criterion-
referenced tests. Whilst these may well have some
use in diagnosing particular cognitive gaps or
difficulties experienced by individual pupils,
there are no grounds for believing that tests can
be compiled which establish criteria to match the
level of difficulty of subject knowledge to staged
levels of learning by pupils. Even less can we
assume measurable levels of ability which provide
the basis for the establishment of national norms
in a pluralist society.

Commenting on a recent attempt to focus
research on to the issue, with the aim of
developing grade-related criteria in eight subjects
for the new Secondary Education Council, Peter
Dines, the deputy chief executive of the Council
was reported as saying (TES, 1984a):

> ... no one yet knows how grade-related
> criteria can work, no one understands them.
> This will be really genuine research, and if

the idea really is fruitful, then it is
something that we would have to do in every
part of the curriculum.

Yet the terms of reference of the working parties
who will be setting out on this task are not far
removed from what the NFER attempted back in 1966.
That is, to take the subjects of the curriculum -
initially English, mathematics, French, Welsh,
history, physics, geography, and craft, design
and technology (CDT) - and to:

identify up to six areas of the subject that
may be assessed; to look at how scores in
these areas could be aggregated; to specify
the skills and competencies related to CSE
grade 4 and O levels grades C and A; and to
ensure that the proposals will have a
beneficial effect on the curriculum.

The search for data to give scientific credibility
to the policy continues, spurred on by the search
for efficiency.
    The 'weasel' word which links curricula-test-
select by ability, in the moves towards efficiency
is 'beneficial'. For if efficiency is defined in
terms of the link between resourcing and achievement of objectives, and if the objectives are
defined as legitimating pupil differentiation by
ability, then anything which aids the jump between
the two ideas is 'beneficial'. The Chartered
Institute of Public Finance and Accountancy are
clear about the links they are making. Their
recent report (TES, 1984b) argues that every LEA's
performance can be boiled down to an educational
balance sheet made up of seven key indicators:

... the pupils receiving free meals as a
percentage of the total school rolls; the
pupil teacher ratio; the gross cost per pupil;
school occupancy rates; admissions appeals
per 1,000 pupils; exam results, and the
percentages of 16-year-olds staying on or
going into further education, training or
employment.

According to the DES account, the report accepts
that 'some indicators, notably that dealing with
exam results will require further refinement'.
Although the report has the status of a discussion
document, the members of the institute 'had no

doubt (that the indicators) could and would be used for making comparisons between authorities and within authorities over time'.

What we have here, is evidence of powerful interests behind the search for the criteria which will provide a measure of efficiency applicable to local authorities, schools and individual teachers. Yet what we also have is an unequal society where differential schooling experiences are organised for different groups on the basis of their ability and potential. Uniting these economic and political structures are the individuals, each duly measured by technical criteria, according to their socio-cultural worth, at the least possible and most efficient cost. It is a neat, managerial model, which engages teachers and pupils in the goals of the enterprise by the competitive measurement of their success in achieving the managerial goals. The problem with it, is that it takes no account of the substantive problems of either teachers or pupils in classrooms, where life is not like that at all.

In order to demonstrate this, and to cover a sufficiently broad spectrum of events to show how the technical concerns of the policy makers for 'efficiency' intermeshed with the socio-cultural relationships which characterise any inter-personal negotiations in intersubjective contexts such as schools, I shall consider three aspects of the process of schooling. These are the questions of pupil evaluation and selection for differential curricular experiences, the issue of testing, and the problem of the relationship between teaching method and the pupil attainment of testable objectives. Whilst these issues have been brought together in the management model, teachers interpret them in different, but overlapping discourses, each of which holds within it the post hoc rationalisations which justify the schooling process in the intersubjective terms of 'helping' pupils. These rationalisations of the substantive situation, unlike the technical rationales of the managerial perspective, leave teachers to mediate the contradictions of a society which assumes a logical connection between the cooperative sociality of wealth production and the competitive egotism of private appropriation (Carter, 1976). Teachers must struggle to hold together both the interests of pupils-in-general and the interests of the most able in particular. The tensions were clearly observable in the middle schools where the

research on which this chapter is based was
conducted.

COMPREHENDING THE INCOMPREHENSIBLE: '... BUT AS IT
ISN'T IT AIN'T ...'

Middle schools were first established in the late
1960s in the context of a rhetoric,framed in the
discourse of the 1967 Plowden Report. As such,
they were part of the policy era which stressed the
importance of delaying selection of pupils for
differential curricular experiences, whilst
broadening all pupils' opportunities in order to
develop their full potential. More pragmatically,
they were part of a general shift towards incorporating the disadvantaged pupils into the
ladder of 'opportunity' whilst allowing local
authorities to make the best use of their existing
buildings in the move towards comprehensive
secondary schooling and the raising of the school
leaving age to a universal 16 years (Blyth and
Derricot, 1977; Bryan and Hardcastle, 1977;
Hargreaves and Tickle, 1980; Hargreaves, 1983).
     The most recent, and long delayed report on
middle schools by Her Majesty's Inspectorate (DES,
1983), reflects the changes in policy which have
occurred since the mid 1970s, and highlights new
links at teacher level. Explicit connections are
made between curriculum, standards and accountability of teachers. The 'areas' of the curriculum
appear as synonymous with subjects and teachers
are urged to monitor pupil progress and pass on
records so that 'on transfer pupils are not held
back and made to cover the same ground'. A further
association is made between subject specialist
teaching and 'standards', although the apparent
scientific gloss given by the statistical tables
to this item of information largely obscures the
fact that subject grades depended on HMI who
awarded the grades on a six point scale by estim-
ating the 'general standard' in each subject.
The same figures demonstrate that resources varied
widely and that, even on HMI rule-of-thumb, the
differences in resource provision were by far the
most important factors in explaining differences
in standards of work (pp. 138-140, 149). No attempt appears to have been made to measure the
consequences of different forms of ability group-
ing, and we are assured that 'whatever the
ability group', the work was directed towards the

average, rather than the able pupil. 'Giftedness' has vanished; the 'able' have taken their place. What emerges from all this is that it is the continuing belief at the DES, that the linear model of pupil progress through sequenced levels of work, can be made to fit the efficient process of schooling, if only teachers work harder at it. The Inspectorate note:

> Progression is easier to manage in those parts of the curriculum where activities can be ordered according to clear logical sequences, but it also needs to be sought in areas of subjects where it is not possible to be so precise.

We are not, however, merely concerned with logical sequences. We are also concerned with logical sequences which can be specified as behavioural objectives with measurable outcomes. Bearing these points in mind, I will present data on the way in which the managerial pressures were affecting teachers' work with pupils in six middle schools in a single local authority, between 1979 and 1981.

The rationale behind my research derived from the view that changes in policy were not merely conducted at a rhetoric level, but involved managerial interventions into all schools. The general hypothesis, therefore, was that changes in policy since the Great Debate would be observable in similarly manifest forms across different schools, regardless of such factors as size of school, age range and type of building, social class characteristics of catchment area, and the stated philosophical position of the headteacher. The general idea was to scrutinise policy documents and policy making processes at government and local government levels, in an attempt to relate these processes to the changes negotiated intersubjectively in the schools studied in the field research.

The methodology for the field study involved two periods of work in six (9-13) middle schools in one local authority. The first period was between November 1979 and April 1980 and the second between November 1980 and April 1981. As well as gathering data using participant-observation, the research included two sets of interviews with teachers, with an interval of about twelve months between interviews. The same, semi-structured schedule was used on each

occasion and more than sixty teachers were interviewed altogether. Forty-nine of these were
interviewed twice and most of the interviews were
recorded on tape. Five of the six schools had been
used in earlier research, as part of a project
undertaken by the Department of Educational Enquiry
at the University of Aston (Ginsburg et al 1977,
1979; Wallace, 1980a,b). These schools had been
chosen for their differences in all of the respects
noted above. By 1979, all of these schools had
become well established and all but one were
suffering to some degree from the effects of
falling rolls. A sixth school was therefore added,
in order to provide an institution of recent
origin which faced problems of overcrowded buildings, unfinished building work, and rapidly rising
rolls in a growth area of new building and new
families. Some of the work from this project has
been published already elsewhere (Wallace et al,
1973; Wallace and Tickle, 1983). In this account
all respondents take the feminine pronoun.
     In Wallace and Tickle (1979), it was shown
that by 1979 there had already been a swing away
from mixed-ability teaching in these middle
schools. Pupils were being formally differentiated
for mathematics and some English work soon after
entry at the age of nine. There had also been a
considerable increase in testing, and the county
had been encouraging annual tests using the
Richmond Tests of Basic Skills. A variety of
other tests were in use, but teachers generally
found them of little use for setting purposes,
particularly in the broad middle bands. The
problem came to a head in January 1981, when cuts
in staffing threatened to disrupt the setting
patterns, as all but one school lost at least one
member of staff. In two of the schools, teachers
opted to give up non-teaching time, rather than
'upset' pupils. In one school a whole year was
re-tested on the whole Richmond battery, before
boundaries were redrawn around larger groups.
Where rapidly falling rolls had led to a considerable loss of specialist teachers, the staff
fell back onto teaching their own classes in mixed-
ability groups. By April 1981, the uncertainties
in the schools regarding the next round of cuts,
or the next set of rules which might affect their
rolls, or even their existence, was encouraging a
debate on the desirability of reverting to mixed-
ability teaching by class teachers for much of the
time, in order to create a more settled environ-

ment for the pupils. The major problem was not
merely located in the difficulty of responding to
moves made at short notice by the local authority,
but in making a response which was justifiable in
the substantive situation of the school. Underlying this was the difficulty of setting pupils on
the basis of technical criteria alone. Two teachers who endeavoured to explain this to me in the
staff room, in April 1981, show the problems they
found in attempts to use tests for setting:

> Originally we had two top English ...
> (Interruption: The English setting didn't
> work very well ..) .. No. (Interruption:
> because to set the middles we couldn't
> decide a criterion for setting them and
> therefore, when we tested, we only tested for
> certain things and it wasn't sufficient
> information for changing the sets ... so we
> ended up not knowing why we were setting the
> middles, what criteria we had for setting them
> and so on). And the groups .. we had four
> joint middles and this group that's in between
> the middle and bottom now .. (Interruption:
> has evolved .. has evolved during the year).
> We discovered that we've got roughly a middles
> group but there were certain ones in every
> group that had these problems ...
> (Interruption: They were good orally and
> they've got a good Richmond comprehension
> score ..) But they couldn't (Both teachers
> together: .. get it on to paper ...) So we
> abandoned ... (Interruption: So we abstracted
> about 15 .. sorry .. interfering aren't I?)
> It's working better now.

The solution adopted in this school was to have
two top groups, 'three joint middles, a group that
need extra help in certain areas and a bottom
group'. The head moved in to cover teaching areas
lost by cutbacks in staffing. This kind of problem
was common across all of the schools and there was
considerable evidence that teachers who had tried
using the tests for setting purposes had reverted
to judgements based on work in class and on
'knowing the child'. 'Joint middles' solved some
of the problems.
    Ball (1981) claims that teachers liked
mixed ability teaching because it enabled them 'to
inhibit the development of anti-school peer groups
by moving key personnel into other forms (p. 257).

However, there was also evidence that teachers
liked to spread 'the motivated ones' across more
than one form if possible as this helped them to
get oral contributions from pupils when they were
class teaching. In addition there was some
evidence of ethical considerations in line with
teachers' own value systems. Pollard (1984)
suggests that such value systems may lead teachers
to 'sponsor' certain pupils, even at the infant
stage. Evidence from my research suggested that
teachers had problems justifying the setting
process because of the association of 'bottom' with
bad. It seemed wrong to put well-behaved pupils
into the lower sets. A coordinator in a school
which had collapsed six sets into five to cope with
loss of staff rationalised the problem thus:

> We felt it was wrong for the children in the
> next to bottom set to suddenly think they
> were in the bottom set, when in fact what we
> were going to tell them was that the bottom
> set were going to come up and join them ...
> ... we tried to make the children feel they
> had not been demoted ... through no fault of
> their own ... just because we were one teacher
> short.

The associated, and pragmatic problem, came from
pupils who could react uncooperatively following
such a move. Assuring them that they had not
been put down was, tactically, a useful negotiating
point in retaining cooperation (Woods, 1979).
We have then a situation in the schools where
testing had lost credibility as a means of
differentiating between pupils. Yet differentiation, even with moves back to mixed ability teaching by class teachers, remained crucial, particularly at the point of transfer between middle and
high schools. Although, again, practices varied
between schools, the high schools were demanding
that pupils be ranked in order of general ability
on transfer, to assist rapid deployment of pupils
to the option 'bands' which increasingly
corresponded to the 16+ examination levels. These
bands covered O level, CSE and 'practical' subjects, with pupil options limited to those
available to their ability band. Although the
process of ranking pupils caused middle school
teachers considerable anxiety, the discussions
between staff took into account, not only the
standardised test results, but also class tests

and teacher recommendations. The teachers concerned did develop a rapport with the high schools
over the two years, so that recommendations were
accepted 'irrespective of those test results', as
one head put it, but the fact that two or three
middle schools contributed to a single high school,
left high school staff drawing lines between
middle school lists on the basis of standardised
test results. It was this practice, together with
the unpredictable consequences of the 1980 Education Act in providing parents with the right to
'express a preference' for one school against
another, that set schools in competition with one
another to improve their results on the standardised tests. Heads appeared to be convinced that
parents would opt for middle schools where a high
proportion of pupils were getting into the top
band of the high schools, even though the local
authority had not decided how it would implement
the provisions of the Act. It was this factor
which induced teachers in the one middle school
that was still resisting the introduction of the
Richmond Tests of Basic Skills, to give the pupils
'experience of an exam sort of situation' once a
year, in the hall:

> really thinking that um if they've not
> experienced this .. this could be a dis-
> advantage when they arrive at the high school.
> And they find themselves in competition with
> children who have already experienced it ..
> but it's the first time we've ever done it.

The problem thus became defined as 'helping'
pupils, whom teachers 'knew' had the 'ability', to
do the tests. Having defined the problem thus,
teachers had three possible reasons why pupils
were not doing as well as they might in any of the
tests. One was that they were not focussing
accurately enough on the question or problem; the
second was that they were not retaining what they
had been taught, and the third was that they
lacked practice. The scapegoats could be anything
from television to the 'ability not to remember
anything'.

The following extract from an interview with
a year group coordinator who taught science
demonstrates how the test issue was affecting her
practice. This teacher used class tests in an
attempt to examine the process of learning:

> In science I try to test ... not always
> successfully ... but I try to test .. not the
> actual material .. but the using of the
> material. I try to take broad questions
> round experiments that they've done and apply
> them to a different situation and see if they
> can follow it.

GW

> And when you've done the test, how would you
> react to the results? What are you looking
> for when you see the results?

Coordinator

> When I actually see the results I'm more
> interested in having a look at the answer
> paper rather than the numerical score; to see
> which ones they were getting right and which
> questions they were getting wrong and try to
> find the reasons for it.

Now all of this sounds like commendable practice.
The tests appear to be used as a means of understanding the process of learning in pupils and of
finding better ways to teach. However, the tests,
according to the doctrine of sequential learning
through a logical programme, are not means but
ends. Correct answers signify that an objective
has been achieved and that pupils may progress to
the next stage. The intervention of this doctrine
into the process, is therefore a corrupting one.
The interview continued:

GW

> And did you come up with any answers on that?

Coordinator

> Yes .. It seems to be the age old story with
> kids .. The more words, the less likely they
> are to get it right. That was the only thing
> I could find that was common to all the
> questions. If I used a long spiel beforehand
> then they were more likely to lose the gist
> of the question I think. And get it wrong.
> Comprehension type questions is one they
> found very difficult. Questions where you
> supply them with some information and then put
> in a sentence 'using this information only ..'
> and they still go back to what they've done in
> the past. They can't restrict themselves to
> what the question says. But I generally find
> .. our children here .. they have great
> difficulty answering a question accurately.

From a concern with process, this teacher switched
to a concern with accuracy; a concern which involves the problem of getting pupils to give the
right answer. My next question took up the
coordinator's reasoning on process. Her response
focussed back onto accuracy.

GW
    Is that because of the language?
Coordinator
    No .. practice, practice. If you look at
    the old primary/secondary situation .. they
    got plenty of practice .. for the testing at
    11+ and answering the questions. Well that's
    gone .. and the high schools **find the** same.
    They can't answer a question accurately.
GW
    Is that a written question?
Coordinator
    Yes .. so what we do now is tend to set them
    some written questions occasionally .. and let
    them have a go at them .. rather than .. you
    know .. do topic work. We try and give them
    some structured questions .. especially next
    term .. the last term.
GW
    So they'll be better at the high school doing
    them?
Coordinator
    That's right. We actually make a positive
    effort to set them questions rather than
    anything else.
GW
    And would they be the sort of questions that
    require a written answer .. like an essay?
Coordinator
    They can be all sorts of questions. In
    science I tend to go for multiple choice ..
    um .. In humanities I require a longer
    answer. Not necessarily an essay .. a para-
    graph .. a few sentences. But certainly with
    an emphasis on answering questions properly.
GW
    And what do you think they are getting out of
    that that they're not getting out of project
    work and that sort of thing?
Coordinator
    Well project work is very much child centred.
    But I feel that our system of education in
    the high schools is not. I think it's very
    much examination geared .. examination

centred .. although a lot of the Boards are
now allowing project work as part of the
assessment. It still requires you to answer
questions <u>accurately</u> at the end of it .. and
I feel that unless we prepare them for that
soon enough .. early enough .. they're
going to find great difficulty.

I have quoted this at length because it shows how a
teacher, trained in the child-centred rhetoric of
the Plowden era has adopted the practices of
objectives-based learning, where those objectives
are defined as teaching pupils to answer questions
accurately. What it also shows is that, contrary
to Kay's apparent intention of distinguishing
methods from objectives, the objective of getting
the right answer has absorbed the method.
Accuracy demanded practice at accuracy.

A head in another school,who blamed television
for the difficulties in getting pupils to be
accurate, argued that television affected pupils'
listening and their observational faculties. 'And
this shows up in science and art'.

GW
>   And you think you can actually detect this ..
>   in science and art?
Head
>   Yes we think so .. we've discussed this ..
>   very much so in art. I think more in art
>   than in science .. much more .. but if you're
>   looking at an object .. virtually .. They
>   don't really see it. They're so used to
>   seeing things .. moving things .. going before
>   their eyes, they don't look and say, 'Well is
>   that line straight? Is that an acute angle?,
>   You know they just don't .. don't look ..

An HMI had visited this school the previous day and
had apparently agreed that the problem was one of
accuracy. Some idea of HMI reasoning in this area
can be gleaned from a recent report on art in six
(9-13) middle schools and three (13-18) comprehensive schools in Kent (DES, 1984). Praise is
reserved for work such as 'pastel paintings of
textured objects such as rope, hessian, bricks and
wood', and for pupils who closely followed a design
brief 'to make a complex tessellated pattern using
a limited number of colours'. Such work 'reflected
careful observation and sustained interest and
concentration' (pp. 9-10).

In another of the six middle schools that I studied the head was turning to rote learning as a solution to the problem of getting pupils to remember what they were taught in mathematics:

> I don't know if we're taking steps backwards
> .. I'm sure we are at times .. but it's
> because we see that certain children's prog-
> ress is being hampered because we're sticking
> in maths .. for example .. to the conceptual
> approach. Now we are fairly certain and we're
> looking into it at the moment .. We're making
> various assessments based upon various tests
> the head of maths is carrying out on children
> in the 4th year .. but we think .. and if our
> tests prove us wrong then we'll think again ..
> but we think that there are certain children
> who will get on faster .. for instance .. just
> being made to learn by rote .. As an example
> .. various formulae on for instance volume of
> a cylinder. Never mind how you work it out ..
> it is pi r squared .. That's what you use ..

I have left the response as it appears on tape, although the omission in the formula was indicated non-verbally, with the stress on the problem of getting pupils to remember the area of a circle, rather than grasping the volume of a cylinder. The basic problem, however, remained that of getting pupils to answer test questions accurately. Precisely the same problem exercised the mathematics specialist in the school, who had responsibility for advising other staff. Her concern was with 'retention problems'. The solution was more frequent practice.

> There's two days a week when the children are
> doing no maths at all theoretically. Throw in
> the weekends .. that's four days um .. when
> quite conceivably they could forget about it
> altogether. I think this is one reason for
> the retention problems. Whereas if we had it
> five days a week, at least you would be getting
> over that constant practising of the subject
> which is missing at the moment ..

Not surprisingly, a young class teacher in the same school was also concerned with pupils' problems in retaining what they had been told. She claimed that 'Children in (this locality) have got this ability not to retain anything from one day to the next', and explained that she was trying to get pupils to learn how to memorise material by giving them practice with 'a nice short rhyming poem'. With regard to mathematics, she argued:

> You see you can teach something one week ..
> one day and they remember the technique the
> next day .. but give them a week and it's not
> just a matter of revising .. you've got to
> reteach. This is what we're discovering. If
> it was just revision .. well that's fair
> enough. You don't expect everybody to
> remember .. but it's not. You're reteaching.
> So from one year to the next .. when they're
> supposed to .. I know the (Head of Mathematics)
> will say, 'Right you should have done this ..
> We'll do a quick ..' and she'll think, 'Well
> they don't .. and it's not revision. You've
> got to reteach.' And they go back and back
> .. so they're right .. They're reteaching.

The examples given so far come from three schools at the more progressive end of the continuum as far as the general philosophical orientation of the headteachers was concerned. In the more traditional schools, where teachers had always been concerned with techniques such as spelling, comprehension and mental arithmetic, they were still finding it difficult to reconcile any concept of pupil 'ability' with test performance. The humanities specialist quoted below, was struggling to reconcile the two notions:

> You see you get articulate children who
> obviously have the English there .. It's
> ridiculous to say they haven't .. and you get
> dyslexic children. You know that they can
> express themselves .. yet they're having this
> dreadful difficulty of putting it down. You
> have some children who .. well for instance,
> they're very imaginative .. their eyes perk
> up when they hear poetry and creative work ..
> When it comes to the bread and butter
> English they're not so interested .. so how
> do you sort of say?'

Faced with the view that it should be possible to rank pupils according to their progress through programmes of work, teachers could make little sense of it all.

We can illustrate this by returning to the

subject of mathematics. Campbell (1984) has provided evidence of the considerable range of the curricular and interpersonal skills required of teachers with responsibility for curricular development in middle schools. Working on a project with these curriculum postholders in another local authority area, he noted how the responsibilities of such teachers were first outlined in the primary education survey (DES, 1978), and later specified in detail in the Cockroft Report (1982, pp. 354-358). In brief, a successful curriculum postholder was required to be up to date in the conceptual structure and methods of the subject; to be able to draw up, implement and assess for effectiveness a programme of work; to be able to select from and 'manage' different materials and approaches in order to achieve a 'match' between pupils' developmental stages and the work programme; to be able to work with and advise colleagues and also to be able to present and justify all this to outsiders, governors and local authority advisers (Campbell, 1984, p.4).

Although the Cockcroft Report was not published until 1982, it is reasonable to assume that the ideas within it were part of the general thinking of HMI the previous year. We can then see how the following headteacher was struggling to come to terms with the general shift towards this kind of expectation. An HMI had also visited this school, the day prior to the interview.

> I am currently, in the 4th year, using the Head of maths as a floater. Now that may sound wasteful. I don't particularly think it is because of who she is .. but um .. she really has by this floating role .. trouble shooter role, even managed to increase the pace of us all .. all who teach maths in the 4th year .. because she visits us regularly every week .. each of the six sets and sometimes does lead key lessons on particular aspects for us .. and really I think we're beginning to feel the strength of this .. and if only I could do it with other people .. you know .. the rest of the school .. I feel certain that I could increase the whole level and pace ..

Now this sounds a sensible move, given that the Head of mathematics is clearly in a better position than non-specialists to teach her subject.

However, the reason for this policy is directly related to the problem of developing a curriculum which corresponds to pupil progress through sequential programmes of learning necessary for the setting of testable objectives at different levels of attainment. It is this part of the exercise which troubles this respondent. She continued:

> .. Er that preoccupies me at the moment .. this pace of learning .. um .. largely because people are finding difficulties over direction .. over the direction they should be aiming at. I don't mean overall direction .. I think we've got a fair idea of that but er direction over certain elements .. And we just haven't got the staffing to go and visit them and talk about it with them often enough.

GW

> There's two things there .. pace and direction. I'm not altogether clear .. er .. what the increased pace is aiming at, if you see what I mean.

Headteacher

> Yes I do .. I hope (laugh)   I do anyway .. um .. If we set out at the beginning of a half term .. say with certain objectives that we wish to cover .. not saturate necessarily .. but to cover within that half term, we are more or less giving flexible guidelines for people to work along.

This respondent has again found it difficult to distinguish between the achievement of objectives as measurable ends, and the process teachers engage in of 'covering' certain aspects of work. As teachers facing a class of thirty or more pupils tend to take the latter approach, the measurement of achievement rests on the measurement of how much pupils can 'retain' of what they have heard. Given the common teaching experience, this teacher found it difficult to understand how 'pace' came into it, except as differences between setted groups; and it was not all that easy to draw lines between sets. She accepted that 'mainstream' children might have suffered because too much time had been spent on pupils with difficulties but continued:

> You set in maths after all .. and here we have the great irony of tremendous ability range within the sets! That too we're finding

> confounding. It may be that we've got some
> sort of inexperienced staff .. which is why I
> should have .. a little bit more liberal staff
> so I could try and improve things.

Preoccupied with the idea of pace, and confounded
by the idea of a wide ability range, she had not
grasped that curricula must embody the assumption
that a potential 'match' is possible between a
course which is structured according to a logical
sequence of cbjectives (each of which offers
progress to a higher level of skill) and the level
of mental processes in individual pupils. Pring
(1976) provides a suitable critique of the view of
'knowledge' presupposed by such an approach. He
calls it the knowledge 'how', which **assumes that**
pupils can have techniques 'stuck on' to them,
without engaging their 'imaginations and aspirations, their questionings and puzzles, their values
and concerns' (Pring, 1976, p. 52). Pring argues
that such knowledge is just as easily 'unstuck';
an idea born out by the evidence of teachers' lack
of success in the schools.

However, even supposing that it is possible to
teach individual pupils to progress to some kind
of understanding of subject knowledge by teaching
them measurable techniques each more complex than
the last; and even supposing that subject knowledge
can be broken down into such a structure of
sequenced techniques, there remains the question
of pupil 'pace' through such a structure. Either
we assume that pupils can progress alone and
virtually unaided through such programmes in a
class of thirty or more pupils similarly engaged,
or we assume that the lone teacher can provide the
necessary individualised teaching to assist
individual pupils through the sequences. Furthermore, there is built into the managerial model,
the view that progress through the sequences will
demonstrate the spread of ability amongst pupils.
Now, either it must be supposed that some pupils
will work harder than others and get through the
programmes faster, or some pupils will find the
progression easier than others because they already
have some kind of advantage. The general idea
gained by the head interviewed above, was that
teachers could get every one to work faster, the
spread would broaden, differentiated achievements
emerge. As resources and staffing declined, the
pupils who could get to the top would get
preferential treatment. This squares well with the

comments of another head who was a member of a
county working party on assessment procedures. We
may thus assume that she is expressing county
policy as she understands it: (Compiled from notes)

> The most important thing is to make them
> realise we're all different. The problem
> going through the school is to make them
> realise their own potential .. I would rather
> see more emphasis from employers on individual
> school write ups than exams. It's stupid for
> non-academics. It's much more important for
> a child to do things relating to responsib-
> ilities. I think this is what employers are
> looking for rather than that ABCD grading ..
> which is all right for the brighter ..
>
> Say you're doing maths, or for the second year
> fractions. You introduce it to them
> altogether and the ability would depend upon
> the class you've got and what you're aiming
> for. With the bright class you know you're
> going to get a lot further. This is what
> worries me about science. The teacher puts
> them in groups .. and the bright ones lead
> the others and the others just chug along ..
> The only way to teach is individually ...
>
> Most of us are too sensitive, not objective.
> We're frowning on Richmond now. It's going to
> be more on the ones we do here now. (i.e. an
> NFER battery of verbal reasoning, mathematics
> and English taken in the 1st and 4th year).
> Richmond's not so popular because of the time
> factor and then it doesn't tell the correct
> things and people have been accused of
> teaching to the test. We want to be sure the
> children have got the ability. Richmond is
> giving the teacher a pat on the back. If you
> know a child has got a good IQ the teacher
> will jump on poor work. The new tests will be
> for English, Maths and reasoning. It will be
> introduced at various stages. In the whole
> country we'll have a good idea where we're
> going.

There are several ideas we can sort out of this.
Firstly, there is a clear reference to more formal
differentiation than that of setting, a fact which
underlines the previous head's concern for
proposals to differentiate between 'mainstream' and

what he called 'complicated' pupils, so that the pace of the former could be increased. Secondly, we have the notion that pupils can be differentiated according to their competitive pace through programmes of work. Thirdly, we have an idea that appears to contradict the whole idea of teacher accountability, namely that pupils have a generalised form of ability which can be tested in ways which circumvent the problems of teachers teaching to the test. Teachers are there to keep up the pace.

Even so, one of the staff commented on the NFER tests in this school:

> .. when you're talking about 2% of the school population .. I think they have a certain validity to play .. but they are indicative of the child who is very much above average .. or as I said before, the child who's very much below average, but I think their interpretation's rather suspect when the ball's in the middle.

Standardised against the normal curve of distribution, these tests are no more than an updated version of the kind used in the discredited 11+ examination. Teachers in this school, as elsewhere, refined their selections on the basis of long deliberations on the many other 'desirable' and 'undesirable' characteristics of pupils, keeping as many as possible in the top sets in order to maximise the chances of 'their' pupils in the high school stakes. On the timetable, English lessons were itemised into periods for spelling, comprehension, reading and essay writing; under mathematics, periods of mental arithmetic were specially identified. The emphasis was on drilling pupils in the 'basics': on attempting to instil the techniques necessary to answer test questions accurately, under the threat of teacher accountability for standards. The ideological apparatus was in place. It was the teachers who had to legitimate the process of selection which linked individual pupils to the economic and political order. The order itself had been restored: the expectations limited to the reality.

SUMMARY AND CONCLUSION: 'THAT'S LOGIC'

In the face of chronic economic decline in the mid

1970s, the government has had to react to a crisis
of expectations generated by the 1960s policies of
expanding the ladder of opportunity in order to
incorporate areas of relative social and geographic
deprivation. The shift has taken the ideological
form of a switch from 'opportunity' to 'efficiency'.
However, the meaning of efficiency in this context,
is one which relates the resources provided for
schooling in some corresponding form to the
political ordering of an unequal society. The
ladder remains but positions on the rungs must take
account of decline rather than expansion.
Aspirations must be aligned more realistically to
prospects.

With the progressive decline in the belief in
fixed mental faculties, difficult to reverse,
alternative forms of justifying differential
resource distribution are necessary. The revival
of a view that subjects can be structured into
sequenced programmes of work centering on skills
of varying levels of complexity, which may be
learnt by practice, offers the possibility that
grade-related criteria can be established which
link curricula, testing and selection by ability,
into a technical package. In an unequal society
this process could establish differential standards
of pupil ability, label them neatly and efficiently
ready for their rung on the ladder, and offer a
measure of teacher accountability, with pupil
success made dependent upon teaching. Establishing
such criteria would obviously be beneficial to
society, in terms of efficiency.

Data from schools suggests, however, that the
differences between individuals are not differences
which are readily interpreted as differences in
pupils' ability on the basis of test criteria. Yet
pupils have to be fitted into an organised order
which assumes that some kind of ladder of general-
isable ability exists. This order is also supposed
to fit the normal curve of distribution. However,
as the organisational order itself changes in
periods of decline, as well as periods of expansion,
there can be no 'match' between defined pupil
'level' and the organisation. As the competition
for top set positions increased with the cuts and
the unpredictable consequences of county policy,
teachers came under pressure to match what they
believed were pupils' abilities, to ever high
levels of performance on test scores, because that
was what seemed to count in the competition. As
they were all doing it, during a period of

184

continuing cuts, there were no defined levels of
attainment which gave pupils any rights to move to
higher levels of provision. The high schools drew
their lines when their ability bands were full,
duly taking into account the middle school
recommendations as well as the test results.
Nothing had changed in the order of things, but
instead of contesting the decline, teachers had
become its managers, answerable for the curricula,
the criteria and the consequences within a logic
which made little sense to them in terms of the
managerial model, because their interests also lay
in maintaining the intersubjective relationships
of cooperation in the classroom. They had to
mediate the tensions.

However, if we take into account the fact that
teachers were supposed to be developing a logically
sequenced curriculum, and that their task was being
redefined not in terms of teaching it, but in terms
of maintaining the pace of individual pupils
through it, then we can see moves towards the deskilling of teachers which Apple (1982) has
identified in the American system. The teachers
who came closest to this model were those who were
pushing pupils through series of graded comprehension texts. In the context of declining resources,
there was not much opportunity to restock with
materials necessary to do much else. Teachers
remained with their skills.

>"I was thinking," Alice said very politely,
>"which is the best way out of this wood: It's
>getting so dark. Would you tell me please?"

>But the fat little men only looked at each
>other and grinned.
>(Lewis Carroll, 1872).

ACKNOWLEDGEMENTS

Thanks are due to the SSRC for the Award which made
the fieldwork possible and to Henry Miller for help
and support in supervising the research. I am also
grateful to the hardpressed teachers who gave me so
much of their time and to the many others who have
encouraged me to continue trying to sort it all
out.

REFERENCES

Ahier, J. and Flude, M. (1983) Contemporary
    Education Policy, Croom Helm, Beckenham.
Apple, M.W. (1982) 'Curricular form and the logic
    of technical control: building the possessive
    individual' in Apple, M.W. (ed.) Cultural and
    Economic Reproduction in Education, Routledge
    and Kegan Paul, London and Boston.
Asubel, D.P. (1967) 'Crucial psychological issues
    in the objectives, organisation and evaluation
    of curriculum reform movements', Psychology
    in Schools, 4 (2), 111-120.
Ball, S. (1981) Beachside Comprehensive, Cambridge
    University Press, Cambridge.
Baron, S., Finn, D., Grant, N., Green, M., and
    Johnson, R. (1981) Unpopular Education,
    Hutchinson, London.
Bloom, B.S. et al. (1956) Taxonomy of Educational
    Objectives: The Classification of
    Educational Goals. Handbook 1: Cognitive
    Domain, Longman, London.
Blyth, W.A.L. and Derricot, R. (1977) The Social
    Significance of Middle Schools, Batsford,
    London.
Bryan, K.A. and Hardcastle, R.W. (1977) 'The
    Growth of Middle Schools: Educational
    Rhetoric and Economic Reality', Journal of
    Educational Administration and History, 11,
    (1).
Campbell, R.J. (1984) 'In-School Development:
    The Role of the Curriculum Postholder', Mimeo,
    University of Warwick.
Carroll, Lewis (1872) Through the Looking Glass.
Carter, M.A. (1976) 'Contradiction and
    Correspondence: Analysis of the Relation of
    Schooling to Work' in Carnoy, M. and Levin,
    H.M. (eds.) The Limits of Educational Reform,
    Longman, New York.
Cockroft Report (1982) Mathematics Counts, HMSO,
    London.
Department of Education and Science (1977a)
    Curriculum 11-16, HMSO, London.
DES (1977b) Modern Languages in Comprehensive
    Schools, HMSO, London.
DES (1977c) Gifted Children in Middle and
    Comprehensive Secondary Schools, HMSO, London.
DES (1978) Primary Education in England, HMSO,
    London.
DES (1983) 9-13 Middle Schools, HMSO, London.

DES (1984) A Survey of Art in Six 9-13 Middle
    Schools and in Three 13-18 Comprehensive
    Secondary Schools in Kent, Report by HM
    Inspectors, DES Publications, Stanmore.
Evanden, I. (1979) 'Assessment across the ability
    range', Secondary Education Journal, 9 (3),
    18-20.
Evans, K. (1979) 'Pupil Profiles: A Rationale',
    in Secondary Education Journal, 9 (3), 21-23.
Ginsburg, M.E., Meyenn, R.J., Miller, H.D.R. and
    Ranceford-Hadley, C. (1977) The Role of The
    Middle School Teacher, Aston Educational
    Monograph, No. 7, University of Aston in
    Birmingham.
Ginsburg, M.B., Meyenn, R.J., Miller, H.D.R. (1979)
    'Teachers, the "Great Debate" and the educa-
    tion cuts', Westminster Studies in Higher
    Education, 2.
Goldstein, H. and Blinkhorn, S. (1982) 'The Rasch
    Model Still Does not Fit', British Educational
    Research Journal, 8 (2).
Halsey, A.H., Floud, J. and Anderson, C.A. (eds.)
    (1961) Education, Economy and Society,
    Free Press, New York.
Hargreaves, A. and Tickle, L. (eds.) (1980)
    Middle Schools: Origins, Ideology and
    Practice, Harper and Row, London.
Hargreaves, A. (1983) 'Conflict and Change in
    Education', Open University Course E205, Unit
    20, Open University Press, Milton Keynes.
Hirst, P.H. (1965) 'Liberal education and the
    nature of knowledge', in Archembault, R.D.
    (ed.) Philosophical Analysis and Education,
    Routledge and Kegan Paul, London.
Holt, M. (1981) Evaluating the Evaluators, Hodder
    and Stoughton, London.
Hunter, C. (1983) 'Education and Local Government
    in the Light of Central Government Policy'
    in Ahier, J. and Flude, M. Contemporary
    Education Policy, Croom Helm, Beckenham.
Husen, T. (ed.) (1967) International Study of
    Achievement in Mathematics: a comparison in
    twelve countries, Almqvist and Wiksell,
    Stockholm, Wiley, New York.
Jackson, B. and Marsden, D. (1963) Education and
    the Working Class, Routledge and Kegan Paul,
    London.
Kay, B. (1974) 'Links Between Subjects', Trends in
    Education, 3, 5-10.
Kay, B. (1975) 'Monitoring Pupils' Performance',
    Trends in Education, 2.

Kogan, M. (1971) The Politics of Education,
    Penguin Education, Harmondsworth.
Kogan, M. (1978) The Politics of Educational
    Change, Fontana/Collins, Glasgow.
Lawton, D. (1980) The Politics of the School
    Curriculum, Routledge and Kegan Paul, London
    and Boston.
National Union of Teachers (1979a) Annual Report,
    NUT, London.
National Union of Teachers (1979b) Secondary
    Education, 9 (3).
Organisation for Economic Cooperation and Develop-
    ment (1965) 'Investment in Education', OECD,
    Paris.
Organisation for Economic Cooperation and Develop-
    ment (1976) Use of Credentials in Employment,
    OECD, Paris.
Phenix, R.H. (1964) Realms of Meaning, McGraw-Hill,
    London.
Plowden Report (1967) Children and Their Primary
    Schools, Report of the Central Advisory
    Council for Education, HMSO, London.
Pollard, A. (1984) 'Coping Strategies and the
    Multiplication of Differentiation in Infant
    Classrooms', British Educational Research
    Journal, 10 (1), 33-48.
Pring, R. (1976) Knowledge and Schooling, Open
    Books, Shepton Mallet.
Ranson, S. and Walsh, K. (1982) 'For the Greater
    Good of the Few', Guardian, 12 January.
Salter, B. and Tapper, T. (1981) Education,
    Politics and the State, Grant McIntyre, London.
Taylor, W. (1980) 'Education: A Redefinition',
    Talk given at a conference of local authority
    inspectors and advisers, London Institute of
    Education, September 1980 (Mimeo).
Times Educational Supplement (1984a) 'SEC acts on
    criteria', 20 April, p.3.
Times Educational Supplement (1984b) 'Accountants
    find LEA's yardstick', report on Performance
    indicators in the education service
    Chartered Institute of Public Finance and
    Accountancy, 20 July, p.1.
Wallace, G. (1980a) 'The Constraints of
    Architecture on Aims and Organisations in Five
    Middle Schools', in Hargreaves, A. and
    Tickle, L. (eds.) Middle Schools: Origins,
    Ideology and Practice, Harper and Row, London.
Wallace, G. (1980b) 'Architectural Constraints
    on Educational Aims and Organisations: with
    particular reference to middle schools.

Journal of Educational Administration and
History, 12 (2), 47-57.
Wallace, G., Miller, H. and Ginsburg, M. (1983)
'Teachers' Responses to the Cuts', in Ahier,
J. and Flude, M. (eds.) Contemporary Education
Policy, Croom Helm, Beckenham.
Wallace, G. and Tickle, L. (1983) 'Middle Schools:
the heart of schools in crisis', British
Journal of Sociology of Education, 4, (3),
223-240.
Wood, R. and Skurnik, L.S. (1969) Item Banking,
NFER, Slough.
Woods, P. (1979) The Divided School, Routledge
and Kegan Paul, London and Boston.

Chapter Eight

TEACHING THE UNTEACHABLE: TEACHER STRATEGIES IN SPECIAL UNITS
FOR DISRUPTIVE PUPILS

Rod Ling

'Look Graham no-one objects to you having problems -
so long as you're prepared to talk about them!' Owen,
head of the Victoria Centre.

'We get curious pride, you know, working with these
kids...it's rather like the kind of pride and
fascination you get when you persuade a wild animal
to eat from your hand...a curious feeling'. Roger,
head of the Delphi Centre.

INTRODUCTION

In this redeveloped wedge of the inner city, monotonous tower
blocks dominate the sky-line and encircle a cluster of public
and commercial buildings; the shops, pub, community centre
and local primary schools. The latter, built of brick and
glass in the functional and unelaborate manner of the early
1970's, were originally planned to occupy adjacent premises
but the numbers of infant children were such that another
larger building was needed which now stands a few hundred,
wind-swept, yards away. The original, redundant infant school
comprising two flat-roofed, one storey blocks subsequently
became the home of the city's first disruptive pupils' unit,
the Delphi Centre.
     Approaching these buildings one begins to notice the
signs of wear and tear; the cracked window, peeling paintwork
and doors in which the original toughened glass panels have
been replaced by more serviceable ones of sturdy plywood.
Inside one of the two classrooms in the 'teaching' block, we
may see twenty or so young people seated behind individual
formica-topped tables. About half these pupils are black and
more than third are girls. They are of different ages and
wear a variety of clothing. There is no noise. On the tables
lie opened books, magazines, and, in one or two cases, comics.
One pupil, sitting in the coveted position alongside the

radiator, is gazing through the window and into the distance.
The majority however are reading. At a desk by the window
the head of the Delphi unit is seated, surveying the classroom.

At the same time, on the other side of the city centre,
but still within the inner zone where industry and housing
are entangled, other pupils are attending another special unit.
The buildings occupied by the Victoria Centre are more typical
of special units and have a much longer history. Built in
the revivalist Gothic style, popular in the Victorian period
as a Board school, they are located on a rise in the manner
of the medieval churches the architecture celebrates. Over-
looking the railway line, the new dual carriageway that runs
alongside it and the surrounding housing development these
buildings look even more dishevelled and uncared for than the
Delphi Centre. The many tall ogival windows provide the
classrooms with a great deal of light but they have proved
more difficult to protect. A number of them are patched with
squares of the ubiquitous plywood which is also employed to
board up the now empty, adjoining, caretaker's house.

Inside the building the atmosphere is more inviting.
Pupils are to be found in a number of rooms and there is more
noise here. Some children are chatting across the desks
whilst working unsupervised in their project folders, a few
others are constructing a 'trolley' and making table tennis
bats in the craft room and another group is involved in
another classroom in a range of art activities. In the office,
some girls have engaged the secretary in conversation. A
boy with 'pool' cue in hand is hoping that his presence in
the games room will not be noted by the staff.

Scenes such as these may be witnessed in many of the
special units for disruptive and disaffected pupils which have
been established in the last ten years. There are now more
than four hundred off-site units (Ling and Davies, 1984) and
an unknown, but probably similar, number of on-site units
i.e. located on the campus of an orthodox school. Not all of
these off-sites units are administered and funded exclusively
by LEAs although this is so in the majority of cases. In
addition referral procedures and working methods exhibit
considerable variation. Taken as a group however their
expansion, in a period of considerable financial difficulty,
indicates the 'success' of their operation and, by extension,
the 'failure' of popular schooling.

This success raises some important questions. Given the
long-standing behavioural problems that the pupils attending
these sites have set the teaching staff in schools, how is it
that they can be brought together in a seemingly improbable
admixture with the results, orderly and controlled, as
described above? When each pupil's deviant career embraces
many hours of chastising, cajoling and counselling, how do
unit teachers succeed in teaching the unteachable? What
skills and strategies do they employ and what, if any, are

implications for schools?

It is the purpose of this paper to explore these questions through a detailed examination of the two units to which we have already been introduced. Both units, catering for a similar age-group and facing similar pressures and demands are part of a sizeable unit provision established by education and social services departments in one large urban authority. The data presented here is drawn an ethnographic study of the meaning and practice of a small number of these units.

'COMMONSENSE' ACCOUNTS

The questions posed above can hardly be considered new or original. They are after all, the natural concern of all the parties involved in the management of disruptive behaviour. In conversation with parents, pupils and teachers two different sets of answers have emerged. One emphasises the importance of the different conditions which obtain in the special unit and the advantages thereby afforded to the staff. The most important factor is seen to be the preferable staff-pupil ratio (SPR) but the freedom to relax certain behavioural and curricular demands is also frequently mentioned. The other type of explanation focusses upon the qualities of the staff in the units; upon their perceived abilities and personalities. On occasion the essence of such individualised accounts is distilled in terms of 'charisma' and thereby rendered impervious to further analysis.

There is little doubt that both sets of answers contain elements of accuracy. Both the Victoria and Delphi Centre have an SPR which seldom rises above 8:1 and on many days is less than this. Moreover, in the provision of a shortened working day with extended breaks, frequent 'trips out', a greater emphasis upon practical activities and the opportunity to play 'pool' and table tennis, the staff are permitted both to reduce demands which may prove the source of conflict and grant privileges which encourage co-operation. On the other hand, staff also demonstrate certain skills and abilities which enable them to secure positive relationships with their pupils and avoid or defuse sources of potential conflict or disturbance.

The point is, however, that neither of these explanations will suffice on its own. The 'structural' account understates the problematic nature of the containment and control of difficult and disruptive pupils. Conflict and disturbance remain a constant possibility even in the most successful units (see for example Jones 1977) and would continue to do so even if the SPR was improved still further. In fact, if the pupil considers referral to a unit as punishment (Ling 1982), then the greater the structural differences are perceived to exist the greater the possibility that these differences, which recreate the possibility of control, may also become a source of disturbance by signalling the abnormality of the pupil's new environment.

A change in structural conditions cannot, in other words, guarantee specific changes in behaviour. Insofar as such changes are achieved within the new setting they are always the outcome of an interactional process. The staff must, in other words, work for these outcomes. However, accounts which rely exclusively upon the skills and abilities of the staff are equally insufficient. Staff and pupils do not meet 'anew' in the unit; they confront the meanings attributed to past experience, to their personal and collective biographies. The work of the unit staff entails the shaping of this meaningful, as well as the physical, environment.

Thus I wish to examine the question of how 'teachers teach the unteachable'through a perspective which concedes the importance of structure whilst remaining sensitive to the creative and spontaneous elements in staff-pupil interactions. I want to suggest that the way in which staff can organise this engagement is heavily constrained by the nature of the unit's and their pupils' relationship to the wider school structures but that sufficient space exists to permit a range of possible responses. It is the tracing of the parameters of these responses in which I am interested.

It is for this reason that the paper concentrates upon the work of two special units who confront very similar conditions and yet whose approaches demonstrate, and are perceived by the staff and others to demonstrate, considerable differences. It will be argued that an examination of the daily activity of these units reveals the existence of alternative approaches which are themselves contingent upon the location of the special unit within the range of schooling provision. Between these relatively pure forms of response lies the space within which the staff have the capacity to 'make' their choices, to construct their social world.

TEACHING STRATEGIES AND SPECIAL UNITS

The means by which we can link interaction and structure is through the concept of strategy or more specifically, that of coping strategy. The use of this concept in the sociology of education has been developed by a number of writers but, most notably in recent years, by Woods (1979, 1980a, 1980b), Hargreaves (1978, 1979) and Pollard (1982, 1984). Briefly we may view teacher (and pupil) strategies as the creative solutions of individuals to situations which are substantially constructed for them in both psychological and material terms, by others. As Pollard (1984) has written,

'The concept of coping strategy has linkages to the
macro concerns of history and social structure and to
micro concerns of the biography and the unique social
contexts which exist in classrooms.'

Quite evidently a major vehicle for the translation of
structurally determined needs into the day-to-day behaviour
of teaching staff takes place through the setting of the
strategic goals. In orthodox schools these are generally
taken to be twofolds; to maintain control and facilitate
learning (Stebbins 1980). In the case of the special unit we
must ask how far these objectives are modified by its location
within the range of LEA provision.

The special unit remains subject to the normal definitions
of what is entailed in the enterprise of education, but in
accommodating a specially selected intake we must consider the
particular demands which the staff must seek to satisfy.

These demands emanate from a number of different sources
and are by no means uniform or unit-directional. Firstly the
demands of schools (which are not the only referring agencies
but by far the most significant) are that the unit staff prove
responsive to their requests for the accommodation of problem
pupils. Secondly the demand of the LEA, particularly in the
case of the Victoria and Delphi Centres which were designed
to cater for the lower end of the secondary school age range,
has been to emphasise the importance of returning pupils to
the orthodox school. This may be seen to both legitimise the
operation of the units (subject to criticisms that they offend
the comprehensive principle) and moreover improve their 'cost-
effectiveness'. Unsurprisingly the referring school and the
pupils themselves may be less than enthusiastic about meeting
this demand.

Parents also, of course, have expectations of the units,
although these are likely to differ according to whether they
share or resist the referring school's definition of the
situation. Whatever their views however the parents of
disruptive pupils are generally reluctant or unable to involve
themselves closely with their children's schooling.

Finally the most persistent demands made upon the staff
derive from the pupils themselves. Since almost all the
pupils attending our two units have at some stage openly
challenged the authority of teachers and subsequently
resisted attempts to reassert it the staff are confronted
with the immediate and pressing problems of containment and
control. In this situation, where the pupil may well perceive
his or her referral as a further punitive measure, the staff
must stress the advantages of attendance and co-operation
whilst asserting the disadvantages of a failure to do so.
They are assisted in this process by an ability to relax
certain demands, grant additional privileges and experiment in
new approaches.

There are, however, real limits to the extent to which the staff can go in redefining the school day and the nature of its social relations if only because their pupils face two ways on schooling. On the one hand they have rejected much of what it has to offer. On the other hand the mainstream school continues to represent the common experience of their peers and families; it is part of the fabric of normality and as such retains a powerful attraction. Moreover if the units propose to return their pupils to school then the need to maintain some continuity with its practice is of consequent importance.

This brief exploration of the demands and pressures that confront staff in units suggests that control and containment of pupils becomes more important within units, because it is the pupils resistance to this in the orthodox school which has occasioned referral. As we have seen this does not mean that the unit staff are free to experiment in any manner they may wish. Pupils, parents and schools impose important constraints upon these processes.

The teaching or learning goal of the unit staff is thus explicitly a behavioural one. The replication of the traditional curriculum and its attendant pedagogy and assessment practices are important only insofar as they advance behavioural objectives. In the special unit, as in the special school (Tomlinson 1982) the hidden curriculum emerges from cover and assumes an undisguised priority.

There is one further consideration which must be explored before we proceed to examine the actions of teachers in special units in strategic terms. As the quotation from Pollard above confirms, writers have invariably had the orthodox school and its classrooms in mind when describing their ethnographic research. However in the special unit the timetabled lesson tends to lack clear boundaries. The activities that take place during lesson and break times (particularly in the afternoon) may well be similar, as will teacher and pupil behaviour, and there are no bells to regulate their commencement and end. Furthermore in the special unit the individual classroom teacher can no longer be viewed as the most appropriate agent of strategies. Special units do not have the extended hierarchies of schools, the majority having no more than three or four teaching staff and a secretary. A high degree of social and ideological cohesion is made both necessary and possible if the staff are to work closely together. It is this feature that makes the identification of a 'collective strategy' largely shaped by two strong-minded head-teachers possible.

Owen and Roger, the two Heads of Centre, can therefore be seen to have developed their respective strategies in response to the broadly similar sets of expectations and demands that confront them and which have been outlined above. I shall argue however that in attempting to satisfy these demands, with all their inherent contradictions, each employs a distinctly different strategy. This comparative analysis is assisted by the fact that although their individual biographies are different, both are motivated by a similar ambition - they wish to secure a position of deputy headteacher in one of the city's comprehensive schools.

THE ELEMENTS OF STRATEGY

Paisey (1975) suggests that the identification of distinctive strategies is made possible by the existence of 'logical relationships between acts'. The 'act' however is a term which tends to collapse the different elements entailed in interaction into specific verbal and bodily behaviours. In identifying control strategies within the unit I want to suggest that there are three distinctive but interactive features that must be taken into account.

The first of these concerns the use of procedures and the organisation of regular activities which serve to reduce uncertainty and provide a framework for the regulation of staff-pupil relations. These processes and procedures not only regulate the cycle of a pupil's career within the unit from admission to departure but also on a daily, weekly and termly basis.

Within these regulated processes staff are engaged in momentary decisions as to the appropriate way to act, that is how to present themselves both audibly and physically to their pupils. Such acts may or may not be temporally specific; they entail the usage of what Stebbins has called 'strategic aids'. Those that I shall concentrate upon are the use of physical contact and, to a lesser extent 'verbal skirmishing' between staff and pupils.

The third and final element is not considered by Paisey though it remains an important source for the identification of strategies. This consists of the articulated and conscious attribution of meaning to an act of uncertain significance.

An important assumption here is that although rhetoric may often serve to mask the true meaning of the act at other times it helps to provide the means and the impetus by which future action is made possible and thus becomes inseparable from it. Act and attribution are, in this sense, interactive. Rhetoric in other words, cannot be ignored for as Willis (1977) has written,

'Consciousness is a privileged source of information and meaning if properly contextualised and ultimately the only stake in the struggle for meaning.' (p 122)

Nevertheless rhetoric is not simply accepted at face value. The discrepancy between rhetoric and practice or 'doctrine and commitment' arises says Selznick (1949) from the distinction between the interrelation of ideas and inter-relation of phenomena'.

OWEN AND THE VICTORIA CENTRE

Owen is in his middle thirties and his working background is in education. Over ten years ago he was teaching in a school, that was to become one of the LEA's first comprehensives. Even then his interests lay with the disadvantaged groups. He was active in the fields of multiracial education, pastoral care and curriculum innovation for the 'ROSLA' pupils. After a period teaching abroad he returned to the U.K. and worked in one of the city's newly opened centres for suspended pupils. Three years later he became the head of the Victoria Centre.

For Owen the resolution of the conflicting pressures and the demands made of him and the unit staff takes place through an education philosophy that reconciles the interests of the child, the school and the LEA. Such a resolution emphasises an egalitarian and humanistic view of the society and the place of schools within it. Its main contention is that there is no irrevocable conflict of interest between the different parties. Disruption in school is epiphenomenal and dysfunctional. The interests of the child reside in obtaining the best possible education, something that only regular attendance at school can bestow. Certificates are one outcome of schooling and will enable the pupil to compete effectively in the labour market. If children approached schooling in this manner schools would have no wish to 'lose' their pupils, the throughflow of children with genuine adjustment problems in units would be assured and the 'moral order' re-established. A child-centred philosophy which for many free schools in an earlier period, was part of the justification for an alternative educational provision has been transformed. Units, in some ways the descendants of the free schools (Francis 1979, Macbeath 1977), are not seen as alternatives to schools but as supplementary. A child-centred approach has become pupil-centred; the interests of the child, particularly the working-class child, are seen as being compatible with and not antagonistic to, those of the school.

This approach does not reduce to a simple acceptance that the child or the family are deficient and in need of 'treatment'. Schools cannot escape criticism. Many are considered to be ineffective and contribute to the problems of disruptive and disaffected behaviour - but for unstructured and individualised reasons - an uncaring and insensitive teacher here, an inappropriate and irrelevant syllabus there. Owen, significantly, makes repeated reference to the work of those (e.g. Rutter, Renolds) who insist that 'schools do make a difference'. For Owen therefore there is then no 'philosophical' objection to the

goal of returning a pupil to school in the manner that the
LEA is eager to encourage.

> 'School is where these kids should be. If they are
> not going to fit into school then they must be placed
> somewhere more suitable. It makes no sense for them
> to stay here; that's been tried and it didn't do them
> any good in the long run.'

It is only within the context of this 'world view' that
particular features of the Victoria Centre and the
attribution of meaning given to them can be understood.

PROCEDURES AND PROCESSES AT THE VICTORIA UNIT

The emphasis upon the consensual nature of school and pupil
interests which is symbolised by Owen's adherence to the
'return goal' can create real difficulties for staff-pupil
relations within the unit. It means that pupils must both
want to come to the unit and eventually, to leave it.
Engineering this balance of aspirations is inherently
difficult. The former is usually approached by the
promotion of close personal relationships made possible by
the structural factors referred to above, but such
relationships may be threatened by an insistence that the
placement is temporary. In order to ensure that pupils who
have come to enjoy the advantages of the unit do not
deliberately fail on a return to school, Owen refuses to
readmit them once reintroduction has taken place. Such
pupils may then be left outside the school system for a
considerable period of time, perhaps indefinitely. This may
be distressing not only to the child and his or her parents
but also to the unit staff who have got to know the pupil well.
In order to reduce the possibility of failure of this
kind, with all its implications for staff and staff-pupil
relations, Owen seeks to systemalise and formalise the process
of referral. He stresses the importance of establishing rules
and procedures that will govern unit-school relations. Data
is collected with a view to determining which 'kind' of pupil
'succeeds' and which does not. This data is incorporated in
publicising of the unit and its work; in articles, meetings
with other professional groups and in a display on the wall
of the head's office cum staffroom where it is often referred
to in the course of interviews with parents and pupils.

Owen: 'Well Kevin, we are trying, and we'll be working
with your parents on this, to get you back to school
and up onto that list up there...see...that's a
list of those who've returned to school. It won't
happen until you've done a term here but it will be
within the year.'

Referring schools are expected to assist in the collation of information by providing a case history, attending meetings and co-operating in assessments (using the Bristol Social Adjustment Guide and the Rutter Scale). This information is supplemented by reports requested from the Education Welfare Service and Schools Psychological Services. Pupil files contain these records together with the brief notes recorded daily by the staff, copies of termly reports, and completed conduct forms which accompany the pupils when they commence a programme of phased re-entry to school.

The collation of this information and its subsequent analysis is seen to be central to the procedures within the unit. In referral meetings attended by all the staff, an educational psychologist, and an Education Social Worker, decisions on particular cases are taken according to a broad consensus which operated around two major and related considerations. The first of these concern a judgement as to the likelihood of the pupil returning to school which in turn is seen to be crucially influenced both by the nature of the pupil's case history and the record of the school in re-admitting pupils. The second entails a projection as to how the pupil will behave in the unit but this is often obliquely expressed and reworked in terms of the first. The 'ideal' pupil is one who is thought to require a period of adjustment coming from a school which has expressed a willingness to take the pupil back.

It is of interest to note that in seeking to systematise referral procedures Owen has begun to undermine the principle of flexibility which was one of the advantages such provision was thought to have over special schools. One senior teacher in a referring school has bluntly informed Owen that if he continues to insist upon the adherence to detailed procedures and referral criteria 'they will be forced to lie'. Though he is aware that there is another, more common accepted, way of working Owen is reluctant to compromise,

'Some people do this I know; they say "if you take this one then we'll help you out over another" - deals in other words. I couldn't do that.'

Another feature which brings us closer to the issue of the control of pupils within the unit is the 'unit contract'. This arrangement comprises a documented exchange of obligations between the unit staff and the pupil. It is signed by all the parties present at the pupil's initial interview. Whilst the pupil agrees to be polite, attend punctually, behave considerately and ask for permission before leaving the premises the staff agree to provide specific curricular inputs requested by the pupil and to secure a place for him or her back in an orthodox school. Establishing this agreement with its quasi-legal status does not ,of course ,spare the staff the continual difficulties of maintaining control. Its significance is symbolic; it represents a tangible token of the consensual nature governing the pupil's attendance and in so doing attempts to counter the punitive and coercive meaning which accompanies referral.

These elements are also present in other features and an important one concerns the operation of what Owen terms 'participatory democracy'. Group meetings are a regular daily event. Staff and pupils are usually seated in a circle in the games room. The meetings are often prolonged, ungoverned by the timetable and the bell, ending when the staff feel it to be appropriate. An obvious and important feature of these meetings is the way in which Owen makes the personal and the private, public and a subject for general discussion. Individual pupils are praised for their achievements and transgressors have their sins exposed.

This is not to say that staff do not seek to ensure that an apparently open exchange concludes with the 'correct' decision. On one occasion the group were being asked about their thoughts on the question of how pupils who disrupt lessons by walking out should be disciplined.

Owen: 'When George, or you Robert...or you Carol walks
           out and slams the door that means the teacher
           has to give up time they could be giving to the
           others in the class, the ones who need the help.
           Now how do you think they should pay back the
           time wasted?'
Several: 'Detention, give 'em detention.'
Chris (member of staff): 'No, not detention.'
Owen: 'Not detention.'
After some conversation and the usual smattering of frivolous
suggestions, one pupil interjects,
Steven: 'Stay in at break.'
Owen: 'That's what we were thinking, not detention... but
           why should the people who misbehave have the nice
           things here like pool and table tennis?'
After further comment Owen sums up,
Owen: 'It's agreed then people who misbehave and cause
           the teacher to waste time must pay it back at
           break.'

This notion of 'paying back time' is yet another example of the way in which the pupil-teacher relationship is couched in moral terms, on this occasion in the language of 'consumer ethics'. This leads the staff into some contortions since logic would suggest that those who 'consume' more than their fair share of 'teacher time' should lose some in the future rather than take up still more as the monitoring of the punishment will entail.

The purpose of group meetings is not just the
demonstration of those aspects of 'negotiation' and 'making
the private public' that have already been referred to.
They also function as a focus for the generation of collective
values and a group identity which is considered desirable
given the fragmented and impermanent nature of pupil attendance.
This desire is also reflected in the encouragement given to
pupils to undertake group projects, perhaps in making a
display, organising fund-raising events or planning for an
excursion or residential experience. Lunch periods are also
intended to be a group activity. All pupils and staff are
encouraged to eat together around a U-shaped arrangement of
tables.

An additional feature of the unit's organisation is the
administration of a Behaviour Modification or 'points'
system. This can be viewed as a fairly powerful mechanism
for exerting control over a number if not all pupils in a
situation where few sanctions exist. In fact, because the
pupils have exhausted the range of sanctions available to
a school, new and additional ones can only be created by the
granting of rewards and privileges. The removal of these
then constitutes a sanction. In this sense the privileges and
goods that pupils can 'purchase' with the points they earn
provide for an effective degree of control. Rhetorically
the points system is also designed to reinforce specific
identified behaviours that will be 'learnt' and carried over
into other (school) situations.

A further feature, implicit in much that has already been
said, is the emphasis given by the staff to 'openness' and
'accessibility'. Owen operates what he terms an 'open door'
policy that permits pupils access to the staff at all times.
Moreover he welcomes the involvement of other agencies in the
work of the unit. These and others; schoolteachers, students,
the police, media, and even researchers, are welcome, if
only,

'To show kids that there are other adults besides
teachers around the place prepared to talk with and
listen to them.'

THE USE BY STAFF OF PHYSICAL CONTACT

The distinction that has been made with regard to the use of
rhetoric and strategical aids such as physical contact is in
many respects an artificial one. These elements are all
embodied in the interaction between staff and pupils in an
attempt to reproduce specific and logically connected
meanings.

Nevertheless physical contact as part of the presentation
of self is considered separately here because it is considered
to play a unique role in staff-pupil relations within the unit.

The absence of reference to the teacher use of physical contact
in school ethnographies suggests that it is relatively rare
phenomenon. Its usage is possibly restricted by the
culturally oriented meanings that surround it to highly
ritualised ceremonies such as the annual staff/pupil football
match, hand-shaking at speech days, incidents of caning or to
highly unstable moments such as those entailed in explosive
moments of physical conflict. There are of course particular
taboos relating to cross-sex contact but these may be present
in same-sex interactions as well.

     In special units, in the absence of an extensive range of
formal sanctions, the imperative to personalise relationships
is even greater than is in schools. In these circumstances
the staff in both the Victoria and the Delphi Centres place a
greater emphasis upon the use of physical contact and are
prepared to take the attendant risks.

     Just two examples are given here of the nature of physical
contact in the Victoria Centre. Chris and Owen often indulge
in brief physical exchanges apparently designed to communicate
acceptance and friendliness and thereby reinforce the
consensual nature of social control. These exchanges may take
the form of 'mock fighting' in which a clear set of rules may
be said to operate. Firstly the teacher must 'win' or at the
very least not 'lose' in a manner that would result in a loss
of face. No real violence may be done, intentionally, to
either party and as accidental injury may cause the
definition of the situation to change quite radically, it must
be avoided. These encounters are for this reason accompanied
by a great deal of laughing, smiling and verbal exchanges.
This continuous flow of information may be seen as maintaining
the equilibrium in a situation which entails considerable
risks, particularly for the teacher.

     The secretary at the Victoria Centre in conversation with
staff referred to this behaviour as 'joshing' and when
questioned confirmed both its frequency and importance,
'Oh yes, they like it - especially the black kids'. Female
staff are less likely (though not unknown) to adopt such
approaches largely it is assumed, because they have less
confidence in their ability to control a potentially harzardous
interaction. In this context it is of interest to note that
male staff in the city's special units often have sporting
interests and a significant number are former PE teachers.
Not only then do they come from a professional sub-culture
which permits and often encourages a range of physical contact
(quite apart from the obvious sporting activity, PE departments
in schools often administer their own disciplinary code) but
they also have the physical self-confidence to undertake the
risks that are present in these encounters.

     Physical contact of a different yet similar nature is
also entailed in the sporting activity at the Victoria Centre
known as 'murderball'. The onset of this 'game' is often

triggered by instances of behaviour during the lengthy lunch break which is likely to be seen as 'boisterous' and 'high spirits'. The object of this activity is for one side to carry a 'ball' from one end of the assembly hall to the other. The opposition's task is simple - to prevent this and attempt to 'score' their own 'goals'. Both sides are permitted considerable licence to achieve their aims and in ensuing melee, where there is little prospect of administering rules, many old scores are settled.

The effect of this activity is cathartic. In an environment where considerable emphasis is placed upon the regulation of behaviour by reference to a moral code the playing of murderball is an anarchic act. Underlying it however is the demonstration by the staff of their superior physical strength. Pupils and staff meet in direct physical confrontation. Pupils may well score goals but the staff assert their strength and in addition their willingness, given the shared knowledge of the event's unusual nature, to indulge in unteacherlike behaviour.

In summary, the use of physical contact in the Victoria Centre, the organisation of the daily cycle of activities, the regulation of the pupil's unit career and the attribution of meaning to these events demonstrate continuities which are also evident in the educational philosophy which Owen articulates. The underlying connection reflects an adherence to a moral solution to the configuration of demands which he and the staff must confront. In asserting the common interests of schools, pupils, LEA and parents, Owen does not of course escape the consequences of the inherent tensions and contradictions. In many respects the adoption of this approach increases the problems of containment and control and thereby demands a greater degree of commitment. The 'high profile' that this gives Owen provides the satisfaction that he requires and in addition holds out the prospect of career advancement.

ROGER THE DELPHI CENTRE

Within the Delphi Centre, although it is possible to identify the employment by Roger of a distinctive strategy for resolving the demands that are made of him, it is radically different from that of Owen and the Victoria Centre. This alternative strategy is in many respects less coherent than Owen's and it is this which helps to explain the fact that Roger's approach is often misunderstood by those outside the unit. He is seen by colleagues in special units including Owen, as reluctant to pursue the 'return to school goal'. He is considered, partly as a result of this, to be particularly child-centred, willing to keep pupils for longer because he is unwilling to make the potentially painful decision to insist that a child should have an environment to which he or she has

grown accustomed. 'They love him' says Owen ruefully, 'but
it's very short sighted'. On this issue Owen and Roger have
come into open conflict but, although the observation that
Roger lacks commitment to the aim of returning pupils to
school is a correct one, the implications drawn from it are
not.

Roger's background, unlike Owen's has been in social
services establishments. Prior to his appointment as head of
the Delphi Centre he taught for a number of years in an
Observation and Assessment Centre. Roger sees himself and the
unit not as child but as school-centred.

'Only after we have helped the schools are we child-
centred. If we can do things for the kids then that's
fine, a bonus, but otherwise we are trying to help the
system, to respond to what it wants of us.'

It is Roger's belief that the cause of a substantial
amount of disruptive behaviour is due to the size and
impersonal nature of many schools. The solution to this
situation revolves around a celebration of 'variety' which
contains an element that is hostile to the principle of
comprehensive education and considers it ill-conceived.

There should be a variety of schools. Too often they
are forced into being the same. There should be
schools of different sizes with different disciplinary
procedures; not all children respond to the same
approach.....and even different kinds of curriculum.
This would cater for the variety of children that
exist.

The argument is extended to the work of the units themselves each of which is felt 'to have its own strengths' and
which, at a time when some pressure was being exerted by the
LEA, should be permitted to retain its distinctive and
separate character. Roger has little interest in the
development of a local association for those working in
education and social services units. He and his staff rarely
attend their meetings which he tends to view as an extension
of the interests and personalities of those to which he is,
to some degree at least, in opposition. This would include
not only Owen but the Education Officer responsible for the
administration of the units. Roger does not share the
commitment to a 'return to school' or the educational
philosophy on which it is founded.

PROCEDURES AND PROCESSES AT THE DELPHI CENTRE

The processes entailed in referral and admission are less
accessible at the Delphi Centre because they tend to be

concentrated in the hands of Roger himself; decisions are
often made instantaneously, without consultation and
frequently in the course of a telephone conversation. More
emphasis must therefore be placed upon Roger's explanation of
events.
    A feature closely related to the celebration of variety
referred to above is Roger's scepticism towards any attempt to
systematise the operation of the unit. The identification and
espousal of appropriate regulations and procedures is
considered to be an illusory goal. It is more important in
his view to give unit staff the freedom to respond to the
particular circumstances that exist with each pupil. Allied
to this is the tendency to work closely with those schools
which share this unstructured and flexible approach to
referrals.

    We work with kids from schools which treat us properly.
    I've taken someone this afternoon from Highdown just
    until the half term when they should go to a special
    school. Some schools abuse us and once a kids in they
    leave them here - but if I think a school understands
    us then I'll fit in with them.

For the Delphi as with the Victoria Centre it is
important that schools recognise their needs but for Roger
this is based upon a mutuality of interest which is
unimpeded by the operation of specific criteria. When pupils
return to school from the Delphi unit it is because the
pupils themselves wish to (in Roger's words 'the problem
solves itself') or because the staff are anxious to 'relieve
the pressure' in the unit rather than as part of a schedules
policy of reintegration.
    The pragmatic nature of this relationship with referred
heads is exemplified by the absence of almost any interest in
the collation of information about the pupils attending the
centre. None is required of schools and only the barest
details are maintained on the files.

    We don't believe in keeping information. I tell the
    kids that they start afresh here. I don't wish to know
    what has gone wrong in school.

In the almost total absence of information there can be
no interest in systematising procedures in the manner of the
Victoria Centre. Similarly other features such as the
Behaviour Modification System are considered to be of little
value. Roger has also dismissed the use of 'contracts':
'As if you can hope to put relationships down on paper'.
    In interviewing pupils and parents Roger is not
constrained by the need to ensure that 'acceptance' of a place
is conditional upon a future wish to leave. The formal and

contractual element between the staff and the pupil is not present; conditions are laid down, but verbally and not on paper. In an interview attended by a newly referred pupil, his parents and the head and year tutor of the referring school Roger was blunt and uncompromising,

> 'We aren't a unit that believes in giving kids a lot of freedom. They have to follow school routines, can't swear, smoke, or call the staff by their first names and we will use physical means of punishment if we have to, if they're naughty. If they are verbally aggressive to staff they will be dumped unceremoniously in this room. If you don't want me to touch your child then I would not take him.'

> 'I should say as well that we are mostly concerned with behaviour here, not academic progress. You must realise that we cannot provide all the subjects when they are all at different stages.'

There is no attempt to persuade the pupil that his perception of the experience of schooling is in need of readjustment, only his behaviour.

At the Delphi Centre pupils are told that whatever happens they will never be suspended (except in the case of persistent truancy). The impression given to those outside the unit is that the staff are prepared to tolerate misdemeanours that others would not. The reality is different. In effect the staff, in making this statement, are erecting a 'fence' around the unit which excludes those agencies that might otherwise expect to be involved. There was very little evidence at the Delphi Centre of the involvement of the EWS or the SPS. The events within the unit are privatised, pupils and staff must be left to establish their own solutions to problems.

> 'I want my staff to sort out their own difficulties with the kids. Jean Gray (the former head) ran this place like a headmistress. If the teachers had a problem they sent them to her. I won't do that. I won't have staff justifying themselves to me.'

This approach means that the task of establishing and maintaining control takes on a different form at the Delphi Centre, the deliberate employment of 'control periods'. Two examples can be given of this.

Lunchtimes at the Victoria Centre are intended to be a communal affair but at the Delphi Centre they are strikingly different. In Roger's words, lunch provides an opportunity in the middle of the day to exercise control over all the pupils in one group. The partaking of the meal is compulsory.

Pupils are seated in groups of up to four around a number of evenly spaced tables. Silence is established before the meal is served, the staff patrolling the perimeter of the room, affecting indifference as to how long the pupils continue to talk. Compliance to the often unspoken demand for silence is eventually forthcoming, though the dignity of the pupils necessitates that this is not given immediately.

When Roger feels that the group is sufficiently quiet he will ask for someone to say 'Grace'. This brief ritual has little or no religious significance. It is a symbolic episode echoing the experience of the primary school (an experience which is generally thought to have been more successful and with which all units make connections; most notably in the organisation of an 'academic' morning and an 'activities' afternoon). The pupil who says 'Grace' earns for him or her table the privilege of being first in the queue. I asked one pupil if he ever said Grace. He replied, 'Sometimes, yeah, if it's fish for dinner'.

The staff have no illusions as to the secular nature of the 'trade' being made here. When the meal is over Roger once again insists upon a 'satisfactory' degree of silence before pupils are dismissed. Compliance on this occasion is advanced by the pupils desire to enjoy the recreational facilities, most importantly the 'pool' and table tennis.

A further example of the use of 'control periods' is the one illustrated in the introduction and described on the time-table as a 'reading lesson'. With all pupils gathered together in one room always with Roger supervising, at the end of the day, control is enforced in a highly visible and audible manner. At the same time Roger demonstrates his unique position in relation to the other staff, a distinction that Owen with his emphasis upon 'staff democracy' attempts, with only limited success, to blurr.

> I really don't mind if they're not reading. Graham spent a lot of time staring out of the window - did you see him? - but it was very quiet. It's good to end the day like this - they often don't get the opportunity to experience this at home. It might be thought of as repressive but they actually enjoy it.

I asked Roger how he managed to establish this kind of control, to reproduce with twenty or more disruptive pupils the semblance of a 'model' lesson.

> It was difficult at first. In my first six weeks here I had lots of battles - taking on the bigger ones. But when that was won it was much better. I now occasionally have to look fierce but generally its fine. The other kids will warn the one who is going too far.

At the Delphi Centre there is no equivalent of the group meeting. Problems are individualised or even suppressed rather than openly explored with all the possible difficulties that this entails.

> 'Race is a real problem amongst the girls at the moment - not with the boys, they are active and have to mix, but with the girls. We try to keep it under the surface but it's definitely become much more of a problem.'

Pupils are encouraged to establish their own personal accommodation with each other, the staff and particularly with Roger who will play the major role in the decision-making process. Rules and procedures would interfere with this approach but even in their absence an appeal may be made by pupils to a wider understanding of a moral order. In one conversation Roger was accused of favourtism in the placing of some girls back in school. This pupil went on to criticise him for his lack of 'fairness'. 'Fairness' said Roger, 'doesn't come into it, it's a question of what is best for you'.

That 'fairness doesn't come into it' is of considerable significance for Roger. His view is that pupils at Delphi are 'naughty but normal'. Sometimes pupils react to insensitive or even boorish and bullying behaviour on the part of some teachers, but this has to be accepted by the child. His definition of a Delphi Centre pupil is,

> 'One that can't cope with the fact that some teachers are pretty hopeless. Others see this and they do cope, but keep their heads down.'

THE USE BY STAFF OF PHYSICAL CONTACT

Reference has already been made to the preparedness of the staff at the Delphi Centre to use the overt forms of control both in terms of language and physical contact. Many such incidents are of a consensual nature as is illustrated in the following example.

In one of the morning's brief, structured lessons the pupils were told to draw a still life composed of cups, a tea pot and a coffee pot. During the lesson the male member of staff was continually engaged in a physical interaction with a number of pupils. The teacher used a stick to repeatedly tap or prod pupils whenever he felt that they had spoken too loudly or obscenely. The pupils were evidently prepared, despite their protests, to accept this physical means of censure in return for the continued excitement of being noisy and abusive. The pupils probed the boundaries of accepted behaviour, trading the acceptance of a physical rebuke for the freedom to enjoy verbal skirmishing of a kind that would be generally unacceptable in school.

When one boy attempted to impart some sense of movement to the still life by pouring himself an imaginary cup of tea the teacher lightly but firmly kicked him back to his seat, smiling and talking in a manner that confirmed for the pupil the 'naturalness' of this action. Physical contact of a different nature was employed by another member of staff when during a break period he enquired disarmingly of a pupil whether he'd ever seen an 'Irish whip'. When the pupil replied in the negative his wrist was seized and swung violently up behind his back. 'You have now' said the teacher.

Roger was observed to favour during one period an indirect form of physical contact but one that remains based upon the demonstration of a superior strength, ability and resolve. At the end of an outdoor games session Roger encouraged the pupils to risk themselves by attempting to catch a cricket ball he would throw into the air. No one could be persuaded to attempt this feat until Roger offered the pupil a momentary inducement. Three or four pupils danced at a distance of thirty or forty yards and occasionally sprang forward to catch the ball. None were successful. The fifty pence went unclaimed and all had been witness to the head's control of events. It appears that underlying these and other instances of physical contact is the staff's preparedness to inflict physical discomfort and to demonstrate quite openly the nature of their authority. This does not mean that they are in continual and open conflict with their pupils. Some pupils did, on occasion, object to the behaviour of the staff but many derived considerable excitement from these exchanges.

MORALISM AND PRAGMATISM

The common sense view expressed by those who know the work of both Owen and Roger is that they adopt radically different approaches ; I would wish to argue that this difference is best seen in terms of the use of alternative strategies designed to resolve the inherently conflicting demands that are made of them. In other words whatever differences exist can be examined in a way that asserts the importance of the similar conditions which each of them faces. Their responses to these conditions draw upon the existence of two distinct principles themselves contigent upon the nature of schooling in society.

In their phenomenological account of deviance in classrooms Hargreaves et al (1975) remind us that such behaviour in school as in society generally is essentially about the problem of order. When order is threatened teachers must intervene and in so doing draw upon 'two potentially conflicting justificatory principles'.

These principles underpin and provide the rationale
for the rules of the classroom; and they are also
used for formulating reactions to breaches of the
rules.
The first principle we shall call the moral
principle. A rule can be established and justified
by an appeal to this moral principle on grounds that
the regulation of social order enjoined by it promotes
and reflects certain moral values. Such rules, and
the values from which they are derived, are seen by
members to be inherently 'right', 'good' and 'just'.
The second principle we shall call the pragmatic
principle on the grounds that it provides an
efficient and effective way in which teachers and
pupils can realise their goals, carry out their
activities or perform their roles within the classroom.
Such rules appertain not because they are 'right'
but because they 'work'.

These principles I would argue, sometimes in tension,
sometimes not, arise from the legal and ideological status of
schooling. Not only is attendance at school to be in receipt
of that which is 'good' and intrinsically worthwhile but it
is also compulsory, enforceable by law. Moreover the
compulsory nature of schooling is justified by its 'goodness'.
Those children who truant or misbehave and thereby challenge
the 'goodness' of schooling can be exhorted to behave
correctly and the action designed to bring this about
justified, by recourse to either the moral or pragmatic
principle or, because social interaction permits of some
contradiction, a combination of both.
     It is important to note that the identification of a
strategy based upon one of these principles can not be
identified solely from an observation of the 'act', from the
verbal and bodily behaviours of staff toward pupils. Rather
such identification necessitates the situating of the 'act'
within a wider culturally and historically specific 'moral
order' and the determining of the degree of continuity that
exists between this culturally located act, the setting
within which it occurs and the justification made of it.
Thus the same act may be seen by different actors to be
either moral or pragmatic. For example this might apply in the
case of corporal punishment. For a full understanding as to
the nature of this act we should need to know not only something about the culture and period within which it was
administered by other features or 'interactive elements' as
well, how the actor explained his or her behaviour, how
frequently it occurred, how pupils responded to it and how it
related to the use of other repeated behaviours.
     It is as a result of an analysis of this nature that the
claim to have identified two distinctive strategies in two

similar units, is made. The response of Owen and the staff of
the Victoria Centre to the demands that are made of them
represents in a relatively pure form the fashioning of a
strategy based upon the moral principle. Not only do the
staff react to the deviance that takes place within the unit
but also to that which has already occurred in the moral career
of the disruptive pupil.

A wish to re-orient behaviour through a process in which
the pupil's world view is challenged always contains the risk
of additional tension, a type of deviancy amplification. This
is something that Owen is prepared to tolerate because it is
through this moral reconciliation of conflicting views and
interests that he renews his commitment to work. This
reconciliation creates the conditions upon which a return to
school is justified and the status of the unit elevated above
that described by the term 'sin-bin'. Without this commitment
Owen is unable to project a future career that will make sense
on a personal level.

The features that serve to distinguish this essentially
moralistic strategy are, briefly, celebration and practice of
a 'participatory democracy' with its emphasis upon negotiation,
'openness' and collective enterprise, the assertion of an
external moral authority which orders human relations and
which detracts, at times, from that of the teacher, and the
search for rules, procedures and systematic approaches which
will promote the achievement of a 'success' which reconciles
hitherto conflicting interests.

In Roger's case, on the other hand, we are presented with
a less clearly defined strategy. Although there is a very
personal element to his rejection of the LEA's interpretation
of the unit's role, there remains a belief that this cannot
be reconciled with the wishes and needs of schools, pupils and
ultimately, rate-payers.

Given the inevitability of conflict Roger chooses to focus
upon meeting the needs and expectations of schools. Many
schools face severe problems with a number of pupils they have
attempted to control in a variety of ways over a lengthy period.
They view the placement of a pupil in a unit as an opportunity
to gain a 'breathing space' and at the same time to reassert
the schools ultimate authority to control the physical
environment of the child. They are unlikely to consider that
the unit can effect real behavioural change in difficult pupils
though they may willingly suscribe to the view that a younger
pupil must eventually return to an orthodox school. Many
however will be most immediately concerned to use the unit as
an extension of a range of sanctions at their disposal and
will favour those staff who see their role in terms of
supporting their authority or at the very least, doing
nothing to undermine it. The acceptance by Roger of this need
on the part of at least some schools shapes the internal
arrangement at the Delphi with its emphasis upon containment,

control and the individualisation of solutions to pupil's problems.

The deviant career of the pupil is not an issue because the staff do not challenge the interpretation of past experience simply the judgement of the pupil in resisting the school's authority. Hence the lack of interest in information and liaison with other agencies. Surveillance replaces observation because self-regulation is not worked for and is not expected. The response to deviance within the unit is a simple and pragmatic one, to suppress it. Staff must respond in a manner that they see as being appropriate, employing the resources that are available.

It is this kind of justification couched in a moralistic vocabulary that creates the lack of clarity referred to earlier. Despite this and other examples we must see Roger as acting largely in a pragmatic fashion. He adapts to problems as they arise and is largely unconcerned with the wider issues that surround the work of special units. It is this uncomplicated and down to earth approach which he feels will secure him the position that he wants.

> 'I would like to be the deputy in a normal school who
> is seen as hard and unapproachable - the one who makes
> it possible for the rest of the staff to relax with
> the kids and get on with the job of teaching. When the
> discipline is there then it is possible to do that -
> if not you're running around patching up one crisis
> after another.
> 'I won't go looking for this job. A head who knows the
> way I work will approach me - if it doesn't happen in
> a couple of years then I'll relax the pressure here in
> the unit and settle things down.'

CONCLUSION

In summary, Owen and Roger present fundamentally different approaches to the similar situation in which they find them-selves. This difference cannot be understood simply in terms of pupil and child-centred approaches. The difference between them stems from the choices made in the context of organising a provision for those who have challenged the authority of their school teachers. The creation of special units as an administrative response to disaffection heightens the tension between the principles that operate when deviant behaviour is perceived and subsequently acted upon. Owen's aim is to repair the moral order breached by the challenge to the teacher authority and the assumptions of intrinsic worth upon which it is founded. This repair entails the reconstruction of the child's experience of schooling. Control at this level is likely to be difficult to establish but when it is achieved it will be deep and self-sustaining. Roger on the other hand does

not attempt any such reconstruction. Those who contest
authority may be genuinely unable to 'cope' in school and may
therefore need alternative provision. The majority, however,
are simply in need of a demonstration that 'authority' cannot
be challenged with impunity. The acknowledged and exclusive
aim of the unit is to control and contain. In many respects
this releases the staff and pupils from the moral imperative
and may well come closer to an authentic understanding of the
pupil's experience. It provides for a sense of continuity and
is not invasive of the pupils private and meaningful 'world-
view'. It permits the pupil to derive unfettered satisfaction
from the excitement of 'skirmishing' and the release from
school-like demands. The paradox is,of course,that this may
well enable the staff to establish relationships with some
pupils which would not be possible in school or in the
Victoria unit. Although control is, in these circumstances,
more easily established it is unlikely that it will be
generalised to other sites. The reintroduction of pupils to
school is therefore given less emphasis in the Delphi Centre.

It is not my intention to argue that the strategies
identified here are necessarily exhaustive of those that
pertain in other units. They are shaped by the nature of the
particular circumstances in these two units and the
biographies of the staff and particularly their heads.
Nevertheless it is hoped that this analysis will provide a
framework within which the detailed practice of other unit
staff can be examined. The other aim is to suggest that in
order to understand 'how teachers teach the unteachable' one
must recognise the manner in which they are engaged in
managing a delicate balance of perceptions - that they be
like and unlike schools. As with all institutions they must
find ways of working which attempt to shape perceptions and
therefore behaviour, and work to absorb the challenge that
deviant behaviour poses to their authority. Largely then,
unit staff, in the position of those in the Victoria and Delphi
units have some choice in the way that they organise their work
and respond to their pupils but this is heavily constrained by
the circumstances, the structural conditions and meaningful
environment within which they operate. Innovation is possible
but it takes place within parameters laid down by schools and
is to be seen largely in the sphere of social relations. One
element which does provide some basis for fruitful
re-examination of the work of teachers in orthodox schools is
the way in which the staff in both units 'listen' and respond
to their pupils in a physical way. Here at the very least are
some important lessons to be learnt and acted upon.

REFERENCES

Francis, M. (1979)   'Disruptive pupils: Labelling a new
        generation', New Approaches in Multiracial Education,
        8, (1), 6-9
Hargreaves, A. (1978)   'The significance of classroom coping
        strategies' in L. Barton and R. Meighan (eds.)
        Sociological Interpretations of Schooling and Classrooms,
        Nafferton, Driffield, Yorkshire
Hargreaves, A. (1979)   'Strategies, decisions and control:
        Interaction in a middle school classroom' in J.
        Eggleston (ed.) Teacher Decision-making in the
        Classroom, Routledge and Kegan Paul, London
Hargreaves, D. Hester, S. and Mellor, F. (1975) Deviance
        in Classrooms, Routledge and Kegan Paul, London
Jones, N. (1977) 'Special adjustment units in comprehensive
        schools', Therapeutic Education, 5, (2), 17
Ling, R. (1982) 'Punishment or cure?', Times Educational
        Supplement, 9 July, p 19
Ling, R. and Davies, G. (1984) A Survey of Off-site Units in
        England and Wales. A research report by the Social
        Education Project, Birmingham Polytechnic, Birmingham
MacBeath, J. (1977) 'Goodbye free school, hello special
        unit', Times Educational Supplement, 9 December, p 3
Paisey, H. (1975) The Behavioural Strategy of Teachers,
        NFER, Slough
Pollard, A. (1982) 'A model of classroom coping strategies',
        British Journal of Sociology of Education, 3, (1),
        19-37
Pollard, A. (1984) 'Coping strategies and the multiplication
        of differentiation in infant classrooms', British
        Educational Research Journal, 10, (1), 33-34
Selznick, P. (1949) T.V.A. and the Grass Roots: A study in
        the Sociology of Formal Organisations, University of
        California Press, Berkeley and Los Angeles, California
Stebbins, R. (1980) 'The role of humour in teaching: strategy
        and self-expression' in P. Woods (ed.)
        Teacher Strategies, Croom Helm, Beckenham, Kent
Tomlinson, S. (1982) A Sociology of Special Education,
        Routledge and Kegan Paul, London
Willis, P. (1977) Learning to Labour, Saxon House,
        Farnborough
Woods, P. (1979) The Divided School, Routledge and Kegan Paul,
        London
Woods, P. (1980a) (ed.) Teacher Strategies, Croom Helm,
        Beckenham, Kent
Woods, P. (1980b) (ed.) Pupil Strategies, Croom Helm,
        Beckenham, Kent

Chapter Nine

SUBJECT TEACHERS UNDER STRESS

Bede Redican

INTRODUCTION

Much of the debate about educational arrangements,
like the policy decisions that eventually determine
to some extent how schooling is experienced, are
carried out at a distance from the process itself.
Armchair rhetoric about the distribution of educational opportunity and more recently about the
assessment of both pupil and teacher performance,
a rhetoric that has emerged in contrasting perceptions of the economic climate, has questioned
the simple assumption that education is a good
thing in itself and criticised our inept management of the process. It has largely ignored the
lived experience of those teachers daily involved
in the schooling process. The purpose here is to
explore beyond the secret garden of the curriculum,
beyond the externally imposed parameters of school
size and resource allocation, and to examine "the
back room of school administrative procedures".
The focus is the career and workplace perceptions
of teachers as individuals or as groups with similar conditions of service, and the internal
dynamics of the school as perceived and sustained
by them. How do they see the reality of schooling
from the inside, "the back region", and what tactics
do they employ to change or sustain procedures that
they regard as worthwhile, despite the external
parameters determined by economists, politicians or
armchair theorists? Such tactics may have important consequences for both educational distribution and standards of performance. An examination of this kind requires form and this is
sought by adopting ethnography as an appropriate
research method (Hammersley and Atkinson, 1983) and
by seeking to operationalise some aspects of a

social theory proposed by Giddens (1979).

The data on which this chapter is based is
drawn from an ethnographic study of two large
comprehensive schools. Ethnography is selected as
the research method because it involves participation in the lived experience of those under study.
It asks the researcher to recognise the reflexive
character of the research and it involves the
watching, listening and recording activities
required to collect data. The definition of ethnography, preferred here, is the broader definition
that includes a wide range of sources of information - in fact collects whatever data are available
to throw light upon the issues involved (Hammersley
and Atkinson, 1983:2). This study includes both
interviews and participant observation, and it
explicitly recognises that all social research has
a reflexive character. We can neither escape the
world in order to study it nor avoid having an
effect upon it in the study process. No data may
be regarded as 'pure' data and consequently a more
realistic aim, adopted here, is to seek to interpret the data obtained, acknowledging the foreshadowed problems, anxieties and biases, the
surrounding developing theory and the limitations
implicit in the interview interactions and in the
recording of observed episodes of situated interaction.

As suggested by Giddens (1979:210) the concept
of 'region', Goffman's front and back regions, is
pertinent to small scale institutional analysis of
the kind employed here. The researcher must be
aware that the setting of encounters (in the front
room) may be purposively arranged to hide the
potentially compromising or dangerous features of
such encounters. The penetration of such time/
space settings is a fundamental part of the
analysis. Foreshadowed problems, those issues
anticipated on the basis of reading and experience,
may emerge as real issues or as merely part of a
carefully sustained legend. The objective here is
neither to collect relevant data to test a hypothesis, nor to confirm assumptions by imposing
ideas on the data, but to seek to remain anthro-
pologically strange. This is sought by acknowledging aspects of the reflexive character of the
research while searching for that penetrating
collaboration or contradiction, the issues that
emerge substantiated during the process.

FORESHADOWED PROBLEMS IN THE LARGER SCHOOLS

Published material on the comprehensive school
claims that its arrival demanded some rethinking
especially about organisational factors associated
with the size (Burgess, 1983:10). There was, and
still is, little research in this area (Gray, 1980:
20). What appears common practice in comprehensive
schools is to consider that beyond a certain number
of pupils a headteacher must delegate or dis-
integrate (Watts, 1976:127), that pastoral posts
were created to delegate the heads concern for
pupils in the broader than 'subject performance'
sense (Chetwynd, 1976:27; Burgess, 1983:17), and that
a certain type of person was sought to fill these
pastoral vacancies. Several authors warn against
this division of responsibility between the pastoral and the academic because it could lead to
confusion about school objectives. John (1980:97)
argued that since comprehensive reorganisation,
particularly in merged institutions, the cohesion
of the school had been adversely affected by the
gulf which grew between the curricular and the
pastoral systems. Richardson (1975:69) claimed
that these two areas of work pulled in opposite
directions and encouraged teachers to wear either
an academic or a pastoral hat and to subsequently
abdicate responsibility for the other. Further,
there is the danger that pastoral care systems may
drift into becoming mainly disciplinary agencies.
The reality of pastoral care may differ sharply
from the high aspirations held out for it in the
early comprehensive years. Not only may the
priority given to it detract from the essential
teaching function but many teachers not directly
involved in it feel that it is merely a nuisance,
a thrashing bore, an impossible, impractical and
largely unnecessary diversion from the real job of
teaching (see for example Best, Jarvis and Robbins,
1980). It is argued by Hamblin (1978) and Marland
(1974) and many others, that pastoral work is better
conceived as an integral part of all teaching. Few
schools, however, seem to have rejected the pastoral
care ideology as a legitimate explanation for the
awarding of promotion to relatively non-teaching
staff.
   The roots of this foreshadowed problem lie in
the emergence of the larger school for all, from
the two previously somewhat distinct systems of
grammar and secondary modern schools. Teachers were
trained for and experienced in either selective

schools where high expectations were held by all interested parties for their pupils, or they were trained for and experienced in non-selective schools where quite different expectations normally existed. It is generally accepted that non-selective school teachers better understood and were more accustomed to coping with less parental support, with pupils who had learning and behavioural difficulties and in situations where schooling had to be legitimated in terms broader than examination success. They frequently perceived themselves as more competent in terms of knowledge and capability in this respect than ex-grammar school teachers. Grammar school staff, meanwhile, were acknowledged to be more competent in terms of subject knowledge. Given the opportunities for teachers with these different lived experiences and different perceptions about school objectives, these two groups of staff tended to move into two distinct career patterns within the comprehensive school. The simple convenience of fitting staff to the perceived needs of the larger school, giving some staff appropriate subject work and others more pastoral care work was never fully endorsed by teachers or by educationalists, but within the legend of pastoral needs and the reality of controlling large numbers, its existence emerged as legitimate. John (1980: 90), however, examines what teachers in pastoral posts actually do and concludes that 'guidance' would better describe their activities. It would seem a short step from collating information about pupil learning, assessing pupil strengths and weaknesses, and proposing remedies, to 'the supervision' of the work of other teachers. The extent to which 'pastoral' is now perceived as both 'supervisory' and 'dominant', and how such an unintended consequence of early staff placement decisions has been developed and sustained by the action of teachers in daily episodes of situated interaction is the issue examined here.

THE THEORETICAL CONTEXT

Sociologists from many traditions are currently seeking to bring about a synthesis within social theory. Those who are 'strong on institutional analysis, weak on action theory', from Durkheim to Merton, may now be seen to be seeking such synthesis through general systems theory, or morphogenesis (Buckley, 1967; Archer, 1982). Those who are 'strong on action theory, weak on institutional analysis', from earlier Wittgensteinian to Mead, appeared initially satisfied with a partial accommodation between symbolic interactionism and functionalism, between a micro-sociology that deals with small scale 'interpersonal' relations and a macro-sociology that deals with more embracing economic and political concerns (Giddens, 1979:50). Giddens' (1979) chosen enemy is determinism tout court , stigmatising all those theoretical trad- itions that downgrade human choice at the individual level (Gane, 1983:372). Knorr-Cetina's (1981) chosen enemy is methodological individualism, rejecting all theoretical traditions that renounce any interest in explaining social order in pref- erence to a search for individual meaning and lived experience. Both in their own way identify a deep division between those major perspectives that have been preoccupied with action and found no way of coping with structural explanation and those perspectives that have concerned themselves with such concepts but treated the conduct of actors in society as determined to a greater or lesser extent by social institutional norms (Giddens, 1979:49). The debate is not that a relationship may or may not exist between action and structure: this seems to be fertile territory for both theorising and em- pirical research by both sides, but precisely how is this middle ground construed and this relation- ship submitted to empirical demonstration. The 'duality of structure' theory proposed by Giddens (1979) is one example of an attempt to map out this middle ground. He seeks to offer a framework through which an analysis may be made of how know- ledgeable, capable actors may draw upon the rules and resources embedded in the structure through a process of structuration. Action and structure form a duality, logically entailing each other and structure is both the medium and the outcome of the social practices it recursively organises. The middle ground becomes the arena where it all occurs. Here human action (teacher action) and institution (the rules and procedures embedded in the label school) interact.

Central to the 'duality of structure' concept lies a recognition that to be regarded as a com- petent member of an institution an individual must know a great deal about its workings, its rules and procedures concerning how things are normally done (Giddens, 1979:255). Participants act in terms of tacit knowledge of these rules and

procedures which they know how to apply in specific
situations and which they disregard at their peril.
Such disregard may question their competence and
incur disqualification as a knowledgeable member of
that society (institution) (Knorr-Cetina, 1981:4).
Participants also plan their action carefully. As
Knorr-Cetina (1981:36) proposes, actors impose
constructs upon the world in attempts to make sense
of it and to become knowledgeable about the structure of it. They try these constructs out for size
by experimenting in micro-episodes, and come to be
more knowledgeable and capable as a result of such
approximate representations becoming successively
more accurate. Such activity echoes the perspectives of phenomenologists such as Gray (1982:39).
Most behaviour, he claims, is based upon assumptions
about what is going to happen rather than what has
actually occurred. However, to merely claim that
schools are arenas for fantasy realisation and that
the barganing process may be explained solely in
terms of individual endeavours towards their fantasy
realisation, is to fail to account adequately for
the structural rules and procedures that have to be
learnt, mastered and modified to give reality to
such meaningful activity. Fantasy realisation
(Gray, 1982) and the representation hypothesis
(Knorr-Cetina, 1981) are only partial explanations
in a more total social theory proposed here. To
operationalise the social theory outlined by Giddens
(1979) and supplemented by the representation
hypothesis of Knorr-Cetina (1981), requires this
study to demonstrate the degree of penetration actors (teachers) have of the structuring properties
of schools and how they are able to draw upon this
knowledge in daily episodes of situated interaction
to realise their objectives.

THE ETHNOGRAPHIC CONTEXT

Two Midland comprehensive schools were selected
for the collection of ethnographic data. Both
schools were comprehensive schools, created by the
amalgamation of grammar and secondary modern schools
and had accepted a comprehensive school intake for
seven years at the time of this research in 1981-3.
They were mixed with approximately 1100 pupils and
56 staff in each school at the start of the two
year research period. Access was negotiated through
the headteacher, and the programme of interviews and
observation periods through the deputy heads

responsible for timetabling. All staff interviews took place in the spring terms, during staff free periods. While this may be initially seen as an imposition upon the scarce free time staff have available for planning and marking, it did guarantee that they would not have to 'cover' for absent teachers during that period. There were two clearly defined objectives. On the one hand, staff were to be interviewed formally and informally and, on the other, I was to observe and record incidents of situated interaction. In almost every case, teachers welcomed an opportunity to discuss their problems in a situation where confidentiality and trust had been established, where no consequences for future conditions of work or promotion prospects were involved and where a sympathetic but informed ear was available. Confidentiality was stressed and the interview always took place in a private office, prep-room or work area. The object was to ensure that teachers felt relaxed on their own territory and safe from intrusion. Throughout, an attempt was made to minimise the inhibitors of communication, in particular, the competing time demands, ego threatening or embarrassing questions or traumatic incidents (Gordon, 1975). Initial questions and reactions throughout the interview sought to allow the interviewee to search for meaning in his or her own experience and to see the exercise as valuable for the future of the profession and the quality of the education available to children.

My second objective was to observe, record and analyse a selection of routine or unusual incidents of situated social interaction. This process has three distinct parts, registering, interpreting and recording. The actual recording inevitably takes place retrospectively. In this significant time gap - normally three hours or more, the observer recreates the event and assesses the various participant attitudes and behaviours. There is the search for collaborative evidence, the checking of his own perceptions with those of others. The final account for analysis is consequently a collection of what was registered and what became more apparent during the interpretation and recording process (Schwartz and Schwartz, 1955:345). We therefore only reach an approximate 'reality', the event is potentially distorted and misinterpreted. The presence of the observer means that movements are made and orientations are developed towards him which would not otherwise have occurred (Schwartz and Schwartz, 1955:346). The challenge is to be fully aware of reflexivity, to share the lived experience of staff, but to observe and record their behaviour as objectively as possible.

THE EMERGENT PROBLEM

As the field work progressed, the evidence from both interviews and participant observations indicated that teachers were aware of the reality of so-called pastoral staff activities, of the increasing power and influence of such post holders and of their drift into supervisory staff roles. The legend may be that so called pastoral posts are filled by staff who are more concerned with teaching in the broadest sense, but in reality their occupants drift from petty administration, discipline and control, to the supervision of both pupils and staff in the pursuit of overall school objectives. The challenge was to present sufficient evidence to substantiate this teacher knowledgeability and to propose how the supervisory staff used communication, power and sanction to bring about and sustain this superiority. Sufficient evidence would include a demonstration that the split between those teachers who 'manage' and those who 'do' is not only a teacher perception but also a teachers' representation of how things actually are embedded in the normal rules and procedures of the school. Teachers both anticipate that this is the reality of the backroom and that they have to contend with and actually behave in recognition of it. Necessarily, the interview data and the analysis of an episode of situated interaction must show that those who hold pastoral posts actually carry out traditional management tasks and use management strategies. Managers in any organisation plan, organize, arrange staffing, direct staff, coordinate, report and budget (Martin, 1983:17). Managers take precautions to distance themselves from accountability for 'doing', taking steps to separate conception from execution. They seek to interact with staff in a manner that promotes their superiority, that consolidates their position as capable of legitimately telling others what to do, even or especially, in areas where they obviously can do it themselves and in an occupation where the autonomy of the teacher in the classroom is high.

THE INTERVIEW DATA AND THE IMPLICATIONS EMERGING FROM IT

This section sets out the evidence on which the drift into two career ladders is claimed to have moved from a foreshadowed problem to a sub-stantiated emerging issue in these two large schools. First, teachers are demonstrated to be aware of the fact of promotion opportunities for supervisory positions and to be aware that such positions are supervisory and designed to assist the head with the administration of the school on a day-to-day basis. Secondly, it is sought to demonstrate that supervisory staff actually use management strategies in their daily interactions with relatively classroom subject staff.

(a) Promotion for 'Pastoral' Staff

It is obviously important to know the teaching background of pastoral staff even though it is seven years since the schools became comprehensive and made the initial appointments to fit staff from grammar and secondary modern schools to the new larger institutions. During the two years 1981-83 covered by the field research in these two schools there were fifteen internal promotions and six appointments from external applicants. Thirteen of these internal promotions were attached to pastoral and administrative responsibilities. Ten of the total staff promotions and appointments were restricted to staff who already held administrative staff posts and five were for young staff making their initial move from scale one. Only five staff were appointed and one promoted for classroom subject teaching. One of the staff described the reason for his decision to apply for a year tutor's post:

> I did grab a pastoral post because I really needed to have a scale two, but it meant that I teach my subject less well. To some extent I haven't time to do justice to my pastoral job either. A lot of it is routine administration. The really interesting problems do not conveniently arise when I have my free periods.

Not only did his promotion lead to a perceived reduction in his teaching effectiveness but there is a hint not only that the two 'jobs' are in-compatible, but also that you need more 'free periods' to cope. It is apparent also that it is not the type of pastoral care that Marland (1974) considers an integral part of teaching that is perceived as the new role requirement but the much more extra-curricular counselling, guidance and supervision. The reluctance to leave the real job of teaching was further emphasised by another new year tutor:

> I enjoy my teaching ... but to get on here, you have to sell your soul to the administration ... I don't think I would have got any prom- otion unless I had accepted an administration job.

Senior staff, too, were aware of the need to 'sell your soul' to the administration. 'It is a pity scale four or sometimes senior teacher is the limit for a teacher who really wants to make the connect- ion, subject knowledge - pupil talent - psychic reward' (Head of Department, scale 4). Even a deputy head stated that to get beyond a scale four, a subject teacher must offer to take on some administrative task. However, it may well be too late for a scale four head to switch career ladders. There may simply be too few subject specialists left or more likely the 'pastoral staff' career ladder may have already been colonised by teachers who lack good subject knowledge qualifications. At one of the schools only two of the seven senior administrative staff had graduate qualifications in the curriculum subject areas and all seven had teachers certificates plus additional education degree qualifications. In addition, four of the five young staff making their initial move from scale one were teachers without graduate qualifica- tions of any kind. Rewarding the qualified subject teacher did not appear to be a major feature of either the salary structure or the promotion procedures at either school. Good administrators, not good teachers, were the models (Richardson, 1973, 1975). The system encouraged low, short term commitment to classroom teaching.

(b) Pastoral staff are rarely qualified to teach
'real' subjects but possess delegated headteacher
authority

Staffing procedures and comments made by staff lend support to the proposition that the rise in super- visory staff numbers was a response to the need to

control the complexity of the process (Ozga and
Lawn, 1981). Size and demands for accountability
appeared crucial in legitimising the process but if
those promoted were those who had been less well
qualified to inspire pupil learning, classroom
failures could be found supervising the work of
classroom successes. As the fieldwork progressed I
became increasingly aware that classroom staff
perceived supervisory staff as both unqualified to
do 'real' subject teaching and required to carry
out delegated headteacher activities. One head of
subject for example, asked:

> How can you respect those who are supposed to
> be superior but who can't do anything real?
> It is not as if they were all really good
> classroom teachers either. Some of them, I
> know, couldn't control pupils when they had
> them in a classroom, so how are they going to
> do it now?

A subject teacher with a scale three post echoed
these sentiments:

> So called pastoral staff have the right to
> call in pupils books and staff record books
> for inspection, but they could not do the job
> themselves, they don't know how to do it.
> They are not qualified in any subject ... do
> they just call them in to prove that they can
> do it? ... just trying to see if I'm giving
> homework and marking it?

Such supervision was seen as worse than no supervision at all. It provided no opportunity for
constructive help, allowed really good work to
pass unacknowledged and emphasised conformity to
routine requirements rather than the creative,
spontaneous and innovative aspects of real learning.
There was evidence in both schools, despite the
derisory comments made about pastoral staff competence in subject areas, that some pastoral staff
had been successful subject teachers. It may be
argued as John (1980:87) did, that teaching 'real'
subject courses is now as much the protected
preserve of the classroom teacher as pastoral care
is of the supervisory staff. Supervision by the
head of subject department was not perceived as a
realistic alternative.
 If the qualifications held by some staff
disqualified them from actually doing many of the

structured and progressive courses on the curriculum, what can they actually do? Their main teaching commitment was with non-examination classes. To be seen to teach lower status classes may encourage them to glorify the demands of such remedial and non-examination work. It may lead to their search for recognition in extra curricular drama, music and sporting activities. However, the adoption of certain delegated headteacher administrative and supervisory activities may have most appeal. A preoccupation with 'control' may be discerned as the traditional paternalistic attitudes of the English headteacher (Coulson, 1979; Caspari, 1976). Heads identify with their schools and overemphasise their responsibility for all that goes on in them. Heads in smaller schools were able to control the activities of teachers in a manner more appropriate to workers performing routine skills, than to relatively autonomous professionals(Hoyle, 1969). There is a way in which heads were expected to manage a school. They alone embodied its aims, determined the curriculum, controlled the timetable, distributed finance, selected staff and dominated the communication networks, or in industrial management terms, they directed, controlled, planned, coordinated and evaluated activities. The head did not actually teach, except in emergency situations. The dichotomy between controlling and executing was maintained by distancing himself from the classroom work, by directing and by inspecting the work of the staff. As this authority was delegated to various grades of pastoral/administrative staff, such staff received management trappings: more periods free from actual teaching, more access to confidential information and a private or shared office to deal with pupils and parents as professional clients. All thirteen senior administrative staff in these two schools had their own private offices and some year tutors had found a private space where such consultation would be facilitated. A brief look at the principles of scientific management (Braveman quoted in Martin, 1983) suggests some useful comparisons. Managers (headteachers and their delegates):

  (a) give all 'teachers' only partial
      processes to perform - teaching mere sub-
      jects while they retain responsibility for
      the total education of the child,
  (b) concentrate information exclusively in the
      hands of the management group - only

members of senior conference and pastoral
staff have access to the full range of
confidential information about pupils,
(c) use their monopoly of resources to control
privileges, promotion and working conditions.

A newly appointed head of year was pleased to point
out that, 'promotion to my current head of year
post has meant that I am now told more confidential
information, information not even given to my head
of subject ... about kids generally'. Such access
to confidential information, plus attendance at the
senior management meetings where 'problems' are
sorted out, is part of a whole nexus of strategies
designed to consolidate the supervisory staff
groups dominant position. An analysis of how they
normally deal with their subject colleagues and how
they seek to devalue the classroom subject teachers
role is now attempted.

(c) Supervisory Staff Interactions with Other
Teachers are Predominantly of a 'Commanding Nature'
and Rarely Involve 'Consultation'
Martin (1983:63) suggests that 'contacts with subordinates' are most likely to have the following
flavour. They are rarely of a collegial nature in
which work problems are discussed, mutual input
into the decision making process encouraged, or long
range strategic plans generated. They are occasionally for the purpose of evaluating the performance
of the subordinate and frequently to give orders or
instructions, or to reprimand the subordinate for
some deficiency or delinquency in carrying out past
directives. Martin (1983:63) quotes some evidence
supporting this position, claiming that they found
managers' contacts with subordinates were largely
for the purpose of making requests, sending or
receiving information and occasionally strategy
making. During a period of two months I noted every
interaction between supervisory staff (the thirteen
senior administrative staff) and the teaching staff
that occurred where I could observe it, in the
staff room, corridors, and classroom. I noted
thirty seven such interactions in a random way.
Sixteen of these were clearly 'one way' interactions, giving instructions about new arrangements
for class movements and about duties that needed
doing, including leaving the staff room promptly
when the bell goes. Twelve were eliciting

information about required petty administrative
tasks such as collecting money, completing reports,
collecting permission slips, and relatively public
announcements about 'school wide' activities, plays
and exhibitions. The other nine were significant
because they were accompanied by either the giving
out of typed forms which required some action by
the teacher or they involved interactions of a
humorous kind that accompanied the posting of sub-
stitution lists or revised duty rotas on the staff
room notice board. The contents of these duty lists
could dramatically effect a teacher's plans for the
day. He could find himself losing preparation or
marking periods, doing duties in his lunch break or
covering for absent colleagues. The humour, somewhat 'in group', was only addressed to certain
members of staff, and referred to activities outside
of school, e.g., local soccer team results, holiday
plans, car problems, incidents at staff socials etc.
There was also a large quantity of instructions or
commands that appeared in writing: memos, notes,
weekly events, newsletters, and general information.
Staff also spent some time talking to supervisory
staff in private offices. When I asked about these
private meetings I was told that when such interviews were held at the request of supervisory staff
they were regularly intended for the discussion of
individual pupil problems. When they were requested
by classroom staff they were more frequently to
resolve conflicts between staff or between staff
and pupils. By far the majority of staff interactions in private offices took place between those
who had private offices themselves. They were
places, away from the staff room and out of the
corridor, where discussions regarding planning,
staffing, organising and budgeting, administrative
staff 'doing' activities, could take place. Those
I did obtain access to were predominantly about
circumventing tension or anticipating opposition
to plans they intended to introduce. Coffee and
tea were frequently available and such encounters
could be described as 'places of association' where
supervisory staff belonged and others definitely
did not. They were not as open as other 'hideaways'
such as the science prerooms, CDT offices and HE
kitchens, where other staff associated in cliques,
away from the isolation of the classroom and the
crowded staff room.
    Although supervisory staff were rarely
qualified to advise on subject matters (schemes,
plans, resources required ...) it is clear that to

have sought advice from subject staff would also
have risked the exposure of some inadequacy. No
member of the subject classroom staff could remember when their opinion had been sought. One head
of subject for example put it this way:

> Career is "fame" not "fortune" - fame from
> being "worthy to be consulted" instead of being
> consulted merely because of your position. If
> the head would only consult us, he would
> reduce that craving to get promoted so that
> someone listens to you. To have a say is to
> be respected.

This lack of consultation was a major insult to the
pride and integrity of those classroom subject teachers who were doing a good job. Lack of consultation was perceived as lack of respect, appreciation
and positive criticism. 'Teachers', said one head
of subject, 'are frustrated by having to work in
conditions where they see how classes could be
better arranged, but do not have access to the
decision making that could bring about these
changes'. 'We are unable', added another experienced subject teacher, 'to persuade management
of our priorities - they never ask - if we raise it
they refuse to listen to complaints.'

(d) Supervisory Staff Take Steps to Devalue the Subject Department Heads and the Work they Co-ordinate and Carry Out

The delegation of traditional headteacher authority
to a group of senior administrative staff has not
occurred without struggle and it is a situation
that has to be continually sustained. While the
head's authority may be sufficiently acknowledged
that it is not vulnerable to threat from simple
association with staff, supervisory staff generally
have to employ strategies to limit the power of the
major opposition group, the heads of subjects, and
their power base, their subject knowledge and their
autonomy in the classroom.

The heads of subjects may be regarded as the
only group that seriously challenges supervisory
staff positions. They are normally experienced
and well qualified in their subjects. Twenty-four
of the thirty-four subject heads in the two schools
held first degrees in their subject and a further
nine were heads of subjects where degree qualifications were not available until recently (i.e. PE,

HE, CDT). Only one head of subject was only a
certificated teacher in a subject area where
graduate qualifications would normally have been
available. Heads of subject may thus be perceived
as the leaders of the 'doers'. They have the
capacity to provide academic leadership rather than
administrative management. There was no evidence
that any steps were taken in either school to
support or to promote the influence of these
leaders. The lack of innovation and the poor
examination results were more popular supervisory
staff comments. Meanwhile, the isolation and lack
of support was echoed by all the heads of subject
interviewed.

> Heads of subject, like myself, are not
> consulted about appointments or about the
> promotions of our own subject staff. Members
> of my department are given points of
> responsibility for administrative reasons and
> it is not clear for what and to whom they are
> now really responsible. Scale promotions and
> appointments reduce my 'hold' over staff.
> Why should they listen to me? Doing a little
> 'leg' work for the administration brightens
> their career prospects while working for me
> gets them nowhere.

If supervisory staff had set out deliberately to
reduce the power of heads of subject their success
was overwhelming. Heads of subjects were denied
office space, indeed any secure working area, timetabled in excess of the junior staff in their own
subject areas who had year tutor posts and
scheduled to perform the general duties from which
supervisory staff on lower grades were exempt.
In addition, they were regularly called upon to
cover for absent colleagues in their own subject
areas because lower grade supervisory staff were
not qualified enough to teach pupils. Even a
probationary teacher had noticed that, 'heads of
subject do not have a room of their own - they must
leave their classroom and go to the staff room
during their free periods, just as we do, because
their rooms are timetabled for the use of other
members of staff'.
    To consolidate the decline in status of the
head of subject it appears that the supervisory
staff had to devalue subject knowledge itself and
to reduce psychic rewards gained from classroom
success for those teachers. In the latter case it

was better to risk poorer results than to have
classroom subject teachers with a powerful base
recognised by pupils and parents alike. The
'comprehensive intake' appeared to imply that much
of the subject based expertise and concentration
upon examinations was irrelevant. Many pupils were
suited to alternative courses. However, there was
little evidence that staff, resources and finance
were provided to create and sustain alternative
courses. Those teachers who did initiate new
courses were quickly promoted out of the classroom
and often out of the school itself. Once external
supporting agencies left the schools to carry on
with innovations, after the initial injection of
resources, the programmes faded. In place of
sustained efforts to create viable alternative
courses we discern the labelling of ex-grammar
school subject staff as too narrowly subject-
orientated to cope, while ex-secondary modern school
staff fled the classroom. The grammar school ethos,
that link between the challenging subject, the
talented pupil and highly appreciated achievement,
was rejected <u>toute</u> <u>court</u>. On the contrary it was
claimed that education was a process of personal
education through the medium of subject knowledge
rather than a glorification of the acquisition of
subject knowledge. The task of the new comprehensive school was much bigger than mere subject knowledge and beyond the resources providers were
prepared to lavish upon it. A senior teacher said
that, 'ex-grammar school staff have been sensitive
to a decline in privilege. We began by being
sensitive about elitism but soon gathered from what
new staff were saying that we were somehow not
appropriate, not needed by the new school - many
who could do so, left, of course.' Another head of
subject referred to the perceived decline of
standards: 'Doing really well by hard work is not
appreciated, not even expected by upper echelons
of staff. To get promoted you need to get out of
your subject.'
　　Lortie (1975:168-175) argues that what makes
a good day for teachers is when psychic rewards
gained in the classroom situation are high. 'Good
things' are always linked to classroom matters.
Negative events include any incursions on teaching
time for petty administrative or clerical tasks.
They resent interruptions. Programmed lessons
should take priority over other activities.
　　'I regret', said one subject teacher, 'any
interruptions of the classroom lesson, however

important. The sanctity of the lesson is inter-
rupted too easily and eroded daily.' A head of
subject identified a relationship between examination failures and the number of interruptions.
'When I was asked why there had been so many examination failures, I replied at length, stating how
many lessons had been missed or cancelled without
request or advanced notice ...' Supervisory staff
in both schools appear to have established, by
practice, the right to interrupt lessons to give
non-essential messages, to withdraw pupils for
trips, drama, sport or religious activities that
are rarely timetabled in advance - just reported
in weekly newsletters. A subject teacher on a
scale 2 summarised by claiming that, 'little
priority is given to loss of lesson time ... pupils
are withdrawn, lessons are cancelled at the drop
of a hat ...'
    Weekly newsletters are just one example of the
exploding quantity of paperwork. Keeping classroom
subject staff at a distance and increasing their
inert time may be helped by producing and demanding
paperwork. 'There is no doubt', claimed one member
of staff, 'that more administrative work is created
by having special people with responsibility for
it. This is because they create work for others
rather than serve the teachers working at the chalk
face.' Both the larger school and the allocation of
responsibility for certain delegated administrative
jobs is recognised as a cause of the paperwork
explosion, but some question the depersonalisation
and distancing effects of this. Subject staff
commented that 'as paper work explodes, personal
contacts die'. Another said 'that there is too
much bureaucracy - even staff are given numbers.
The paperwork reduces you to a cog in a wheel and
divides you from the people you are working with.
The personal touch is missing.' Many staff
considered the required administrative tasks menial
and a serious distraction from the real job. A
head of year admitted that, 'staff are asked to do
too many menial tasks, a great deal of paperwork
should be done by a good secretary or teachers'
assistant. I don't need all the training I have had
to do these tasks.' A newly qualified teacher
observed that 'paperwork is just one more way of
misusing teacher time ... others include doing
extra detentions, missing lunch breaks, searching
for trouble makers, collecting absence slips,
registers, etc.'

A SELECTED INCIDENT OF SITUATED INTERACTION
DESCRIBED AND ANALYSED

To study an incident or a series of connected
incidents in search of some interpretation of how
institutions normally run and transform themselves,
is to seek to operationalise structuration theory.
This section outlines an analytic technique based
upon structuration theory and processes one example. A number of such incidents would require
similar analysis before substantial conclusions
could be reached. It is necessary, as claimed
earlier, to demonstrate how structuration occurs in
the middle ground where human actors draw upon and
consolidate the rules and procedures available to
them. A model for the analysis of an episode of
situated interaction is offered here (Figure 1).
It has the three aspects, human agent, middle ground
and institution. The middle ground refers to a
process, at the level of social integration where
the teacher draws upon structuring properties in
the institution as he communicates or signifies,
using the power he has from authorisation and/or
allocation and appealing to his legitimate rights.
However, prior to giving some substance to the
model, it is necessary to describe the incident
itself.

The Incident
Mark, a fourth form pupil, had recently received
a succession of poor reports in a particular subject, but his parents had discovered at a careers
convention that he needed, a GCE pass in that
subject at 'C' level in order to pursue the career
they had in mind for him. Mark had been assigned
to a CSE class in the subject and, according to the
head of that subject, this was a generous allocation
because his progress barely merited this and he had
a reputation for disruptive behaviour due in part
to lack of interest in completing work assignments.
The parents sought an interview with the head of
middle school, explained the situation and asked
for Mark to be reassigned to an 'O' level class.
The head of middle school reviewed Mark's grade
profile in all subjects and decided that in Mark's
best interests he should be assigned to an 'O'
level class. The parents were promised that this
would be done immediately on the clear understanding
that Mark would work hard and behave exceptionally
well. The parents were invited to visit the school

Figure 1   Episode of Situated Interaction

MIDDLE
GROUND

1. HUMAN AGENCY
   BRINGS TO EVERY
   EPISODE

a) RELATIVE KNOWLEDGE-
   ABILITY

b) RELATIVE AND ROUTINE
   CAPABILITY

c) A NEED TO TAKE
   ACCOUNT OF THOSE
   ABSENT AND PRESENT

d) A CAPABILITY TO MAKE
   SUMMARY REPRESENTA-
   TIONS

e) A COMMITMENT TO SOME
   IDEOLOGICAL STANCE

f) UNACKNOWLEDGED CON-
   DITIONS OF ACTION

STRUCTURATION PROCESS

2. STRUCTURING
   PROPERTIES THAT
   CONSTRAIN OR
   ENABLE, THAT MAY
   BE DRAWN UPON

a) SIGNIFICATION
   (LANGUAGE CODES)

b) DOMINATION,
   AUTHORISATION
   (ALLOCATION)

c) LEGITIMATION
   (NORMATIVE
   REGULATIONS)

again the next term for a progress report.
     At this stage no consultation with the head of
subject had taken place. The head of school was
not qualified to teach this subject at all. A memo
was sent to the teachers concerned, not to the head
of subject, noting the decision to reassign Mark to
the 'O' level group with effect from the following
Monday morning. Mark was told of the arrangement
and of the conditions attached to it. He agreed to
his side of the bargain.
     The head of subject, who is responsible for
producing the graded lists of pupils for examination
preparation in his subject, found out about the
arrangement on the Monday morning when the
'receiving' class teacher asked why the reassignment
had taken place, as Mark had demonstrated his lack
of ability to cope with this standard of work.
This happened in the crowded staff room at break -
time and I was fortunate to be there as it happened.

Why did you transfer Mark to my GCE class?
I thought we had agreed he couldn't cope!

I didn't know anything about it - when did
this happen? Who did it? - not the head of
middle school again?

The head of subject was obviously very annoyed and
left his coffee to go in pursuit of the head of
middle school. I followed at a discrete distance
hoping to find out first hand what had happened,
but aware that I would probably have to follow it
up in conversation with the relevant staff later.
The conversation I caught before the matter was
followed up behind closed doors went as follows:

Head of subject X: Who's idea was it to
transfer Mark to the GCE class? No one
consulted me about one of these moves again.

Head of middle school: I meant to see you
about that. His parents have asked for the
change. I've looked at his grades profile
and your subject is the odd one out. He is
doing GCE in other subjects. They insisted,
so I decided to give him a trial run ... I
hope you don't mind ...?

Head of subject X: I put him in a CSE class
because I know he couldn't cope with GCE
work ... my staff agreed. He disrupts the
class and will be lucky to get a CSE pass
nevermind a GCE. What is the point of me
placing them in the proper class if you
change them at the whim of a parent? What
do they know about the subject? ... What
do you know about it for that matter? ...

At this point the head of middle school got the
message and began to direct the head of subject
into his private room out of the earshot of myself
and several others in the corridor. The last thing
I heard was the head of middle school saying 'I
thought you would support my decision ... it's just
for a trial period after all ...'
The head of subject was not with the head of
middle school for long. He later told me that he
had gone straight to the school headmaster but got
no satisfaction. The head supported the right of
the head of middle school to make such a decision
provided he had studied the grade profile for the

pupil and decided that it was in the best interests
of the pupil as a whole to be assigned, for a trial
period, to a GCE class. After all, if he is GCE
quality in other subjects, maybe all he needs is
encouragement, a fresh start, a bit of cooperation
between parents and the staff to produce the right
attitude. The head of subject X said that he told
the head that without proper consultation he could
not see how his subject staff could be expected to
cooperate in this situation. In their opinion, in
this subject, he was simply not GCE material. A
fail grade was inevitable and his presence in the
group would simply distract the pupils and disturb
their concentration. The head had agreed to ask
the head of middle school to consult with the head
of subject before making similar assignments and
to review Mark's position in four weeks time rather
than wait till next term.

In conversation with the head of middle school,
I sought his view of the situation. He disagreed
with ability banded classes in the fourth year
anyway. He felt that all teachers should be able
to teach mixed ability classes. There had been a
lot of complaints about the subject teachers in
subject X and these referred to their lack of
ability to control classes. It may not be all the
fault of the pupils. The head of middle school
also complained that books were not marked on a
regular basis and parents would not be pleased
should such information come to light. The trouble,
he claimed, with some subject teachers,was that
they had too narrow a perspective on their job and
failed to see the pupils education as a wholistic
exercise.

The Incident Analysed in Terms of the Content of Figure 1

1(a) Human agency brings to every episode relative
knowledgeability. The head of middle school
perceives himself to be senior to any head of subject in the staff hierarchy. In terms of tacit
knowledge it appears from the incident itself and
from subsequent interviews that he was aware
that:
i)   he will obtain the head's support for his
      action despite his failure to consult,
ii)   the parents will support his action,
iii) he is paid a higher salary to make controver-
      sial decisions of this kind,

iv)   even if the head of subject complained, he
      lacked the power to make his complaint stick,
v)   he may appeal to staff loyalty to administra-
      tive decisions to protect staff from direct
      confrontation with parents,
vi)   he has to demonstrate his competence to make a
      decision in the face of potential opposition
      from the head of subject.

The head of subject, meanwhile, made a feeble
complaint because he knew that:
i)   the head of middle school considered him so
      unimportant that he had not even received
      notification of the reassignment, nevermind
      been consulted,
ii)   he had no supporting peer group; heads of
      subjects did not form a body that could
      collectively embody their leadership potential
      or protect their interests,
iii) another spectating member of staff commented
      that he would probably not have complained at
      all had his subject staff member not raised
      the subject in a public place (the staff room)
      and he appeared to be making as much of a
      point about the powerlessness of the head of
      subject as about the cause of the pupil con-
      cerned.

(b) Relative and routine capability. The head of
middle school could have acted differently. Con-
sulting the head of subject was an option open to
him but he saw it as a professional expectation of
supervisory staff to be able to make routine
decisions of this kind. To handle the subsequent
tension was part of his conditions of service as a
middle management supervisor. To have consulted
would have delayed action and he would have had to
take the decision eventually. He said that he
preferred to defend a decision he believed he had
every right to take, than to risk consultation
where such a right may be questioned and to lose
the advantages of a quick solution to a potentially
dangerous parent/school confrontation.

(c) A need to take account of those absent and
present. Actors need to consider reciprocity,
resistance and challenge in their approach to any
situation. The head of middle school has had to
take account of the interests and expectations of
the head, the parents, the pupil and the teachers
concerned. What the head would expect him to do

(to make the kind of decision a delegated head
should make), the parents wish to arrange the best
subject provision and the pupils contract to good
behaviour and hard work as a result of his action,
are his clear priorities. There was no doubt that
the head of subject or class teacher's right to
be consulted was a very low priority. The head of
subject challenge could be easily resisted and the
head of middle school saw reciprocity more in terms
of those above him in the hierarchy and parental
approval of the school procedures than in terms of
his relationship with the head of subject. He had
simply made a decision and handling the consequent
resistance was merely routine.

(d) A capability to make summary representations.
Incidents of this kind are incidents in a series of
similar ones and the head of middle school is able
to review the way he acted, to anticipate the way
he will act next time and to adjust his fantasy
about such practices. Parental complaints can be
dealt with in this way. Decisions can be taken
with impunity without consultation. He is capable
of taking them and of handling the subsequent
tension. To manage implies no less. The head of
subject, meanwhile, reviews the same situation in
terms of what he can anticipate will happen next
time and adjusts his fantasy about such practices.
His professional and academic judgement has been
ignored. Subject studies and subject teachers have
been devalued. His authority to lead his subject
classroom teachers has been eroded by their perception of his lack of power to make his definition
of the situation actually count. There will be
difficulties next time he requests staff assistance
to place pupils in appropriate ability groups or
bands because they will question the value of an
exercise that can be overturned as easily as the one
Mark was involved in.

e/f A commitment to some ideological stance and the
unacknowledged conditions of action. The unacknowledged conditions of teacher action can
include misread communications, fears, grudges, and
sectional interests that may be unacknowledged.
Perhaps the legend of the comprehensive school
suggests that opportunities should be open to all
and selection based upon performance is somehow
undesirable. To tell a parent that a pupil has no
more right to sit for an examination now than he
would have had before comprehensive education is

merely to shift selection from the 11+ to teacher
judgement. To demonstrate that such judgement can
be overruled may be better than to demonstrate that
the system hasn't really changed. There was no
forum for the discussion and the arrival at some
consensus about school policy in either of the two
schools. Senior conferences were restricted to
staff holding administrative responsibilities and
excluded heads of subjects. A sectional interest
in the continuation of management in the absence of
consultation and consensus appears to be an unacknowledged condition of action by administrative
staff.

2a) Interpretative scheme, significance and
communication. This refers to what the head of
middle school intended to communicate (what he
meant to say) and what his utterence actually
meant (by deferment to established language codes).
By drawing on language codes (signification) the
actors in an episode communicate and reproduce
these codes. The head of middle school has drawn
upon language codes to indicate what consultation,
assignment procedures and parental concerns actually
mean.

'I meant to see you about it' implies that
consultation means to let you know about my
decision. 'His parents have asked for the change'
implies parental concerns that head of middle
school has to deal with and has to protect the
teachers from. 'I've looked at his grade profile,
your subject is the odd one out ... I've decided to
give him a trial run' implies that if all the other
subjects have classified him as GCE material, the
fault may lie in the subject rather than with the
pupil. 'I thought you would support my decision',
implies a certain reciprocity: your loyalty in
return for my protection.

2b) Facility, domination and power. This refers to
the head of middle school's capacity to draw upon
the rules and resources (due to authorisation and
allocation) and in doing so to exercise his power
to secure outcomes where their realisation depends
upon others. In the same moment, these authorisation and allocation structures of domination are
reproduced and modified. The traditional power of
a headteacher, delegated somewhat to the head of
middle school, is embodied in professional convention. The middle school head's success in making
his definition of the situation actually count by

drawing up domination resources, stores this power
to make such decisions for middle school and other
delegated headteacher posts in general and for this
middle school head in particular.

2c) Norm, legitimation and sanctions. The system of
norms (claims to certain rights and the acceptance
of certain obligations) has to be sustained in the
flow of episodes of situated interaction. The
operation of sanctions is a chronic if not subtle
process of adjustment in all interactions. The
head of middle school implies that he has protected
the head of subject and his staff from parental
pressure, a sanction he should beware of because
books are not regularly marked and the pupil
appears to be making good progress everywhere else.
Meanwhile, the head of middle school has the right
to assign pupils to classes and expect staff
respect for his ability to make decisions of this
kind on the basis of all the information available
to him.

CONCLUSION

The danger in using this structuration analysis in
the middle ground lies in assuming that 'all' is
necessarily embroiled in chronically recursive
reproduction. While it may be demonstrated, even
from a single episode of situated interaction, that
actors using communication, power and sanction may
draw upon and reproduce signification, domination
and legitimation rules and resources, there will
always be some consequences that slip from the
totally inclusive explanations. These are referred
to as the unintended consequences of such episodes.
These may lie beyond the discursive penetration of
the encounter by these involved. They contribute
to the complexity and contradictory nature of many
of the rules and resources systems. They may also
contribute to the summary representations that all
actors employ in building their perceptions or
fantasies about the way things are normally done
within their institutions, since it is proposed
that every episode is one in a stream of relatively
similar and broadly related episodes. This final
paragraph attempts to summarise by claiming that
incidents such as the one analysed and the evidence
from interviews is sufficient to substantiate the
fruitfulness of middle ground analysis in the
pursuit of understanding how institutions differ

and how arrangements within them are sustained and modified by pressure groups.

On the evidence that emerged from the analysis of the interviews and the selected episode of situated interaction, it is claimed that the distinction between relatively classroom based subject teaching staff and relatively non-classroom based supervisory staff is upheld. The teachers perceive it as such and act in recognition of the existence of this division. Those in dominant supervisory posts act in incidents of situated interaction to reproduce this distinction. The unintended consequence is that the quality, disposition and status of the teacher programmed to interact with pupils in the classroom is devalued.

But management has no other purpose than to facilitate the creation of the most effective teaching/learning situations (Gray, 1980:22). Such a purpose may have become more difficult as schools have become larger, their precise objectives less clear, their resources restricted and their internal dynamics devoid of adequate consultations. However, the evidence presented here substantiates to some extent how one group of teachers who began in a less favoured position academically, were able to exploit the pastoral care legend, and now continue to have the major say about how things will normally be done in schools. Tactics used to retain their right to the dominant decision making processes, have eclipsed their care for establishing effective teaching/learning situations and promoting the self esteem and disposition to their task of those teachers who interact with pupils in classroom situations.

ACKNOWLEDGEMENTS

I wish to thank the headteachers and staff of the two West Midlands schools and Dr G.Walford of Aston University, without whose support, encouragement and critical comment, this study could not have taken place.

REFERENCES

Archer, M.S. (1982) 'Morphogenesis versus structuration: on combining structure and action'. British Journal of Sociology, 33, (4), 455-483

Best, R., Jarvis, C., Robbins, P. (1980)
    Perspectives on Pastoral Care, Heinemann,
    London
Buckley, W. (1967) Sociology and Modern Systems
    Theory, Prentice Hall, New Jersey
Burgess, R.G. (1983) Experiencing Comprehensive
    Education, Methuen, London
Caspari, I.E. (1976) 'Roles and responsibilities
    of head teacher and teaching staff in primary
    schools' in Peters, R.S. (1976) The Role of
    The Head. Routledge and Kegan Paul, London
Chetwynd, H.R. (1976) Comprehensive School, the
    Study of Woodbury Down, Routledge and Kegan
    Paul, London
Coulson, A.A. (1976) 'The role of the primary
    head' in R.S. Peters (ed.), The Role of the
    Head, Routledge and Kegan Paul, London, pp.
    92-108
Gane, M. (1983) 'Anthony Giddens and the crisis of
    social theory', Economy and Society, 12, (3),
    368-399
Giddens, A. (1979) Central Problems in Social
    Theory: Action, Structure and Contradiction
    in Social Analysis, Macmillan Press, London
Gordon, R.L. (1975) Interviewing, Strategy,
    Techniques and Tactics, Dorsey Press, Illinois
Gray, H.L. (1980) Management in Education,
    Nafferton, Driffield, England
Gray, H.L. (1982) The Management of Educational
    Institutions: Their Research and Consultancy,
    Falmer Press, Lewis
Hamblin, D. (1978) The Teacher and Pastoral Care,
    Blackwell, Oxford
Hammersley, M. and Atkinson, P. (1983) Ethnography:
    Principles in Practice, Tavistock, London
Hoyle, E. (1969) 'Professional stratification and
    anomic in the teaching profession',
    Paedegogica Europaea, 5, pp. 60-71
John, D. (1980) Leadership in Schools, Heinemann
    Educational Books, London
Knorr-Cetina, K. and Cicourel, A.V. (1981)
    Advances in Social Theory and Methodology.
    Toward an Integration of Micro and Macro
    Sociologies. Routledge and Kegan Paul, New
    York
Lortie, D.C. (1975) School Teacher: A Socio-
    logical Study. University of Chicago Press,
    Chicago
Marland, M. (1974) Pastoral Care, Heinemann,
    London
Martin, S. (1983) Managing Without Managers,

Sage Library of Social Research, SAGE, London

Ozga, J. and Lawn, M. (1981) Teachers, Professionalism and Class: a study of organised teachers, Falmer Press, Lewis

Peters, R.S. (1976) (ed.) The Role of the Head, Routledge and Kegan Paul, London

Richardson, E. (1973) The Teacher, the School and the task of Management, Heinemann, London

Richardson, E. (1975) Authority and Organisation in the Secondary School, Macmillan, London

Schwartz, M.A. and Schwartz, C.G. (1955) 'Problems in participant observation', American Journal of Sociology, 60, 343-353

Watts, J. (1976) 'Sharing it out: the role of the head in participatory government' in Peters, R.S. (ed.) The Role of the Head, Routledge and Kegan Paul, London

Watts, J. (1977) The Countesthorpe Experience, George Allen and Unwin, London

Chapter Ten

UNIVERSITY CUT AND THRUST

Henry Miller and Geoffrey Walford

July 1st, 1981, is a date that many university academics will find difficult to forget, for on that day the University Grants Committee (UGC) announced its decisions on the distribution of government financial support for individual universities for the following three years. The government had already announced that there were to be major cuts in overall provision for universities, but the UGC had decided that the cuts were to be distributed unevenly between the 43 universities dependent on its support. On that fateful Wednesday in July 1981, several universities found themselves thrown into confusion and turmoil.

There are now several accounts of the ways in which the financial cuts were imposed at the national level and responded to by universities (Kogan and Kogan, 1983; Shattock and Rigby, 1983). It is necessary to review some of the national features to provide a context for our account; but the main purpose of this chapter is to take a more micro perspective and examine some aspects of the turmoil that resulted in one of the universities most badly hit - the University of Aston in Birmingham. The chapter looks at the nature and extent of some of the problems that this university had to face, and at some of the ways in which it rapidly responded to maintain financial equilibrium. It will be seen that financial equilibrium was achieved, but at severe non-financial costs.

THE BACKGROUND TO THE CUTS

The Kogans claim that the 1981 cuts were unprecedented. They state that:

244

> Although ministers may have been ignorant of
> the implications of their policies, it is now
> certain that between 1981-1982 and 1984-85,
> when the number of 18 year olds seeking places
> in higher education will be at a peak, 18,000
> undergraduate and graduate home and EEC places
> in the universities will be lost. This is in
> addition to the 5300 places held by overseas
> students which were lost between 1979-1980 and
> 1981-83. Some 5600 academic and academic
> related posts will be disestablished in the
> universities in the next two years.
> (Kogan and Kogan, 1983)

Although the scale of these cuts was certainly
unprecedented, the authors rightly go on to point
out that the wind of change was blowing many years
before 1981, it was just that the universities
chose to treat this warning as a "bad spring"
rather than a change in climate. The warnings can
be traced back to 1973 for, from then onwards,
there was continued uncertainty about future
financial support. As the economic recession
deepened the former quinquennial system of grants
to universities was abandoned. From 1975 grants
were expressly fixed by a cash limit imposed by
government which, as it only partly took inflation
into account, meant that the grant was gradually
reduced in real terms. By 1981 some 10 per cent
per student had already been cut.

The 196Cs was the boom period for expansion
of university provision. In that decade, the
Robbins Report proposed and legitimised a virtual
doubling of the number of universities in Britain,
backed by the assumption that the expanding
economy would continue to expand and that education played a part in that expansion. It was the
hope of Robbins and successive governments that
the major expansion would be in science, engineering and technology, but this did not materialise.
The system responded in piecemeal fashion to student demand, and much of the expansion of student
numbers was in the humanities and social sciences.
In the mid 1970s the Labour government, faced by
an energy crisis, capitulated to the demands of
the International Monetary Fund and started the
process of cuts in education and social services.
Britain failed to keep pace in education with the
expansion of nearly all other industrialised
countries (Edwards, 1982). The Conservative
government of Mrs Thatcher brought in a new

monetarist doctrine, and had a clear mandate to
"roll back the boundaries of the state". There
was a commitment not only to a free market economy
but also to a reduction of public expenditure in
order to curb inflation and direct resources to
private wealth-creating enterprise. Expenditure
on education was no longer seen as it had been in
the 1950s and 1960s as contributing to economic
growth, but as part of the public sector which was
too large and which should take its share of the
cuts (Baron et al., 1981).

The relationship between the number of eight-
een year olds in the population and the required
provision for university education is a complex
one. It was certainly known that there would be
a peak in the number of 18 year olds in 1983 and
that by 1994 there would be only 67 per cent of
the number at this peak. The various projections
given in the Brown Paper by Oates (DES, 1978)
suggested that even if the age participation rate
was to increase dramatically during the 1980s, it
was highly unlikely that it would be able to
compensate for the requirements of 1983. In short,
it seemed that the major alternatives facing
government were whether to expand higher education
to take account of the 'hump' or to 'tunnel through'
the hump by fixing the age participation rate at a
lower level than demand would justify.

In practice the situation was even more
complicated than this for, during the 1970s, the
number of 18 year olds leaving school with
qualifications entitling them to enter higher
education (two A levels) rose steadily, but the
percentage seeking and going into higher education fell. Further, the decline in birth rate
was not even for all social classes and least for
the middle class which provided the bulk of
university students. With so many variables,
predictions are extremely difficult and have been
the subject of much debate (DES, 1983; Royal
Society, 1983) mostly to little avail as, by 1980,
the government had admitted that the system was to
be 'expenditure led' rather than 'demand led' (DES,
1980; Shattock and Rigby, 1983; DES, 1984). The
government was determined simply to spend less
money on higher education and the results of this
determination cut across the different aims and
logics of other sections of government. Actions
were not clearly thought through in any detail, and
the period from 1979-1983 saw wild swings in policy
as the unintended consequences of actions became

clear. While the cuts were the result of dogma,
the dogma itself was not coherent.

The cuts were imposed by a sword with two
sharp edges. On one side the cuts were purely
financial. The budget of June 1979 announced
reductions in university recurrent grants, student
awards, funding for building programmes and for the
Research Councils. The UGC warned universities in
August 1979 that they should reduce their intake
of students by 5 per cent because further cuts were
anticipated. The second sharp edge, however, was
directed at overseas students. It was announced in
October, 1979, that their fees, which accounted for
about 13 per cent of all university income, would
have to be drastically increased such that they
paid the 'full economic fee' for their courses.
Where overseas fees had been about 30 per cent
higher than home student fees, they were to rise to
between 90 to 150 per cent higher depending on
discipline (see Williams, 1984, for details). No
one knew how many students would be able or
prepared to pay such fees, but all predicted major
losses.

This particular cut was unfair to universities
and to overseas students alike. Overseas students
had not been evenly distributed throughout the
system, but were heavily concentrated in a number
of large centres. The University of London, Aston
and UMIST, for example, had built up a large proportion of overseas students, and were thus badly
hit through no fault of their own, and with no
judgements being made about the academic quality
of the courses being offered. Little thought had
been given to the effects of potential losses in
student numbers on the universities, nor had
thought been given to the effects that such increases of fees might have on Britain's relationships with foreign governments who had regularly
sent students to Britain.

The notion that the full-economic fee was to
be calculated quite simply by taking the total cost
of higher education in that academic area and
dividing by the total number of students was in
itself, of course, nonsense. As Edwards (1980)
argued, more than half the cost of universities is
associated with their research output, rather than
their teaching. Overseas students were thus being
expected to pay a share for the research output of
the universities as well as their teaching. It has
been argued (Walford, 1983) that research students
make a major contribution to the research output of

universities, especially in the sciences and engineering, through their involvement in ongoing research. Under the new scheme foreign students would not only be contributing to British research through their work, but also through their pockets.

In practice the losses were not as large as had been predicted. The fall in the value of the pound after 1981 reduced the effect of the fees increases for many overseas students, and the loss of some 5,300 places between 1979 and 1982, was large enough to hurt, but not as dramatic as had been feared. The government, too, had second thoughts on the affair for, in early 1983, under pressure from foreign governments and even its own Members of Parliament, an overseas student scholar-ship scheme was introduced. Money was given to students from specific countries in line with the government's foreign policy commitments, thus mak-ing explicit the political nature of support for higher education.

By 1979 the decision had been taken that there would be no expansion of provision to take into account the peak in the age distribution - the best that could be hoped for was a 'tunnelling through' the peak. As the year progressed estimates of future expenditure got more and more bleak, and in November 1980 a three and a half per cent cut below level funding was announced. The Expenditure White Paper of March 1981 deepened the cut by a further eight and a half per cent for the period 1981/84.

> For home students in higher education the plans provide for a progressive reduction in expenditure so that by 1983/84 institutional expenditure (not of tuition fee income) will be rather more than 8 per cent below the level planned in Cmnd. 7841. This is likely to oblige institutions to review the range and nature of their contribution to higher education. It is also likely to lead to some reduction in the number of students admitted to higher education with increased competition for places.
>   (Expenditure White Paper, 1981)

The total cut in funding to universities during the period 1980-81 and 1983-84 was thus to be somewhere between 11 and 15 per cent in real terms. No one knew exactly how large it would be for no one knew how many foreign students would still come to Britain. We now know that it was about 13 per cent in a period of just three years.

Having decided how much money was to be spent on universities the government then did not at that time take direct responsibility as to how that money should be spent. Various Ministers and MPs made political statements about the need for greater 'relevance', more science, computing, engineering and management. Sir Keith Joseph, Secretary of State for Education and Science, made very clear his dislike of social science. But, though the hints were there for all to take, the government left responsibility to the UGC. The Committee's task was one for which it was singularly unsuited (Ashworth, 1982). Committees composed of academics may be well suited for handing out an ever increasing bounty to universities, where all current activities were continuously funded and bids were made for the icing on the cake. Cuts in funding, however, caused damage. Choices had to be made about the relative worth of activities that had previously been funded, and courses and departments would have to close.

The UGC quickly made two major decisions. It decided that it would not simply share out the cuts between universities and give 'equal misery', and, at the other extreme, it decided that it would not try to force the closure of any complete universities. The criteria used to determine the final distribution have still not been made completely known. The uproar which followed the announcement encouraged UGC to divulge some general criteria, but the details of how these criteria were weighted have still not been disclosed.

On the 1st July, 1981, the UGC sent two letters to each of the University Vice-Chancellors or Principals, outlining individual allocations of the grant. The first five page letter gave details of the overall strategy for the university sector. In spite of the rise in student demand the UGC announced a decision that,

> It is the Committee's view that the university system as a whole should not be asked, with this reduction in funding, to maintain its home and European Community (EC) student numbers at the 1979/80 levels, and a reduction of about 5% is therefore assumed.

The decision to cut student numbers as such was taken by the UGC, not government. It aimed to worsen the staff/student ratio somewhat, but not as much as would be necessary to maintain (or expand) student intake. The reduced numbers of students were to be distributed in a somewhat different way between the subject areas. In line with government preferences, there was to be a shift in the distribution of students as among arts, science and medicine, from 50 : 41 : 9 in 1979/80 to 48 : 42: 10 in 1983/84 within the reduced student numbers.

The second three page letter of 1st July 1981 detailed the individual grant allocation to the specific recipient university for 1981/82 and gave provisional figures for 1982/83 and 1983/84, along with numbers of students in arts, science and medicine 'that the Committee has used in determining provisional grant for 1983/84'. It then gave general advice on particular subject areas and suggested what changes the university might consider making to achieve the desired numbers and balance its books.

As a pair, the two letters seemed strangely insubstantial. They were the missionaries which were to reshape the British university system, and were to cause three years of disruption and chaos, court cases and in-fighting. They were to initiate or legitimise dramatic changes in the managerial style, organisation and governance of universities. They were to disrupt, damage and bring to a close the academic careers of thousands of staff who would have otherwise continued to be productive members of the academic community. They were, in 2 years, to exclude 61,000 undergraduate students from university education who would have otherwise benefitted from it, (Waldegrave, 1982) yet the letters themselves were brief, unpretentious and unassuming, somehow an anticlimax to the psychological build-up that had preceded their publication.

Yet these letters were very different from any letters that had ever preceded them. For the first time the UGC gave specific advice to reduce student numbers even where the university was recruiting well qualified students in that area. All of the universities had some cut in income, but the range was wide. In three years even the 'luckiest' universities such as Bath or York were to lose some six per cent income, while the "unlucky losers" such as Salford, Keele and Bradford were to lose 44, 34 and 33 per cent respectively. The University of Aston in Birmingham, the subject of special study in this paper, was fourth from top of the

cuts list, losing some 31 per cent income in three
years.

THE UNIVERSITY OF ASTON IN BIRMINGHAM

Although the University of Aston in Birmingham was
only given university status in 1966 it can trace
a direct line of descent from the Birmingham and
Midland Institute of 1875. It became the first
College of Advanced Technology in 1956 and was
raised to university status as one of the group of
new technological universities as a result of
proposals contained within the Robbins Report
(1963).
    The University expanded steadily through the
1970s, always taking in slightly more students than
the UGC grant would justify. The staff/student
ratio was thus rather lower than most other
universities during this time. It maintained links
with the surrounding industrial and commercial
world, and had a special emphasis on courses which
included elements of industrial experience within
them. At the end of the decade there was a total
of 5690 students. Of the 4620 undergraduates, more
than half (2430) were on sandwich four year courses,
where the third year was spent away from the university in industry or commerce. It is worth noting
the irony here that the present government has
highly praised such courses, and has wished to see
them extended. In 1980 there were four Faculties
of unequal size. Engineering had 2390 students,
Science 1180, Management 790, and Social Sciences
and Humanities, 580. The remainder of the students
were on interdisciplinary courses not attached to
a single faculty.
    The University has had three Vice Chancellors.
The first Sir Peter Venables had been Principal of
the College of Advanced Technology and had seen the
university into its new status. Sir Joseph Pope
presided over the expansion of the university from
August 1969 to September 1979. After a brief
inter-regnum Professor Frederick Crawford took
office in July 1980.
    Professor Crawford was in a number of ways an
unusual choice for Vice Chancellor. He was a local
Birmingham boy who had worked for his first degree
in engineering at the College of Advanced Technology, Birmingham, while being a research trainee
in a local manufacturing company. He received a
doctorate from Liverpool and had briefly returned

to the College of Advanced Technology as senior
lecturer. However, his main experience of higher
education was in the United States rather than
Britain. He moved to Stanford University in 1959,
first as a Research Associate, working his way up
to become Director of a research centre at this
highly prestigious private university. It was
after twenty-two years there that he returned to
Britain as Vice-Chancellor. Quite clearly, his
experience of higher education in the States helped
to structure his understanding of how universities
did and should work. His model of a successful
university seemed much nearer the American model
than the traditional British one.

At the immediate surface level, his American
experience was clearly visible as he set about
establishing a Science Park financed by the Local
Authority and a major clearing bank, and in the
building of a Centre for Extension Education, which
was to operate using Tutored Video Instruction
following the pioneering work on TVI at the Stanford
Instructional Television Network. The American
management techniques were not so immediately visible in the first year, but were to prove to be
decisive in the following years.

BEFORE THE LETTER: JULY 1980 - JUNE 1981

Professor Crawford took up his post as Vice-
Chancellor of the University of Aston on 1st July
1980, just as it was becoming clear that the university was facing serious financial problems. He
very quickly recognised that there would be a need
for a revision to the Academic Plan and initiated
'information gathering' exercises to this end.
In November 1980, as Phase I of this Academic Plan
revision, he circulated a lengthy questionnaire to
all members of academic staff to be completed
confidentially and returned to him. There were
two types of questions: factual questions about
personal activities in teaching, research and
administration, and opinion-sounding questions on a
wide range of issues. This second group of
questions invited comments on strengths and weaknesses of the respondent's own department, how it
ranked with similar departments in other universities, how things could be improved, which
activities of the department ought to be phased out
and which strengthened. It also asked for comment
on which departments were thought to be the strong-

est and which the weakest within the university, and which activities the university ought to phase out and which retain.

The Vice-Chancellor put forward the question- naire as an exercise in democracy to enable the resulting Academic Plan to embody the views and aspirations of the greatest number of academic staff, but it also raised a number of doubts and questions. The Local Branch of the Association for University Teachers (AUT) advised its members not to complete the form as they were concerned about how the information might be used in the future. They also saw little need for a new structure of representation responding directly to the Vice- Chancellor, when academics were already represented through trade unions and university official committees. This was an understandable reaction at a time when there was already talk of possible redundancies and many would argue that it was proved justified in view of the later events. The prom- ised analysis and comments from the Vice-Chancellor on these questionnaires have still not appeared.

News of future cutbacks in funding grew as the months passed. Aston had about 20 per cent of its students from overseas. The government announcement that support for these students was to be withdrawn by the UGC, and that universities were going to be forced to ask for a 'full economic fee', thus brought real fears for the future. The announce- ment of a three and a half per cent cut in univer- sity spending was also made in November 1980.

The Vice-Chancellor responded to these threats by setting up an Advisory Group on Budget Adjustment in January 1981. This consisted of a small, ad hoc, group of senior academic and administrative officers which tried to make short and medium range financial forecasts and suggestions as to how the university's budget might be balanced. In the setting up of this group it is now possible to see the beginnings of moving away from the official organisational com- mittee structure of the university and also the greater involvement of senior administrative staff in academic decision making.

In January 1981, Phase 2 of the Academic Plan Revision process was launched. Thirty-five 'task forces' were set up, one in each of the departments and a few in some special areas, to raise questions and debate the future of those groups. Again the emphasis was on enabling junior academic staff to get their views heard and were to discuss new directions in teaching and research, student and

staff recruitment, resources generation and much
more, not only in times of expansion and steady
state, but in the more likely future of contraction. As can be imagined, the response to this idea
from Professors and senior academics was not
generally enthusiastic. The local AUT this time
did not know which way to jump - they liked the
idea of consultation, but were again worried about
misuse of information and the bypassing of official
procedures.

The Advisory Group on Budget Adjustment published widely an interim report which suggested
that expenditure would need to be cut by 18-22 per
cent by 1984, and this would mean 1,000 fewer
students, 120-150 fewer academic staff and 240-
300 fewer non-academic staff unless new sources of
funding could be found. This automatically caused
considerable anxiety. The major problem that
British universities face when confronted with
rapid cuts is that possible responses are highly
circumscribed. About three-quarters of all
expenditure goes on pay to staff rather than on
non-pay items, which indicates that substantial
savings can only be made by staff reductions. The
majority of academic staff, however, hold tenured
positions. Every university has a slightly
different charter and, as it happened, Aston's
Charter was one of the most specific in this
respect. Tenured academics had individual contracts which could only be terminated because of
physical or mental incapacity or immoral or
criminal activity. It was clear that the contract
could not be terminated merely because the university was potentially unable to pay salaries.
Leading counsels for the AUT suggested that breach
of contract claims might give rise to payment of
30,000 - 80,000 pounds and, at this time, the
government was giving no indication that there
would be any help for universities in paying these
costs (Geddes, 1981).

It is important to recognise that it seemed
that no other universities were planning so much in
advance at this stage. Certainly Aston's position,
because of the high number of overseas students,
was bleak, but not necessarily as bleak as some
other institutions. The government was arguing for
more applied research and teaching, and it might
have been thought that Aston would not be very
badly cut when the distribution of UGC money was
finally announced. Perhaps a new Vice-Chancellor,
coming from the United States, was more able to

read the signs than those who had remained in
Britain. In early 1981 all staff vacancies were
frozen, but, much more surprisingly in April 1981,
the University Council introduced an Early
Retirement Scheme for those aged 55 or above, which
was financed from the University's own funds.

The pace of change seemed to be rapidly increasing, for what had started a few months earlier
as an 'information gathering' exercise, had become,
by April 1981, contingency plans for varying
possible levels of funding for the future. The
uncertainty was so great that by May 1981, when the
universities still did not know what their funding
for the coming academic year would be, Aston froze
all undergraduate admissions. The University
Grants Committee finally announced its recommended
allocations to universities for the academic year
1981/82 and projected allocations for the following
two years on 1st July, 1981. It was a day of high
drama.

THE WEEK OF THE LETTER - 1st July 1981-8 JULY 1981

Wednesday is the traditional day for university
meetings, so that when the UGC announced that the
letters would be available on Wednesday, 1st July
1981, it was found to coincide with a previously
scheduled Senate meeting. The Vice Chancellor
scheduled a further meeting for senate a week
afterwards.

> The seven-hour 1 July Senate meeting was held
> in three parts. The first was given mainly
> to the presentation of a strategic document by
> myself on academic planning and Aston's
> response to the impending cuts Looking Forward.
> The Senate then adjourned while the contents
> of the UGC letter to Aston were telephoned
> from London and transcribed. At 5.10 pm, one
> year to the minute from first setting foot in
> Aston to take up my appointment, it fell to
> me to deliver the stunning news that the UGC
> proposed to cut 31% of our recurrent grant
> over the period 1981/84, and 22% out of our
> home population. The dire prediction of the
> Advisory Group on Budget Adjustment in April,
> based on average cuts, had been far too
> optimistic.
> (Crawford, 1982)

Stunning the news certainly was, and stunned were
most of the members of Senate, yet Professor
Crawford sprang into action. Senate immediately
agreed to his plan to prepare a package of course
cuts for discussion at the 8 July Senate meeting.
Within what must have been one of the most
exhausting weeks in his life a "starting point,
rather than a fully-revised academic plan" had been
presented and agreed by Senate.

The University was faced with very severe
problems imposed upon it by government - the ways
in which the cuts were implemented seemed, indeed,
to be designed to cause the maximum amount of chaos
and disruption to the system. University courses
in Britain last for 3 or 4 years, yet the government allocated funding and student numbers on the
assumption that reductions would be made in 3 years,
starting with the October 1981 intake. The announcement was made in July, yet most places had
been offered by that time to potential students,
conditional on their achieving required 'A' level
grades. The Vice-Chancellor recognised that there
was little sense in simply reducing the number of
students on each course - real savings could only
possibly be made if some courses were axed. If
they could be axed for the following session, then
the university could keep in line with the government timing, if not then it would have one or two
years where there were far more students on small
courses than could be justified.

The individual letter to each specific university sent by the UGC to each Vice-Chancellor,
gave specific target student numbers for 1983/84
in so-called Arts, Science and Medicine students.
Aston only had Arts and Science students. A paragraph of 'advice' was available on each category,
indicating which areas the Committee valued and
which areas the UGC recommended that 'the University should consider discontinuing'. It couched
its recommendations in terms of 'significant' or
'substantial' cuts, yet gave overall student
targets to two significant figures. It turned out
in the end that 'significant' meant about 5 per
cent and 'substantial' meant more than 10 per cent,
but there was no time in that busy week for
delicate textual interpretation. It was clear that
with cuts of this magnitude all the Departments of
Aston would have to suffer. Cuts in the areas
indicated by UGC would not be sufficient to balance
the books.

While the bulk of the university was

deliberating, the Vice-Chancellor initiated action.
Meetings were held with Heads of Department, Deans
of Faculty and other senior academics. Many of
these meetings were just with the Vice-Chancellor
alone - none brought all of the actors together
as a group. He worked right through the weekend,
late into the night, and 'bargains' were struck
with each Head of Department and Dean in turn.
There was little, if any, consultation with junior
members of staff, indeed most staff remained
ignorant of the 'deals' struck on their behalf
until after the second Senate meeting on 8 July.
Indeed, most of the senior members and Heads of
Department remained ignorant of the whole 'package'
until then.

As one Head of Department described it in a
memorandum to staff, 'the Department's part of the
'package' to Senate represents the <u>best I can
negotiate</u> bearing in mind all the constraints,
internal and external' (original emphasis). Heads
of Department, fearful of what they might lose if
they failed to agree, concurred within individual
meetings with the Vice-Chancellor to the 'best
deals they could get'. The fate of courses, and
eventually individual academic careers, thus hung
on the negotiating skills under pressure of each
Head of Department. The whole package was presented to Senate at the 8 July Senate meeting with
not enough time before the meeting for anyone to
read the whole document. It was passed as a
'starting point' with only one dissenting vote.
A motion to recruit students as already planned for
1981/82 to allow more time for discussion was
heavily defeated. The part of the 'package' for
each Department was referred back to each Department for comment, but no formal mechanism was set
up to allow any comments to be passed back to
Deans who were to make the final 'adjustments' two
weeks later. In fact, very few changes were made
to the original 'bargains' struck between Heads
and the Vice-Chancellor.

It might be argued, of course, that the
University was in a good position to make decisions
as it had spent the previous eight months con-
sidering possibilities, yet, in the event, as one
senior lecturer wrote 'It was observed that for
many departments across the University the 'package' proposals represented bilateral agreements
between Heads (and/or Deans) and the Vice-
Chancellor and bore little or no relation to plans
submitted by departmental task forces' (19/7/81).

No Faculty or Department escaped unharmed. Within the Faculty of Social Sciences and Humanities, for example, the cuts in student numbers were to be 40 per cent, and, of nine courses offered by the Faculty, three were to close and two merge.

It was thought by some that the constitutionality of the decision making process, whereby decisions were initially made through private and individual discussions, was open to question. When a course had closed before, it had followed lengthy discussion within the Department, consultations with Faculty Board, approval of Faculty Board and finally recommendations to Senate for decision. All of this process was short-circuited and a complete package of cuts presented swiftly and directly to Senate. Clearly, to have gone through the constitutional procedures would not only have taken longer, but might well have saved many of the courses. This taking of power from lower level committees, although in contradiction to claims for greater democracy, was to recur later.

It is reasonable to assume that it is unlikely that the most rational possible solution was found in that week. Academics are essentially part of a 'fragmented profession', where the individual disciplines to which each academic owes allegiance becomes the dominant force in his or her working life. The institution in which the academic happens to be presently working takes on only a secondary importance. At a time of cuts the essentially fragmented nature of the profession becomes clearly visible, and was very evident in the resulting distribution of courses to be axed. Heads of Department wished to protect the 'heartland' of their discipline, so that there was a strong tendency to first try to get cuts shifted elsewhere, and then to consider interdisciplinary courses for closure. At Aston, for example, this was reflected in the closure of two major courses in Social Science and Humanities. Courses in Behavioural Science and Human Communications were to go; both being taught by staff from several Departments, they were somewhat peripheral to the central interests of those Departments.

TWO YEARS OF TURMOIL: JULY 1981 - JULY 1983

The 'week of the letter' left most people involved gasping for breath. The letter itself was not made public until the afternoon of 2 July and term was

due to finish for the Summer Vacation on 3 July.
The UGC had given the University until the end of
December to formulate a response to the letter,
which seemed little enough time to make such
crucial decisions.

Far from being a slack time of year at the end
of the session, the beginning of July sees most
academics involved in marking examination scripts
and serving on Examination Boards. By the time
they were over, so,in fact, were all the decisions.
By the time academics had recovered from the shock
and sent off letters of protest to Members of
Parliament and anyone else they thought might
support the University, they found that the Senate
had already passed draconian cuts which affected
students on courses, prospective students who had
been offered places on courses now axed, and jobs
of academic and non-academic staff.

As the scale of the cuts and threat to the
courses, research livelihoods and tenure of academic staff became apparent an opposition developed.
The Association of University Teachers (AUT) managed to get an Emergency Meeting called for 9 July.
A packed meeting passed a motion of no confidence
in the Senate's decision and advocated greater
attention to alternative strategies to fight the
cuts or to moderate their influence. As staff
began to recognise the implications of the package,
so anger and dismay spread. Even members of
Senate began to openly regret their rapid decisions.
The whole university, students, academic and non-
academic staff rapidly polarised into 'us' and
'them', and an all out attempt was made by Academic
Assembly (the official body to which all academic
staff belong and which transmits their views), AUT
and other campus unions, to get the decision of
Senate sent back for reconsideration, when it was
considered by Council for final approval.

The Council Meeting of 22 July was a stormy
one but, in spite of pleas to reconsider, Council
allowed the drastic cuts in courses to go through.
At the same time Council approved arrangements for
a 'mobility incentive scheme' whereby lump sum
payments were to be made to academic and non-
academic staff below aged 50 if they left the
University's employ. The scheme depended on age
and years of service, but was at least 150 per
cent annual salary as a lump sum and for some rose
to 270 per cent of annual salary.

After an initial flurry of letters there seemed to be very little centrally organised opposition

to the cuts. The main policy that there seemed to
be developing from the Vice-Chancellor and the
senior administration was to make the budget
balance at all cost by 1984, and to do this through
voluntary redundancy and, if necessary, through
compulsory redundancy, even though this latter
step would appear to require the university to
break its own Charter and Statutes.

It seemed that the university wasn't prepared
to wait very long for volunteers to come forward
either. In late September a report from the
Budget Adjustment Advisory Group calculated the
estimated numbers of staff that could be supported.

> It is estimated that the University's financ-
> ial situation can only support approximately
> 350 academic staff by 1983/84; if additional
> income cannot be found, then up to 140
> academic posts and 310 non-academic posts
> will have to go in addition to posts already
> frozen.
> (Aston Fortnight, 30/9/81)

At the same time a table was published which outlined a timetable which it would be necessary to
follow to complete the reduction by July 1982.
'Redundancy selection criteria' were to be form-
ulated by the Council meeting of 27 October 1981,
redundant staff identified, and redundancy notices
issued by 15 December 1981. As the AUT had a
policy of no compulsory redundancies, the reaction
at the beginning of the next term was strong.

The 'us' and 'them' division of the university
was becoming more polarised. Internal committees
and groups within the university directed their
attack on the Vice-Chancellor and a small group of
administrators who they saw as acting against the
best interests of staff and moving too quickly
towards the possibility of compulsory redundancies.
A meeting of Academic Assembly passed a motion
opposing any steps being taken towards compulsory
redundancies during the year 1981/82, and followed
this by a vote of 350 to 21 for a motion of no-
confidence in the Vice-Chancellor's strategy.
Senate itself voted nem con to oppose any compulsory redundancies during that academic session.
A packed meeting of 1500 students also voted to
support campus unions in preserving their members'
jobs.

Yet the Vice-Chancellor, as early as 27
October 1981, still put forward to Council

compulsory redundancies as one of the possibilities.
In the event, and perhaps somewhat under pressure
from the lobby of 400 odd staff and students outside the meeting, Council voted 20 to 12 not to go
for compulsory redundancies that year. Thus,
instead of the university working together to fight
the cuts or to plan together the best ways in which
to deal with the problems that it had been presented with, the situation rapidly polarised into a
destructive internal battle between the Vice-
Chancellor and a few senior academics and administrative staff and the rest of the University.
There was a shift in the mode of authority away
from the traditional British role of having
consultation and democratic decision making being
made through a miriad of official committees, to
a more centralised American model where Vice-
Chancellor and Senior Administrators were active
in making rapid academic decisions.

So that, for example, in the early months of
the 1981/82 academic year visits were made by what
became known as the 'Gang of Four' to all departments and groups in the university. The four -
the Vice-Chancellor, the Senior Assistant Registrar,
the Staff Officer and the Finance Officer - were
not always given welcoming receptions. The anger
was not just over what they actually said, but
over the very presence of administrative staff at
academic staff meetings and concerning themselves
with what were widely regarded as academic issues.
Again it was the gang of four who addressed a
General Meeting of Students in October 1981.

The two years must be remembered as a period
of endless memoranda, planning documents and
notices, and of endless Union, Departmental,
Faculty, Academic and Senate meetings. At the same
time academic work became identified with and
described by numbers - of students, of A level
grades, of staff, of ratios, of contact hours, and
mostly, of pounds sterling. Questions of quality
became submerged beneath the ever dominant pressures of quantification (Walford, 1984).

Pressures were not only from academics fearful
of losing their jobs. Students on courses at the
university were concerned about the quality of
teaching they would receive as their lecturers
left without being replaced. They were also concerned about the standing of their final degree,
especially those who were to be the last year of
degree courses being closed. Closing courses to
which students had been provisionally accepted also

caused considerable problems. Students were, in the end, offered places on other courses at the University instead, but as one student who originally accepted and planned to study Behavioural Science, stated, 'I should be choosing my course and career and not have it chosen for me'. She and another student later took the University to court for breach of contract - and lost.

The main problem was that once the decision to try to maintain financial stability had been taken, the pace of events was largely determined by the tight timetable of reduction in resources imposed by the UGC. Staff had to be 'persuaded' to leave as rapidly as possible. The two years was thus also a time of continued pressure and deadlines. In June 1982 Senate accepted proposed staffing ranges for each Department and after some minor adjustments a target of 350 academic staff was set. Some 140 posts would have to go. In July 1982 Council decided to enact procedures which would result in every member of staff knowing whether 'an application to leave would be considered to be in the managerial interests'. These letters, which came to be known as 'A' or 'B' letters, according to which sort of decision was made, had a considerable effect. The process is well described by Kogan (1983:81).

In October 1982 Council agreed, quite exceptionally, to hold a postal ballot of its members on the question of compulsory redundancies. The final vote was very close with 19 for, 17 against and one abstention. The Council thus chose to act contrary to the wishes of Senate and Academic Assembly and start procedures for compulsory redundancy. Notices were issued to trade unions and the Department of Employment stating that redundancies were to be made, and a 'consultation' process was initiated.

The university erupted, as did AUT and other universities both nationally and locally. It looked as if Aston was going to be the stage on which academic tenure would be broken. AUT imposed a legal writ on the university for attempting to break its own Charter, and imposed a 'blacking' of the university. No AUT member was to come to Aston to give invited seminars or lectures or was to undertake external examining for Aston. A national lobby of some 1000 AUT and other union members silently greeting the next Council meeting in December 1982, where any decision to select individuals was deferred.

Meanwhile pressures had been mounting on individuals and groups within the university. The university engaged in a cyclic process of pressure, release; new pressure, release; further pressure, release. The Early Retirement Scheme was extended to a Mobility Incentive Scheme, which was then increased with an Academic Restructuring Premium. The government-financed UGC scheme eventually brought payment down again, but later new Enhanced Mobility Schemes were introduced, closed, then reintroduced. The December 1982 Council meeting brought about yet another scheme, this time financed by the university itself again, where the university, in practice, declared itself open to negotiation within bounds. This last move was sufficient and in July 1983 numbers roughly balanced and the threat of compulsory redundancies for academic staff was removed by Council.

CONTINUED PRESSURE - JULY 1983 ONWARDS

Recession and sudden contraction in the University caused by UGC imposed government cuts had certainly been a major cause of two years of 'American mode' university management. But there were few signs of any reversal of style when the threat of compulsory redundancies was finally removed. Throughout the two years the estimated number of staff that the university could support had become a moving, but always declining, target - from 350 to 335 to 320. By November it was clear that by August 1984 staff numbers would be nearer 300, yet the senior administration asked Council once again to offer a Mobility Incentive Scheme.

Pressures continued after July 1983, not only because of new cuts threatened in the future by government, but also due to imbalances in the staff remaining. Officially, staff had only been allowed to leave if it was 'in the managerial interest' but, in practice, the level of discrimination had been low and only a very few academics had been refused a golden handshake. Very broadly three main groups had left. Firstly those people over 55 on the staff were put under heavy pressure to leave. They were eligible to take early retirement and, although many had no desire to retire early, some altruistically gave up their jobs in the hope of saving jobs for others. This was a prominent feature of survival of the University of Salford, where 'in late 1981

it invited all members of staff over the age of 50
to retire prematurely. Most agreed' (Wilde and
Stradling, 1982).

The second group of people to leave were those
who thought themselves most vulnerable to the
possibility of compulsory redundancy, some of whom
felt that the offer on the table was likely to be
higher than they might receive later. Some of
these may have been the 'dead wood' that many wished
to see leave the system, but most were simply those
academics unlucky enough to be in the targeted
academic areas.

The third group was simply those able to get
jobs elsewhere. The money offered by the university
acted as an incentive for everyone to scan the
employment pages of newspapers. Those who had
talents that were saleable either in or out of
higher education were often able to take enough
money to buy a reasonable house in which to settle
in their new jobs. Obviously some of the people
within the last group were amongst the most talented
academics in the university, and, while their talents may be used elsewhere, their going was
presumably not an intended consequence of the
financial cuts. It is also worth noting that there
are more opportunities outside universities for the
academics in the very areas it seeks to encourage
in universities than in those it seeks to dis-
courage. The sociologist or historian, no matter
how expert, has few chances of obtaining a comparable
job outside universities, but the computer scien-
tist, engineer, information technologist and
management specialist may well be able to move.
The imposition of an impossibly tight timescale
for financial reductions has meant that all academic areas have suffered, even those which the UGC
and government wished to see protected.

Aston senior administration was well aware of
these problems and, even though financial equilibrium had been reached by July 1983, the Council
continued its mobility incentive scheme. There
were several inbalances between the academic subject areas of the remaining staff and also in the
age distribution. Most voluntary retirements and
redundancies had occurred at the top and bottom of
the age distribution leaving a bulge of academics
in the 35-40 age range. The growing concern about
the effects on productivity of a group of academics
growing old together with few changes of promotion
has been voiced elsewhere (Walford, 1979; Blume,
1982) but the traditional British style of

university administration would have been reluctant
to do anything about it.

Yet at the same time as trying to encourage
more people to leave, there was a desperate need to
try to improve staff morale and to encourage new
developments and enthusiasm. Two years of being
told that one's services are not really required by
the university had a not unexpected effect on staff
morale. This, coupled with continued anxiety about
the future and a growing realisation of loss of
control within the decision making processes of the
university, is likely to have led to a decline in
commitment to both teaching and research. It would
be strange if it had not. Teaching courses for the
last time, even though their quality had never been
questioned, is an experience unlikely to lead to
great enthusiasm. Nor is it likely that academics
will plan long term research when their own future
and that of their departments are in doubt. This
decline in morale has also been noted by Waton
(1984) in his short article on Bradford.

Fighting the cuts internally and externally
led to a tremendous amount of time being wasted in
attendance at meetings, preparation of documents
and internal wrangling. People leaving meant
changes to courses or changes in individual teaching
commitments, both of which take time and energy.
Of greater importance is, perhaps, the degree of
emotional energy expended during extended periods
of uncertainty, for academic work generally is unlikely to be at its most productive under conditions
of stress.

All this was presumably unintended and unexpected by government in its crude calculations of
the effects of a cut in expenditure. But it is
quite clear that the disabling effects of cuts are
not in proportion to the amount of finance cut -
they affect the entire university and then the
entire university system. What has been surprising
in the last two years is that Aston has been able
to maintain the teaching and research output that
it has. It is obviously smaller, but it has sur-
vived.

At first sight Aston might appear to be a
deviant case. It is certainly true that the cuts
at Aston were amongst the deepest and no other
university acted as rapidly as Aston or seems to
have moved so dramatically in its style of management. This setting of the pace in terms of
management decisions has continued, for Aston was
the first university to agree proposals, at a

University Cut and Thrust

Council meeting in July 1984, which would make
university non-academic staff compulsorily redundant.
Further, a small study group of Council and Senate
members, set up to consider a CVCP paper on the
structure of the academic profession recommended
that new academic staff appointments should be
subject to termination on grounds of financial
exigency or programmatic need, thus severely
limiting tenure provisions.

At the national level the Minister of Education
is maintaining pressure to alter and limit conditions of tenure for all university staff, and is
attempting to interfere in the curriculum - particularly with social science courses at the Open
University. Student grants fail to keep up with
inflation and further financial cuts have been announced. While academics at Aston may perhaps feel
themselves to be more the subject of a new managerial style than those at most universities, it is
unlikely that Aston will remain a deviant case for
long. It is more likely to be merely an indication
of the likely future of most British universities
if the cuts in government expenditure deepen.

NOTE

A related paper 'Responses to government cuts in
British Universities: a Case Study', was given at
the Comparative and International Education Society
Annual Conference, Houston, Texas, March, 1984.

REFERENCES

Ashworth, J. (1982) 'Reshaping higher education in
    Britain', Journal of the Royal Society of Arts,
    130, 713-729
Baron, S., Finn, D., Grant, N., Green, M. and
    Johnson, R. (1981) Unpopular Education,
    Hutchinson, London
Blume, S.S. (1982) 'A framework for analysis' in
    G. Oldham (ed.) The Future of Research,
    Leverhulme Programme of Study into the Future
    of Higher Education, Volume 4, Society for
    Research into Higher Education, Guildford
Crawford, F. (1982) Vice-Chancellor's Report for
    1980/81, University of Aston, Birmingham
Department of Education and Science (1978) Higher
    Education into the 1990s, Brown Paper by
    Gordon Oakes, HMSO, London

Department of Education and Science (1980) Letter
   to Select Committee on Education, Science and
   Art, 3 March, 1980
Department of Education and Science (1983) Future
   demand for higher education. DES Report on
   Education No. 99, April, DES, London
Department of Education and Science (1984) Demand
   for higher education in Great Britain 1984-
   2000. DES Report on Education No. 100; July,
   DES, London
Edwards, E.G. (1980) 'Bleeding is no cure for this
   melancholy humour', Times Higher Education
   Supplement, 11 January
Edwards, E.G. (1982) Higher Education for Everyone,
   Spokesman Books, Nottingham
Expenditure White Paper (1981) The Government's
   Expenditure Plans 1981-1982 to 1983-1984,
   Education and Science, Arts and Librarians.
   Para 14, HMSO, London
Geddes, D. (1981) 'Dons' redundancies may cost up
   to £80,000', The Times, 14 May, p. 5
Kogan, M., and Kogan, D. (1983) The Attack on
   Higher Education, Kogan Page, London
Moodie, G.C. (1983) 'Buffer, coupling, and broker:
   reflections on 60 years of the UGC', Higher
   Education, 12, (3), 331-347
Royal Society (1983) Demographic Trends and Future
   University Candidates. The Royal Society,
   London
Shattock, M. and Rigby, G. (eds.) (1983) Resource
   Allocation in British Universities, Society for
   Research into Higher Education, Guildford
University Grants Committee (1968) University
   Development 1962-67, Cmnd. 3820, HMSO, London
Waldegrave, W. (1982) 'Answer to parliamentary
   question', Hansard 16 March
Walford, G. (1979) 'Spontaneous creation: a study
   of a university department', Chemistry in
   Britain, 15, 447-453
Walford, G. (1983) 'Postgraduate education and the
   students' contribution to research', British
   Journal of Sociology of Education, 4(3), 241-54
Walford, G. (1984) 'The numbering of postgraduate
   research', Higher Education Review, 16, (2),
   61-65
Waton, A. (1984) 'The universities: Knee-jerking
   to oblivion?', British Journal of Sociology of
   Education, 5, (2), 173-175
Wilde, E. and Stradling, S.G. (1982) 'Professional
   development in a rapidly contracting university', Paper given at the Eighth Inter-

national Conference on Improving University
    Teaching, July, West Berlin
Williams, P. (1984) 'Britain's full-cost policy
    for overseas students', Comparative Education
    Review, 28, (2), 258-278

INDEX

Index

Index

LIST OF CONTRIBUTORS

Phil Carspecken is a research student at the
    University of Aston and was formerly a full-
    time volunteer teacher at Croxteth Comprehen-
    sive School.
Rod Ling is a teacher working in Birmingham. He
    has been conducting research into special off-
    site units.
Colin A A Marsh is Headmaster of Boney Hay Middle
    School, Staffordshire.
Kristine Mason is Senior Lecturer in the Sociology
    of Education, The College of St Paul and St
    Mary, Cheltenham.
Henry Miller is Lecturer in Sociology at the
    Management Centre, University of Aston.
Bede Redican is Head of the Department of Science
    and Social Science, Newman College, Birmingham.
Lesley Smith is Research Fellow at the Institute of
    Education, University of London. She was
    formerly Lecturer at the Open University and
    Research Fellow on a Preparation for Parent-
    hood Project at the University of Aston.
Richard Thompson is now Head of Sixth Form at a
    school in Birmingham. He was formerly a
    Research Fellow at the University of Aston.
Barry Troyna is Senior Research Fellow at the
    Centre for Research in Ethnic Relations,
    University of Warwick.
Geoffrey Walford is Lecturer in Sociology in the
    Social and Technology Policy Division,
    University of Aston.
Gwen Wallace is Senior Lecturer in Education,
    Derbyshire College of Higher Education.